Spirit Beings in European Folklore 2
Compendium 2: 228 descriptions – Germany, Austria, Alpine regions, Switzerland, Netherlands, Flanders, Luxembourg, Lithuania, Latvia, Estonia, Finland, Jewish influences
Author: © Benjamin Adamah
2022

Lay-out: Sylvia Carrilho
Editor: Orenda Bol

ISBN 978-94-92355-56-0

Publisher:

VAMzzz Publishing
P.O. Box 3340
1001 AC Amsterdam
The Netherlands
www.vamzzz.com
vamzzz@protonmail.com

– 228 DESCRIPTIONS –
Germany, Austria, Alpine regions,
Switzerland, Netherlands, Flanders,
Luxembourg, Lithuania, Latvia, Estonia,
Finland, Jewish influences

SPIRIT BEINGS
IN EUROPEAN FOLKLORE 2

COMPILED & EDITED BY

BENJAMIN ADAMAH

CONTENTS

INTRODUCTION — 8

5

INTRODUCTION

Compendium 2 of this 4 volume-series *Spirit Beings of European Folklore*, focuses on the German-speaking parts of Central Europe and German-speaking Alpine regions, the Low Countries, the Baltic States, Finland, and sporadically some creatures from what is now Poland but used to be German. Initially written as a single encyclopedia of about a thousand pages, we decided to divide this manuscript into four separate compendia and use a cultural-geographical format, describing alphabetically the spirit beings of a more or less coherent segment of Europe. Each compendium is a stand-alone work, but, when purchased together with the other volumes, can also be enjoyed as part of the whole series – see also *From the same series* at the end of this book.

The classification into cultural-geographical formats is not solid, because many creatures overlap with creatures from other areas or are (basically) the same creature under a different name, which however, almost always has elements integrated from the region and culture where it is locally known. This is especially true of *Alp* or *Mare*-like creatures, *Goblins* and dwarf-like spirits, *Spring-spirits*, often rooted in the Greek *Nymphs*, but also a spirit like *Lady Midday, Mittagsfrau* in German, of which there are also Eastern European variants such as the Russian *Poludnitsa* and the Polish *Południca*. When classifying for *Compendium 2*, Prussia was a difficult story because, although the old language in Prussian areas, such as Pommmeren, is West Baltic, later, when East Prussia was assigned to Poland, many creatures discussed in this series were given Polish names. Prussia is therefore assigned – like Silesia, for example – to *Compendium 3*, which mainly maps the creatures in the Slavic areas of Europe.

The 4 volume-series *Spirit Beings of European Folklore* is the result of much translation work. In addition to the books added in the literature list and apart from other online sources, I collected a substantial amount of useful wikicommons-licensed data fragments, which I edited into new, often more complete texts, after translating the texts from German, Spanish, Portuguese, Basque, Polish, Russian, French, Czech, Lithuanian, Latvian, Estonian, Finnish, Swedish, Norwegian, Romanian, Hungarian and other sources. In particular, my knowledge of German and Lower Saxon (the language I grew up with and spoke as a child) proved very useful and made it possible to make accessible much unique folklore that has never before been presented in English. In general with regard to this series, but especially with regard to *Compendium 2*, I owe many thanks to the German folklorist Wilhelm Mannhardt (1831-1880), whose outstanding but forgotten works deserve at least as much attention as *The Golden Bough* by Sir James Georges Frazer, who was greatly inspired by by his German predecessor.

– Benjamin Adamah, Amsterdam, August 6, 2022

Aitvaras

The *Aitvaras* or *Aitvars* is a *nature-spirit* in Baltic, especially Lithuanian, folklore and mythology. In Latvian mythology Aitvaras corresponds to *Puke* or *Pūķis*. In Slavic mythology in general he is akin to the *Fire Snake*. According to one version, the word Aitvaras came from the Lithuanian *aiti* (tramp, twirler, tomboy) and *varas* (very fast movement). According to another version, the name is connected to the word *aitauti* (calm, quiet), but this version is less common. The etymology may also be related to the Iranian *pativāra*, like the Polish *Poczwara* (monster). Other names include *Atvaras, Altviksas, Damavykas, Damavikas, Gausinelis, Pisuhand, Sparyžius, Tulihand, Koklikas, Pukis, Puuk, Spirukas, Atvaras, Zaltvikšas* and others. Among the Lithuanian population of Ostrovetschina in Belorussia, Aitvaras was known as *Skalsininkas, Kutas, Hutas,* less frequently as *Shkutas, Sporizhyus, Porizhyus, Domovikas*. Before the spread of Christianity, *Aitvaras* was probably an upper-order deity, governing the wealth and relationships of people. The creature lived in the sky or in the forests. In some Lithuanian representations, covered for example in the émigré-newspaper *Renaissance*, Aitvaras is *"a forest spirit running as a wind through the treetops. If one throws a knife into the whirling whirlwind, one may injure Aitvaras"*. Legend has it that if you throw a splinter towards Aitwaras, a coin will fly back. But one shouldn't abuse the serpent's generosity – it may get offended and stop helping. The creature moves by flying and is mostly fiery, but it can change its appearance.

An Aitvaras looks like a white or black rooster with a fiery tail like a meteor and can act as a protective and benevolent home-spirit. An Aitvaras is said to emerge from an egg of a 9 to 15-year old rooster, or from the testicle of a black stallion. It can be attracted by egg-rich food, but, according to the general Aitvaras-folklore, the creature can be accessed in only two ways:
• either by selling a soul (not necessarily your own) to the Devil,
• or by breeding it yourself. This is believed to be done by keeping a black rooster (or a rooster with a colorful bright tail) in the house for seven years until he lays an egg. The rooster has then to hatch the egg himself. The Aitvaras will lodge itself in a house and most often refuse to leave.

He brings grain, milk, honey, gold and other kinds of wealth, which he sometimes steals from the neighbors. If he is angered, he burns down the house.

The creature was first mentioned in 1547 by Martynas Mažvydas. Later sources also compare it with the *Incubus*. In some aspects there is a similarity to the *Alp*. Otherwise, it is compared to the snake or, more frequently, to the dragon – the children's toy "dragon" is accordingly called *aitvaras* in Lithuanian. In Lithuanian mythology, Aitvaras is a red flying spirit in the form of a fiery serpent, a dragon leaving a trail of fire in the sky. After the rise of Christianity, Aitvaras began to be counted among a class of devils and witches, presenting them as a black crow, heron, black or fiery rooster, very occasionally a cat, walking unnoticed in the daytime and turning into a dangerous dragon at night. There was a popular fable that such a dragon could steal a human soul and send it straight to hell with a wild scream. The Aitvaras is also described as looking like a bird (usually a rooster) when it dwells indoors and looking like a dragon while outdoors. The Lithuanian linguist from France, A. Greimas, notes that the Aitvaras eats eggs, entertains himself by plaiting horses' manes and sending nightmares to people. It is believed that a mistress in a house where Aitvaras lives will be constantly ill. Getting rid of the creature is possible, but a difficult and very dangerous undertaking. If the Aitvaras becomes a nuisance, he can be driven away or killed. The latter, however, will bring a terrible fire to its murderer's home. According to church beliefs, Aitvaras can return again even after being banished from the house with holy water. If an Aitvaras dies, it becomes a spark. As a genus of the air and fire beings, the Aitvaras is opposed to the chthonic *Kaukai*, *Kaukuchus* or *Barzdukkas* or *Bezzdukken*. In the 17th century Matthaeus Praetorius described these differences as follows:

"Until our time the Nadravians also call the Kaukuchus the Barzdukkas, whom they accuse of stealing crops and goods of all kinds. They distinguish them from the Aitvars also called Alf especially:
- by place of residence, because the Barsdukkas lives on the ground, while the Aitvars lives underground;
- by appearance: the Barzdukken take human form, while the Aitvars appear in the form of a dragon or a giant serpent whose head is on fire;
- by actions: the Bezzdukken do no harm to the people they cling to (and even provide them with goods), while the Aitvars harm them;

*- by food: The Kaukuchen are provided with milk, beer and other drinks,
while the Aitvars must be offered only boiled and roasted foods, novelties
and dishes that no one has yet tasted."*

Baltic snake cult

Via its serpent shape the Aitvaras is sometimes associated with the Baltic
snake cult. This cult is referred to by Matthew Praetorius, who writes
about the *Zaltones*, or Lithuanian snake charmers. The name is derived
from the Lithuanian *žaltys* and Latvian *zalktis* (grass snake). Among the
Baltic peoples, the veneration of the snake has been attested until modern
times. Among the Lithuanians and Latvians, grass snakes were kept as
pet snakes and fed with milk. It was considered the protector of livestock
and could be equated with the Latvian *Piena māte* (milk mother). In a
Lithuanian folk song, the grass snake is called the "emissary of the gods".
A Lithuanian proverb reads: *"The view of a dead Žaltys makes the sun
weep"*. They were sometimes used to interpret the future and were also
otherwise associated with superstitious practices. Keeping snakes and
feeding them with milk is also attested for the Prussians and, according to
Simon Grunau, they have been worshiped as an idol of the god *Potrimpos*.

13
—
A

Ajatar

In Finnish folklore, *Ajatar*, (also *Ajattara, Aijo, Aiätär*, or *Aijotar*) is an
evil *forest-spirit* in either the shape of a dragon or a serpent – comparable
to *Aitvaras* from Baltic mythology and *Tiamat* from Babylonian
mythology – or wild forest-woman. *Ajatar* is possibly derived from
the Finnish word *ajattaa* (to pursue or to drive). The feminine suffix
-tar appears in several Finnish names, including a variation of *Louhi
(Louhetar, Loviatar, Louhiatar)* and *Syöjätär (syödä* "to eat", with the
feminine suffix of *-tar*, means "devourer, Vampire"). Applying this to
Ajatar, the verb *ajaa* is suffixed by the feminine *-tar*, translating as "female
pursuer." However, the name may as well have its root in *aika* "time", from
where *ajatar* would be an equally regular derivative.

It is said that Ajatar is the mother of the Devil. Through her connections
with *Hiisi* and *Lempo*, she is said to spread diseases, pestilence and
snakes. Anyone who looks at her becomes sick themselves. She lives in
the woods located at the mountains of Pohjola and is described as having
a hair-plait reaching to her heels and breasts hanging down to her knees,

similar to the Swedish *Skogsnufva*, Danish *Seawoman*, or the *Wildfraulein* of the Eifel. Ajatar is the granddaughter of Hiisi (master of the woods and spreader of disease) and is the master of Lempo and *Gnomes*. In strong contrast there is another tradition which depicts Ajatara as a beguilingly beautiful female guardian spirit who has the male gods at her feet. She is said to be wrapped in a transparent dress of *Will-o'-the-wisps* and to produce the most enchanting laughter in all of heaven.

Alb or Alp

Alb, *Alp* or *Nachtalb* is a more recent name for a mythical (class of) creature(s) originally called *Mahr(t)*, *Mare* or *Moor(t)*, that preys on people at night, draining their energy. It is usually a small, black creature, that attacks sleeping people by sitting on them and pressing down with an increasing weight on their chest or throat, which for the victim is often accompanied by anxiety, difficulty breathing, nightmares or sleeping paralyses. However, apart from a hairy creature resembling something like a dark ape, the Mahr can take any form – from eel or snake to cat, dog, bear, goat, etc. In the latter case it is sometimes called *Bocksmärte* or *Bockhexe* (*bock* meaning: billygoat). It also attacks pets, and sometimes even trees. It enters houses through keyholes or knotholes and it can materialize and dematerialize rather quickly. In some stories, the Mahr has a distinctly erotic character. Sexual intercourse between humans and Mahren is reported. The peoples of Westfalen and Thüringen believe these entities are much more active and strong, even moonstruck when the moonlight is brighter, though in contrast – and as a unique exception on the rule – the nipple sucking *Schrättele* (its name among the Swabians and Alemanni) is reported to love playing with sunlight that shines on a wall. When the rooster crows for the first time in the courtyard, or the daylight comes back into the house, the Alb usually escapes silently, mostly like a fleeing animal: a white mouse, a butterfly, a magpie, or even only like a wisp of smoke. Or it lies as a harmless feather, a broom circle, a straw on the bedspread, still being held convulsively by the redeemed.

After the reformation the word *Mahr* was more and more replaced by *Alb* or *Alp*. This creature was already known for thousands of years and is still known by all Indo-European (and also the Basque) peoples. The ancient inhabitants of India accused the *Gandharven* – who are comparable to our *Elves* – of dancing in the forest, like dogs or monkeys,

and to place themselves like a hairy child in the throat of a sleeping
person. The Greeks called the Alp *Ephialtes* (the jumper), the Romans
Inuus (the squatter) or *Incubus* (the one who lies on top), the Lithuanians
Aitvars, who has incredibly large hands and feet, the Latvian *Leeton*, who
rides horses until they collaps from fear and exhaustion. Their desire to
ride horses drives the Alp from Norway to Tyrol into the stables of the
horses, like the Leeton, and he hustles them indoors or outdoors to the
utmost exhaustion. The next morning they stand there snorting heavily,
drenched in sweat, their manes inextricably intertwined. He even sucks
the milk out of cows and does not spare goats and pigs – except the pigs
of the Lechrain-region, who remain a horror to the creature. And finally,
when nothing else is left for the Alp, it even clutches a tree and squeezes
it with all its force, probably squeezing itself to death in the process.
The tree, possessed by the creature, gets sicker from hour to hour and
trembles even in the quietest weather.

Until Luther's time the name Alp belonged only to Central Germany
as the name for a creature that causes the so called *Alpdrücke* (preasure
causede by an Alp), but it was originally applied by all Germanic peoples
to a completely different class of mythical beings, the *Elfen* nature
demons. The name was therefore probably only transferred to them at
the end of the Middle Ages, since these *Alben* or Elfen were also able to
cause physical discomfort, even pressure and shortness of breath, but
by means of thunder and whirlwinds. The older and once pervasive
already Old High German and Old Norse name is *Mara*, in contrast to
Ephialtes, Incubus, Aitvars and *Leeton* female, as well as the Rhenish
Franconian Mahr, while the Anglo-Saxon *Mara*, the English Nightmare,
the Low German *Moor* is masculine and in Middle High German *Mar*,
Mare, in Pomeranian *Mahrt*, the gender fluctuates, but in New High
German the female predominates. The Dutch have *Nachtmerrie*, the
French *Cauchemar* and the *Tretmare* from the Latin *calcare* "tread", the
Slavs *Mora* or *Mura*, which are feminine, but the Bohemian *Morous*
is masculine to which applies the other Pomeranian name *Murraue*.
Despite a phonetic-legal difficulty, the multiform word probably goes
back to Old High German *marren, hemmen, hindern*, and the Old Norse
merja pressen, meaning "the (female) presser". Similarly, the expressions
of the Austrians, Bavarians and some Middle German tribes: the *Trŭd,
Trŭde, Drŭde* points to the Gothic *trudan* (treading), as does the Old
High German *truta* (*Trotte*), "press" and *Trutâre* "the jumper". Thus, the

Trade is a *Treterin, Trotterin* (comparable to the English: treading). These three most widespread names: Alp, Mare and Trude are surrounded by numerous dialectal ones. The Franks call her *Trempe* (She who tramples), the Tyroleans *Stempe* (She who tramples). The Swabians and Alemanni have the unexplained word *Schrättele* for it, furthermore *Toggeli*, meaning something like "a small creature exerting pressure", furthermore *Rätsel* (which can mean "riddle"), *Druckerl* (presser) and *Lork* (toad); expressions which leave the gender being undecided. But the people of Zurich say; *'s Nachtfräuli hat mi drückt!* (The Nightwife has pressed me!). This more friendly female name is contrasted with the more serious *Walriderske*, of Oldenburg and East Frisian, which probably means the riding on the *Wal*, i.e. the sleeper stretched out as if dead, hence the synonym *Zutodereiterin* (she who rides until death). The Alp was said to have enough strength to kill its victim. The predominantly sinister character is also expressed by the more general expression: *der Ungeheure* "the monster", which was used in the Middle Ages and lived on until more recent times in Bremen and Pomerania. The main activities of the Alps; kicking, pushing, riding, can already be recognized from the older descriptions.

Protection methods

Against the *trotting of the Trud* an old protective spell was used, which was recommended by widespread magic books, such as the *Romanusbüchlein* and the *Wahren Geistlichen Schild*. The spell was commonly used in Aargau, the Hungarian Zips and in the south and west of Germany, especially in Bavarian homes. In the 19th century it was still written here and there in the bed chamber or on the side of the bed, around a so called *Trudenfuß* or pentagram:

> *"Trudenkopf, ich verbiete dir mein Haus und Hof, meinen Roß- und Kuhstall, ich verbiete dir meine Bettstatt, mein Fleisch udd Blut, mein Leib und Seel, daß du mich nicht trudest. Trude in ein anderes Haus, bis du alle Berge steigest und alle Laublein an Bäumen zahlest und über alle Wässer steigest. So kommt der liebe Tag wieder in mein Haus††† – Amen."*

(Trudenkopf, I forbid you my house and yard, my horse and cow stable, I forbid you my bedstead, my flesh and blood, my body and soul, that you do not press me. Press into another house, until you climb all mountains and count all leaves on trees and climb over all waters. Thus the sweet day returns in my house††† – Amen.)

Sometimes the Alp could be chased off by uttering a loud cry, or by mentioning the name of Jesus Christ or the Holy Trinity. In Denmark people sometimes put a large sieve over their head, whose little holes the *Mahrt* – which could not count beyond the holy number three – had to count first, before it was able to do any harm. If the Alb did not want to leave, even when its victim woke up, he was threatened to be nailed or promised a gift: three alms or the three white gifts of salt, flour and egg, which were handed to him by the victim with his left hand. He or she would also invite him to breakfast the next day, or hastily call out to him: '*Come tomorrow for a Glehet*', that is, to borrow something. In the 19th century in some parts of Germany, the farmers still put a small bowl of curd cheese at the door for the stranger who pressed them the previous night. There is another way to assure oneself of the departure of the Alb. If one has grabbed a straw, a thread or a bed feather upon awakening, one must not be misled by the harmlessness of the object, but must hold on to it, even nail or screw it down mercilessly, so that it may perish miserably, or turn out to be an old woman screaming for help. If the Alb is still in the room, one plugs the keyhole through which he entered with a branch. Mephistopheles says in Goethe's *Faust*: "'s ist ein Gesetz der Teufel und Gespenster, wo sie hereingeschlüpft, da müssen sie hinaus". (It is a law of devils and ghosts, where they slip in, there they must get out). Thus also the Alp is caught.

But one also provides in advance for all kinds of means of defense; water and fire, sharp tools, magic signs and evil things. In the Upper Palatinate, for example, one puts the feet of the bed in water, so that Trude cannot get up there. A burning candle, even an unlit consecrated wax stick of red color keeps the Alb away. Likewise, a flax hack, a hatchet or a knife on the chest. On the Faroer, as in the Norwegian Tellemarken, one drives away the Mare by moving a knife, wrapped in a piece of cloth, three times around the body from one hand to the other, while saying:

> "*Marra, Marra, Minni,*
> *Are you in here ?*
> *Do you not think of that blow,*
> *That Sjurdur Sigmundarson gave you*
> *Once on the nose bone?*"

Sigurd or Siegfried, the noblest of heroes, is mustered here as a *Marenschrecken* (Alb-scare). In Austria mistletoe on the doorstep does the job, in Bavaria a *Trudenfuß* on the mother's breast, almost everywhere a pair of shoes placed crosswise under the bed, in Switzerland and Vorarlberg a "Schrat stone" hidden under the pillow or in the cradle. These stones probably belonged to the thunderstones consecrated to Donar. In East Prussia the horses had to be fed on Thursdays before supper in order not to be pressed by the Mahr. From the Upper Rhine all the way to deep into Russia, people knew that in the stable a black billy goat, with its horns and its stench, repelled the creature most powerfully. In India people scared away the alpine *Gandharvas* and *Apsaras* with the strong smelling herb fenugreek *(Trigonella foenum-graecum)*. In the German Middle Ages, the Alb was smoked out with verbena or white swallow-wort *(Vincetoxicum hirundinaria)*. And in South Germany strong-smelling witch-herbs are still hung up or put on the bed to chase him away. In Hesse, the nipples, endangered by the creature, were still smeared with human excrement up to well into the 19th century.

The Alb of human origin

An Alb could be a nature-spirit, but could also very well be a living person, who projected her or his etheric double to ride a sleeping person for sexual reasons, or it could even be the spirit of a deceased person. Elard Hugo Meyer in *Mythologie der Germaner* tells of a woman in a Silesian village, who died in 1889 and who once came through the locked door like a gust of wind, scurried into a housewife's bed and tormented her until she fled from her husband's scolding. According to the texts of ancient Scandinavian literature, these are persons who can shift their *"hugr"* into another form. The *hugr* is more than the soul in the Christian sense, it is the entire non-corporeal being of a person, thus also his or her thoughts and desires.

The Norse Mahr and Norse law

The Norse *Mahr* is always associated with "riding" and inflicting harm, at dusk or at night. Other spirits never ride. In the old Norwegian Christian laws, *riding as a mahr* is explicitly punished. *"If it is proved that a woman rides a man or other member of his household"* [...] reads § 46 of the *Christian law of Eidsivathing*. The possibility of changing shape as a Mahr and performing a Mahr-ride is presented as a real possibility. The *Eyrbyggja saga* from the mid-13th century is about the jealousy of two women, Geirrid and Katla, with Geirrid then being accused in a trial of having acted as a Mahr. Similarly, in the *Ynglinga saga*, Vanlandi's death is

attributed to a Mahr who had been set upon him by his abandoned wife
in Finland:

> *"Þá gerðist honum svefnhöfugt og lagðist hann til svefns. En er*
> *hann hafði lítt sofnað kallaði hann og sagði að mara trað hann.*
> *Menn hans fóru til og vildu hjálpa honum en er þeir tóku uppi til*
> *höfuðsins þá trað hún fótleggina svo að nær brotnuðu. Þá tóku*
> *þeir til fótanna. Þá kafði hún höfuðið svo að þar dó hann."*

(Then he became sleepy and lay down to sleep. But when he had
slept but a little, he cried out and said that a Mahre was kicking
him. Then his people came and tried to help him. But when they
grabbed him by the top of the head, it kicked his legs so hard that
they almost broke. They now grabbed his feet, but the Mahre was
now pressing on his head in such a way that he had to die there.)
– *Heimskringla. Ynglinga saga.* Ch. 13. Translated by Felix Niedner.

In the Middle Ages, the mythical creature lived on in the form of
various superstitions and was counted among *schwarzen Berggeister*
(black Mountain-spirits), Zwerge (dwarfs) und *Nachtelfen* (Night-Elves).
In *Niederdeutschen* (Low German) legends, the mostly female *Mahrt*
takes over the functions of the *Nachtmahr*, but hardly resembles its
shape. Later, the *Nachtalb* was also equated with the Devil; the idiom
"The Devil rode you" is to be understood as a synonym for *Dich hat der*
Nachtalb geritten (You were ridden by the Nachtalb). Like *Frau Holle*,
who is said to mess up her victim's hair, the Nachtalb is also said to knot
the hair of humans and animals. *Alpzopf, Drudenzopf, Wichtelzopf,*
Weichselzopf, Wüchselzopf, Schrötleinszopf or *Judenzopf, Haarschrötel,*
Trichoma, Cirragra or *Plica Polonica* are the historical terms for a massive
conglomeration of hair matted into an inextricable weave similar to
today's dreadlocks. Between the 13th and 14th centuries, a distinction
was made in France between male *Incubus* and female *Succubus Nachtalb*,
who were said to have magical powers of seduction. In 1318, this was
explicitly confirmed in a witch trial at the Sorbonne (Paris).

Alke

In Westphalia the *Alke* is a demonic *water-sprite* who appears as a wheel
of fire or a kind of dragon and chases anyone who ridicules the creature.

Almgeist

Almgeister (pl.; "Spirits of the Alpine Meadows") are spirits of the
Alpine regions, who live in the forests and ravines during the summer
season. During the winter period however they are believed to inhabit
the abandoned Alpine cabins until the return of the flocks in spring.
Depending on the region they are known by different names. In Germany
this spirit is called *Almbütze, Hüttlebutz or Novabutz; in Tyrol Kasermandl
or Alperer.* These spirits were believed to milk the (ghostly) animals
they protect to make butter and cheese. They are reported as friendly to
humans but noisy, make knocking sounds or whistling.

The Almputz in Hinterdux

A special Almgeist (*Almputz*) is mentioned in *Der Almputz in Hinterdux,
Von einer Duxerin*, 1847 by Eduard Ille – later quoted by Will Erich
Peuckert in Ostalpensagen (1963):

> *"The Almputz, a ghostly horse covered with bumps, whose eyes
> shimmer like carbuncles, gallops around at night at the call of
> an equally ghostly cuckoo on the frozen wall in Hinterdux and
> tears anyone who approaches him 'to leaves and dust'."*

Alpenmännchen

Alpenmännchen (Little man of the Alps) is one of the many local terms
for the *dwarf* or *Goblin*-like creatures in German speaking countries
and regions. *Das Alpenmännchen von Nikolsdorf* is the best known story
about the creature. It was recorded by Johann Nepomuk Ritter von
Alpenburg, in his *Deutsche Alpensagen*, Vienna 1861:

> *"The village of Nikolsdorf, popularly known as Iggelsdorf, lies on the
> post road, only 11¼ hours from Oberdrauburg, the border town of
> Tyrol and Carinthia. The village has an alpine pasture, and since
> ancient times there has been a noise among the cattle at night time;
> the oxen jumped apart roaring; if they were locked in the pen, they
> jumped over the fence or kicked it down. Only when the shepherd
> hurried over and on the one hand made a brave noise and cursed
> according to the shepherd's custom, and on the other hand called and
> lured the oxen, did he bring them to a halt again; they sometimes
> ran to him of their own accord when they heard where he was.*

Once the shepherd, who is still alive, heard the old noise again and the fence of the pen was already cracking, he hurriedly went to the oxen and saw in their midst a little man of about a foot high in a red skirt with a little green hat on his head. When the shepherd saw this little man, it moved away a little and disappeared. From then on things got much better, but peace came only after the discovery of an old protocol in Lienz, by means of which a protracted border dispute between the Nikolsdorf and a neighboring alp was settled."

Alpmutter

The *Alpmutter* is a female *Alpgeist* (Nightmare) that haunts alpine huts and farms. The Alpmutter, *Alpmüeterli* (Little Alp-Mother) in Switserland, is described as a hunchbacked woman surrounded by servant *Kobolden* in animal form. Her appearance was regarded as a herald of bad weather.

Angzrerweibl

In the folklore of the Salzburg region, Austria the *Angzrerweibl* (Little Woman of the Meadow) is a nocturnal *Kobold* who lures travelers to a bridge where she scares them almost to death. At the arrival of daybreak she suddenly vanishes with a sharp cry.

Aufhocker

In German and Central European folklore, the *Aufhocker* (*Huckup* in Low German, *Bubak* in Sorbian) is a *Kobold* or *Goblin*-like *Druckgeist*, i.e. a ghostly creature who jumps on the shoulders or backs of lonely people who are still on their way at night, becoming heavier with every step. The victim is often paralyzed with fear, suffers from anxiety and is unable to turn around. According to folklorist Friedrich Ranke, the Aufhocker remains on its victim's back until the victim is released from his burden by the dawning light, a prayer, or the ringing of church-bells. The nightmarish experience of the Aufhocker usually takes place in three phases. The wanderer is first approached or accompanied by a sinister being, then the demonic companion grows to a supernatural size, and finally it leaps onto its victim's back. Typical haunted places such as streams, bridges, lakes, forests, ditches, crossroads, hollow

roads, churchyards and murder or execution sites are the usual location
for an encounter with the Aufhocker, which can result in physical and
mental illness and sometimes even death for the victim. Sometimes the
Aufhocker first appear as pitiful old women; but they can also take on
animal forms such as dog, bear, calf or Werewolf (as with the *Stüpp*, a
creature akin to the Aufhocker). Elemental beings such as *water-sprites* or
Will-o'-the-wisps can also act as Aufhocker. The decisive factor is not the
shape of the Aufhocker, but the oppressiveness of the situation.

The belief in the Aufhocker has its origins in the fear of Revenants,
the returning dead. The oldest reports of Aufhocker clearly speak of
"aufhuckenden Leichen" (creeping corpses) and not of Goblins or ghosts.
Unlike the *Nachzehrer*, who did not have to leave his grave if he wanted to
harm the living, other undead, similar to *Vampires*, rose out and robbed
people of their life force. This could be done in a sensual, concrete way
by sucking blood, but also in a more abstracted form. As more recent
research shows, this also applies to the Vampires, who in the oldest
accounts are said to have a damaging effect through strangling and
emaciation, but not through sucking blood. In western Germany, the
Aufhocker merges with the *Werewolf* to form the *Stüpp*, a dangerous fiend
that jumps at humans and allows itself to be carried around until the
victim dies of exhaustion.

Aulkes

In Emsland (the northwestern part of Lower Saxony) and the eastern part
of Groningen (Netherlands) the term *Aulkes* is used for *little demonic
spirits*. According to Claude Lecouteux Aulkes comes from *Alveke*,
(little Elf), while the Dutch writer K. ter Laan (and Dr. Adelbert Kuhn
in *Zeitschrift für Vergleichende Sprachforschung auf dem Gebiete des
deutschen, griechischen und lateinischen,* Berlin 1855) translate Aulkes
(also: *Aunken, Oelken, Ulken, Ölken, Ülken*) as "Old Ones" (*die Alten* in
German). Aulkes were notorious for exchanging babies for changelings
and also for causing bruises on the body, making it look like you had been
pinched very hard. They also kidnapped young women to suckle their
dogs until they got unattractively stretched out breasts. Heinrich Lohre in
Märkische Sagen (1921) mentions the varieties *Elliken* and *Öllerken* in the
Mark (a region northeast of Berlin) who live in forests underground and
wear red caps. In Pomeria they were called *Ullerkens* (dwarfs of the hills)

who sometimes visited humans, played violin in cellars and disappeared when someone visited the cellar with a candle as they could not bear this light. They are mentioned by Jodocus Deodatus Hubertus Temme in *Die Volkssagen von Pommern und Rügen*, Berlin 1840.

B

Bachhund

Nikolaus Gredt in Sagenschatz des Luxemburger Landes, Luxemburg 1883, mentions a sinister area near the Stöckelter Moor, which separates the Sandweiler Bann from the Itziger Bann; for in this moor dwells the Bachhund (Creek hound), an evil, treacherous spirit, who has been cursed there and at night roams the heights of Stöckelts in the form of a large, black dog. From time to time, an eerie roar can be heard above the Stöckelt moor and in the surrounding forests, the cause of which cannot be fathomed and which sometimes roars like a rumbling thunderstorm, so that even drunks have sobered up.

Bahkauv

The *Bahkauv* (from *Bachkalb*, also *Badekalb*, dialectally also *Bakauf*, *Baakauf*, *Bahkauf* or *Bakauv*) is a mythical creature, related to the *Aufhocker*. It is associated with harassing drunk men. In legend, the creature would ambush intoxicated men at night and latch onto their shoulders, forcing them to carry it around before attacking them.
The creature has been featured in the folklore of both Aachen and the Rhineland. The Bahkauv is typically described as being similar to an elongated or deformed calf with sharp fangs and is commemorated by the Bahkauv fountain at Büchel. According to legend, the creature often lurks near fountains, streams, and sewers. The Aachen city sewers and the many thermal springs found under the city have been cited as its dwelling places. One legend holds that *Pippin der Jüngere* (Pippin the Younger), Charlemagne's father, fought against the Bahkauv and killed it one morning at a steaming spring with a sword thrust. In 1902 the city of Aachen erected a statue of the Bahkauv over an old well that had been associated with the monster. This statue was melted down for its metal in

World War II, prompting the city to build a second statue in 1967. This statue persists to the present day. According to the legend of Aachen, the Bahkauv lived in the sewers of the thermal springs at Büchel, the so-called Kolbert. Its shape resembled a large calf with a shaggy coat. Its mouth had sharp teeth and its bulky eyes glowed in the dark. Its paws looked like bear paws with sharp claws, and its tail was scaled and trailed on the ground. The Bahkauv wore chains around its neck and legs that rattled when it moved. During the day, the rattling of chains could be heard from the depths at Kolbert, but the Bahkauv did not come up. At night, however, it would attack *Nachtschwärmer* (nocturnal revelers), especially those who were drunk and on their way home. It jumped on them and let itself be carried on their shoulders all the way to their home. It was impossible to shake it off. That the Bahkauv was a devil's beast was evident from the fact that it made itself heavier when its bearer prayed and lighter when he cursed. Once the carrier had reached home, the Bahkauv would jump off and look for its next victim. However, the Bahkauv never killed anyone and never molested women and children. After the Kolbert was vaulted and built over, the Bahkauv was no longer seen.

In the Rhineland there are numerous legends about demonic creatures that squat by a stream at night, lie in wait for lonely or drunken hikers and jump on their backs. In the area around Aachen and Düren these are mainly two *Unholde* (monstrous phantom creatures), a kind of *Werewolf*, which is called *Stüpp* here, and *das Kalb* (the calf). Overall, the *Bachstüpp* and the *Bachkalb* – also called *Grachtkalb* in the border region to the Netherlands – belong to the class of haunting parasitic creatures known under the name *Aufhocker*. In many places in Rheinhessen, the Rheingau and other parts of south-west Germany, the Muhkalb exists as a legendary creature, which sometimes has features similar to the Bahkauv.

Barstukken

Barstukken, Fingerlinge or Berstuken are a type of German/Polish dwarfish *Household-spirits* in Warmian-Masurian (northeastern Poland) folk tales, mainly located in and near the town of Ketrzyn/Rastenburg. They are most concentrated under elder-bushes in a hill near the village of Święta Lipka/Heiligelinde, where in the pagan times an exceedingly large tilia (*Linde* in German) is said to have stood, under which, the gods were worshiped. The Barstukken appear as good and helpful Household-spirits, who watch over the sick when the other family-members are asleep, especially when the moon is bright. To those they are kindly disposed, they bring what they take from those who are not kind to them. One had to prepare a clean little table for them and put simple food on it, bread, butter, cheese, beer, milk as an offering. If however everything remained untouched, this was a sign the Barstukken had left the house. The Barstukken had a god above them, whose name was *Pushkait,* whose dwelling, like that of his dwarfish servants, was under the elder bushes.

Beatrik

Beatrik is a rather peaceful, but when provoked, cruel giant from the Tyrolean legends. He goes accompanied by a pack of puppies and stays friendly as long as nobody looks at him. In Castelnuovo, he would walk around with a bowl of milk to put to sleep those who responded to his cries. Once asleep he would remove their bowels. In winter he haunts the summer grazing lands in the Alps and hunts Alpine witches called Eguane.

Bergmanderl

In Austria *Bergmanderl* (mountain men) is often used as a generic term for dwarfish *Berggeister* (mountain spirits). There are many stories about them. They live in caves in the mountains, are often associated with gold treasures and can become vindictive towards people.

Bergmönch

The *Bergmönch* (mountain-monk) is a complex German mountain-spirit, also known as *Meister Hämmerling.* He often wears a black hooded robe like monks wear – hence his name "Bergmönch". But in addition to his appearance as a monk, he is also described as a hooded giant with sparkling eyes as big as dinner plates, or as a mountaineer with a silver pit light, and further as a horse with a long neck and fearsome eyes. Often he remains invisible and his presence is sensed in other ways. In some legends, he is said to be the ghost of a dead miner who could not part from his beloved work and must now labor in the pits and tunnels forever. When dressed like a miner, the workers called him Meister

Hämmerling (because of the noise he makes, which often sounds like someone hammering on the walls). Quarries and mines in the mountains are usually the residence of the Bergmönch, but occasionally he also appears on the surface. This mountain spirit is said to be very active on Fridays, when he empties one bucket of excavated ores into another. The Bergmönch can manifest as an erratic and dangerous character who loves pranks and is known to be very hot-tempered. He doesn't like being denied or made fun of, and will surely punish those who do so. He collapses mining tunnels or causes water infiltration and fires. His breath is poisonous and, according to legend, can kill twelve people at once. Sometimes he would grab a miner and throw him down at another place with such force that the miner's limbs were shattered. However, it was believed, that the miners who were assaulted this way by the Bergmönch had usually shown no respect for him or for their fellow workers or had failed to observe certain rules. The spirit punished miners for whistling (which he hated), cursing, selfishness, infidelity and lazyness. In one story, the Bergmönch kills an evil foreman of the miners by crushing his head between his knees. On the other hand, he sometimes presented poor and hardworking miners with rich ore and money. Such a miner could become his personal favorite, whose work he supported by digging up ores for him. He was believed to be able to excavate more ores in one hour than miners could in one week. Whenever his favorite miners were shown hidden veins or veins of gold and silver, the miners had to throw some of their mining tools into the offered vein in exchange for this gift, or the vein would be closed forever or made invisible to human eyes. The spirit also had a reputation for supporting the miners with food when they were trapped by a collapse, and renewing the candles in their lamps. For his contribution to the miners' work, he demanded only half of his wages, but giving him the full amount was advisable. When the Bergmönch offered some of the oil from his giant pit lamp to miners whose mine lamps were in danger of going out, this oil mysteriously never diminished and burned steadily for years, provided the miner kept the secret that he received his lamp oil from the mountain-spirit.

Biersal

A *Biersal* (also: *Bieresal* or *Bierasal*) is a type of *Kobold* (house spirit) of German folklore. The Biersal is a special household-spirit that abides in breweries and in the *bierkeller* of inns and pubs. In these establishments,

the Biersal will gladly clean bottles, beer mugs, casks and kegs that have
been used, in return for payment in the form of his own portion of beer.
This association between Kobolds and work gave rise to a saying well
known in 19th-century Germany, that a woman who worked quickly
"had the Kobold". When not properly remunerated, however, the Biersal
would resort to mischief and vandalism by stealing or hiding tools and
causing equipment malfunctions. Apart from German folklore there also
exists an English legend about a Biersal-type *Goblin*, which first appeared
in the late 19th century. It concerns a house spirit named *Hödfellow*
that resided at the Fremlin's Brewery in Maidstone, Kent, England, who
was wont to either assist the company's workers or hinder their efforts,
depending on whether he was being paid his share of the beer or not.

Bilwis or Bilwiz

Bilwis (also *Bilwiß*, *Bilwiz* (Middle High German), *Belewitte* (Middle
Low German), *Bihlweise*, *Bilweis*, *Willeweis*, *Bulwechs* (male), *Bulwechsin*
(female), *Bilmesschnitter*, *Pilwiz*, *Pilwis*, *Pilewis*, *Pilwihten*, *Pilfas* etc.)
are the names for a benign or malignant, female or male demon that
was sometimes described as a *nature* or *field-spirit*, sometimes as a
house spirit and sometimes as a demon or *moon spirit*, depending on
geographical and historical circumstances. In north-eastern Germany,
the Bilwis represents a beneficent demon of the cornfields, whereas in
Bavaria it is a harvest damaging demon as the *Bilwes* or *Bilmesschnitter*.
Gisbertus Voetius (1589-1676) – and also other authors – use the terms
Beeldwit, *Belwit*, *Pilewiz*, *Bilvitra*, *Bilehvit* for benign household-spirits.
Richard Beitl sees in the *Bilwis* a folk-etiological explanation for the
aisles in the grain fields caused by hares and deer. The Bilwis cuts the
aisles with sickles he carries on his feet. Such an aisle is therefore called
a *bilbez-/bilwetz-/bilfezschnitt*. In Carinthia the Bilwis is also seen as the
personification of the whirlwind. Some descriptions show similarities
to the child frightener figure of the *Roggenmuhm* in order to *"warn the
mostly barefoot village child not to enter the cornfield"*: The Bilwis would
cut off the children's feet, or cut the foot tendons.

In the first half of the 15th century, *Pelewysen* (pl.) appears as a synonym
for *witches*. *Pilweise* is also used as a synonym for *witch* in Silesian sagas
during this period, and in the *Gesammelten Sagen aus dem Orlagau* by
Wilhelm Börner (1788-1855) the term *Bilbze* also means witch. In the

Hausbuch des Colerus (Mainz 1656) *Bihlweisen* is found for *witch(es)*. In Martin von Amberg's *Gewissensspiegel* (Confession mirror) (1382) *Pilbis* is used with the meaning of *Devil*.

Etymology

In *Deutsche Mythologie* by Jacob Grimm, no less than six pages of variations of the name and interpretations of the term by various authors are listed – and again questioned. Several authors suggest – especially for the south-eastern part of Germany and in the context of *Bilweichs, Bilweichszopf* and *Weichselzopf* – a "*plaguing, frightening, hair and beard tangling, grain cutting ghost, usually in female form.*" Still further east, in Poland, the term is also used to refer to the *Bialowieszcz. Bialowieszczka* however denotes a *wise sorceress*, which is why speculations have been made about a Slavic origin. Beginning with the earliest mentions of the Bilwis, Grimm already states that "*..die wechselnde Form verräth, dass man das wort schon im 13. 14. jh. nicht mehr verstand;..*" (".. the changing form betrays that the word was no longer understood as early as the 13th and 14th centuries;..."). Geographical and temporal variations are (alphabetical): *Beeldwit, Belewitte* (Middle Low German), *Belewitten* (Lower Saxon), *Bihlweise* (pl.: *Bihlweisen*; Mark Brandenburg), *Bilmesschnitter* (expanded; grain demon), *Bilweichs, Bilwechs, Bilweis, Bilwicht, Bilwiht, Bilbze, Bilwis, Bilwiß, Bilwitz* (Middle High German), *Bilwiz, Bulwechs* (male), *Bulwechsin* (female), *Pelewysen* (pl.; 15th century), *Pelwit, Pilbis, Pilbiszote* (expanded, a kind of *Nightmare*), *Pilbiz, Pilewis, Pilfas, Pilnitis, Pilnihts, Pilweise, Pilwith, Pilwis, Pilwit, Pilwiz, Willeweis, Wilwis.*

Wolfram von Eschenbach describes the *Wilwis* as an "Elven being" who can paralyze people with a magic arrow, the "*Bilwizschuß*". Elsewhere Pilbis/Pilwiz is an elvish being that – like forest-spirits – inhabits a tree (*Pilbisbawm*) and to which sacrifices must be made. It has also been discussed that Bilwis is a folk variant of an older Germanic fertility being and finally there is an association with the mischievous powers of the waning moon. Within this context the name Bilwis could be related to *Bil*, who was originally an ancient Norse moon goddess. Scholar Leander Petzoldt writes that the figure indeed seems to stem from the goddess and over time saw many changes, later developing "*an elfin, dwarfish aspect and the ability to cripple people or cattle with the shot of an arrow*" (such as in Wolfram von Eschenbach's 13th century poem *Willehalm)*. Petzoldt further surveys the development of the figure:

"During the course of the thirteenth century, the Bilwis is less and less frequently treated as the personification of a supernatural power, but becomes increasingly identified as a malevolent human being, a witch. Still later, with the rise of the witch persecutions at the end of the Middle Ages, the Bilwis was demonized; she becomes an incarnation of the Devil for the witch and sorcerer. A final development has taken place since the sixteenth century, especially in northeast Germany; the Bilwis has been conceived of as a grain spirit bringing wealth; yet this latest manifestation of the Bilwis has its harmful side, the Bilwis-cutter, who is blamed for the unexplained patterns that are formed among the rows of standing grain. The cutter is a sorcerer or witch that cuts down the corn with sickles that are fastened to its feet. He is classified as an essentially malevolent Corn Spirit. Thus, the Bilwis is exceedingly polymorphous, taking on many appearances and meanings in all German-speaking areas throughout the Middle Ages. The Bilwis is one of the strangest and most mysterious beings in all folklore; its varying forms reflect the concerns of a farm culture, and it serves to explain the eerie appearance of turned-down rows of plants in cornfields."

Birkenjungfer

A man from Mutfort (Luxembourg) often saw a lady dressed in white in the Birk. She spread a white carpet in front of him, on which then suddenly a little goat appeared. This lady was the *Birkenjungfer* (Birch Maiden), which has its place of residence in the so-called Birkenmoore (Birch bog).

Bisterk Ding

The *Bisterk Ding* is a demon from Helgoland lore of the "Grim-type". (Helgoland is a rocky North Sea-island in northeast Germany, west of southern Denmark). If someone has an accident at sea, this demon is said to emerge from the water, lie down on steps or hide in the corners of barns. It is usually described as a black monster with eyes the size of dinner plates and the fur of a sheep. He is said to move by rolling. A Helgoland saying is: *"Det Bisterk Ding lay auf dem Weg!"* (The Bisterk Ding lay on the road!), which is used when one is struck by misfortune.

Blauhütl

Karl Haupt mentiones *Blauhütl* in his *Sagenbuch der Lausitz* (1862/1863)
as the *Wild Huntsman* of Lausitz (Saxon Lusatia). He was the restless
spirit of the Herr von Biberstein. This landlord, who lived in a castle near
Schönau, liked to go on wild hunts without any consideration for the
farmers and their crops. One day the entire harvest was destroyed, which
led to fury among the people. As punishment, he had to continue his
hunts after he died until the end of times. For those who see him, it means
misfortune. In the church in Schönau the landlord was depicted with his
dogs and his big blue hunter's hat, from which *Blauhütl* got his name.

Blutschink

The *Blutschink* (sometimes also called *Bluatschink*, *Bluetschinke* or
Plutschinke) is a demonic *Wassergeist* (water-spirit). The term is probably
derived from Blut (blood) and Schinken (ham, thigh), which would make
the Blutschink in German mean "blood thigh". It is known only in Tyrol,
Austria and some smaller localities. Richard Beitl assumes that the name
Blutschink has developed from a Slavic word: The *Błudnik*, a Water-
demon of the Slavic world, that would correspond to the *Irrlicht* (Will-o'-
the-wisp) in the German nature saga. The derived verb *błudźić* means "to
seduce, drown, suffocate". Originally, Carinthian Alpine Slavs would have
brought this legend with them when they settled, but when the word was
no longer understood, it developed further through folk etymological
reinterpretation. The strikingly limited regional familiarity of the
Blutschink also supports this thesis. The Blutschink is depicted with its
upper body resembling a coal-black, shaggy bear, but its legs, though very
strong, are human and naked. In addition, his legs are blood red, and he is
said to be literally dripping with blood. It is precisely because of his habit
of eating people that this demon is feared. It is said that it first sucks the
blood of its victims and then eats them afterwards. Supposedly, he is only
found in and around bodies of water, although in South Tyrol there is
also a widespread belief that he lurks in bean and poppy fields to devour
children.

Bombatsche Kätchen

In the forest of Greiweldingen, in the Föllewies (Luxembourg), the
Bombatsche Kätchen came and washed in the brook that flows by there.

Her washing consisted of small pieces of cloth, as big as a hand. People claim that they saw the pieces hanging on the hedges. Therefore, when someone washes torn rags, people say: *"She/He has a laundry like the Bombatsche Kätchen"*. Grown-up people, no less than little children, are afraid to go there for fear that Bombatsche Kätchen might do them harm. The area where the Kätchen stayed is quite barren, not even trees grow there. Recorded by Nikolaus Gredt in *Sagenschatz des Luxemburger Landes*, Luxembourg 1883.

Boreas or Sturmgeister

Many occult writings distinguish four types of *Elemental Spirits* and classify them according to the Element to which they belong: the *Gnomes* (Earth), *Sylphs* (Air), *Salamanders* (Fire) and *Undines* or *nixes* (Water). Most occultists agree, however, that there is another class; that of the *storm spirits* (*Sturmgeister* or *Boreas* in German). Erhard Bäzner, a clairvoyant member of the German Theosophical Society, described the Sturmgeister like this:

> *"The appearance is more animal than human. The naked body, not adorned by any jewel, is disgusting. Shaggy black hair covers the plump muscle-less body, which is surrounded by a blue-green light. Despite the overlong skinny legs, the very massive arms are reaching down almost to the feet. The grotesquely long fingers with the claw-shaped tips are spread excessively wide. They have strange small cat-like heads. Every part of the creature is in dissonant relation to the rest of the body. Feet and toes are cartilaginous or have spurs attached, sometimes with bushy tails, if not webbed or with fish-like fins. Their size is 7 to 12 meters. According to Bäzner, Sturmgeister are not semi-immortal but live from 18 up to 25 years. He locates their habitat on the peaks of ight mountains or some miles high in the sky, while in winter time they reach lower altitudes. They avoid Earth and Fire, as these Elements damage their ether body's."*

Borries

Borries or *Börries* is usually a huge black demonic phantom-dog from the Lower Saxon folklore of Groningen province, in the northeastern Netherlands. Like *Hommelstommel*, the headless horse from this region, it also usually appears on dark nights or during grey windless weather with a soft drizzle. Suddenly standing there in front of a lonely wanderer, it almost scared this person into a freeze, blocking the old sandy road, and making its victim seek shelter in an inn, if available. Typical are its huge eyes, described as *the size of plates* and glowing in the dark. Sometimes Borries appeared in the shape of a puddle and it was by some regarded as an appearance of the Devil himself. Meeting Borries, however, usually had the same meaning as seeing the Scandinavian Grim or one of the many black phantom-dogs in England: a "herald of the persons nearby death"; *Dodeverlüder* in the Lower-Saxon language. Finally I came across two stories about several black phantom-dogs, with huge fiery eyes, pulling an iron wagon that made loud spooky noises. In one case four to six dogs were involved.

Böxenwolf

Böxenwolf (Wolf in Pants) is the name for an *Aufhocker*-type Werewolf that hurls itself on people's backs and forces them to carry him while getting heavier and heavier. According to Lecouteux the Böxenwolf *"designates an individual who has made a pact with the devil in return for a belt that allows him to change into a powerful wolf"*. The stories about the Boxenwolf center around Obernkirchen and the locality Krainhagen in the district Schaumburg in Lower Saxony, Germany.

Busebeller

The *Busebeller* (also: *Busabella* or *Busebella*, *Busemann*) is an East Frisian (Northwest Germany) legendary figure and scarecrow for children. He was used to teach children to stay away from dangerous places such as deep waters. Parents threatened their offspring that the Busebeller would "get" or beat them if they went to such locations. Children were often threatened with a Busebeller "eating them up". In addition to its function as a scaremonger, Busebeller is also a local term for the Devil and a weed. The Busebeller is often described as a tall, dark figure. He carries a hook with which he pulls naughty children towards him and a sack in which he (like Krampus) then takes them away. Alternatively, the Busebeller carries a rod with which he beats the children. Cirk Heinrich Stürenburg describes the Busebeller in his *Ostfriesisches Wörterbuch* of 1856 as a *"spukhaftes Phantom, ein gespenstisch verkleidetes Subjekt, Popanz, ein Mensch zum Bangemachen"* (a spooky phantom, a subject in ghostly disguise, threatening figure, a person to scare.) The East Frisian term *Bussmanns* or *Busemanns Förke* (i.e. Busemanns Forke) for the weed *Dreteiliger Zweizahn* (three-lobe beggartick – *Bidens tripartita*) can also be traced back to the figure of the Busebeller/Busemann. According to popular belief, the Busemann ensures that its fruit, which is provided with two awns, can sow itself everywhere in the form of a two-pronged fork.

Origin of the name

The name is possibly a compound of the name *Butz* (or *Butzemann*) and *Beller* (to bark, to make noise). Jan ten Doornkaat Koolman, however considers it also possible that the name component *Buse* is identical with the name component *Busse* – used in the North Frisian Bussemann. Nicolaus Outzen assumes that this word dates back to the Vikings and that it refers to a type of ship called *Busse* or *Búza*. This was originally a warship, with which the Vikings wreaked havoc on the coasts, stealing people and children. The men who rowed this ship were called bussemen, so that the cry *"Der Bussemann kommt!"* ("The Busseman is coming!") frightened the inhabitants of the coasts, but above all caused them to worry about their possessions and loved ones. The Vikings made all kinds of scary noises during their raids. This is also expressed in the verb *bussen*, which means to roar, rush, storm and possibly also goes back to the Viking Age. Finally, the term Busebeller is said to have been used by the ship's crews to refer to a *Wasserkobold* (water-goblin) who was up to mischief in the water. Etymologically closely related are the mythical figures of the Frisian *Puk*, the English *Puk*, the Swedish *Pocker* (Devil), the Norwegian *Puk* or *Draugr* (a malignant water-spirit) and the Icelandic *Púki* or *Púkinn* (little devil).

Butzemann or Putz

The *Butzemann* (also called *Butz, Bütze, Butze, Putz, Boz, Buz, Butzenmann, Buschemann, Bugimann, Bullebeiß, Busemand, Buhmann, Boesman, Bölimann, Böölimaa* or *Böögg*) is a collective name for terrifying demons and ghosts, especially all Goblin- or dwarf-like ones. The figure is mainly known in southern Germany, Austria, Switzerland, but also in northern Germany and Scandinavia, and was greatly feared. In more recent times, it appears mainly as a child fright figure, similar to the "black man", although this was not its original character.

Linguistically, the name is derived from the Middle High German word *bôzen* (to beat, rumble, knock). Another name derivation is the Early New High German *Butze* (larva, mask, popanz, ghost, spectre). Another name for the Butzemann is *Mummelmann,* i.e. "the hooded man". There are also forms composed of these two expressions, such as *Butzenmummel, Mummelputz, Mombotz* (in Hesse) and *Mumpitz.* In the Black Forest region of Baden-Württemberg children are threatened with a *Bogey* named *Butzengraale.* In Fildern and in Mittelstadt they say: *"The Graale is coming",* where *Graale* can be translated as "little gray man". In Poltringen they scare children with the *Butzemäckeler.* A first derivation of Butzemann is documented in writing dates from 1510: in the *Liber vagatorum* the word *Butzeilman* is Germanized as *Zagel* meaning "tail" or "penis." In Anglo-Saxon, the Butzemann is broadly equivalent to *Boggart* or *Bogeyman,* which is often translated as "black man". He comes out of closets at night or scratches at windows; his appearance is described differently, depending on the household. In Tyrol, Austria, it is believed that there lives a *Putz* on almost every Alm (mountain pasture). In *Sagen aus Innsbruck's Umgebung, mit besonderer Berücksichtigung des Zillerthales,* collected and edited by Adolf Ferdinand Dörler, Innsbruck 1895, a veterinarian who visits some herdsman on the Kematner Alm is confronted with a *Putz,* who manifests itself as a poltergeist and is very noisy:

> *"A veterinarian, who otherwise did not believe in any ghost, was once taken to the Kematner Alm. Since he had to work there for a longer time, he had to spend the night in the hut. He had not been asleep long when he was awakened by a terrible noise. The pans were tossed about, the dishes and bowls were being tampered with, in short, there was a "clattering" such as he had never heard before in his life. The herdsmen nodded mysteriously to each other, but the veterinarian wanted to know what was behind all this. They all rose from their camp, built a fire, sat down around it and stuffed their pipes. The noise in the hut had now died down, but the angrier it got outside, the cattle snorted and roared, and there was such a stomping and "G'steaß" that one could believe the devil was loose. Heavy footsteps approached the door of the hut, and the herdsmen thought for a moment that someone was coming in. As the commotion grew, they left the hut to check on the cattle. But the cattle lay quietly in the enclosure. From now on, the veterinarian claimed for sure, never again, that there were no ghosts.*

Since there is a Putz on almost every mountain pasture, especially when the herdsmen have already left, it is advisable, if you want to spend the night undisturbed, to say when entering the hut: "I wear woll di in Gotts Nommen ibernacht'n dearfn!" ("I want to spend the night in God's presence!") Then even the most malicious Putz can't harm you, and you will be able to sleep peacefully all night."

C

Chlungeri

Chlungeri are spirits with the appearance of a humpbacked women in the German speaking regions of Switzerland. They have long nails and crooked noses, are associated with spinning and live in caves. Chlungeri travel about during the Twelve Days to verify if spinners have spun their yarn properly. They are mentioned by Theodor Vernaleken in *Alpensagen: Volksüberlieferungen aus der Schweiz, aus Vorarlberg, Kärnten, Steiermark, Salzburg, Ober-und Niederösterreich* (1858).

D

Dockele

In the folkbelief of Schwaben and Alemannia the *Dockele* or *Schrättele*
(also: *Dochje, Dockeli, Doggi, Toggeli*) is a special kind of *Mahr* or *Alp*
who does more than just exerting pressure on a sleeping person. This
creature is notorious for its painful sucking of nipples to obtain milk. The
male Dockele or Schrättele sucks in cat form the breasts of children, and
even of men, so that they swell up and one can press milk out of them.
Women, on the other hand, have their milk sucked out completely. If a
child drinks at the mother's breast in the Lechrain-region, the mother
usually had a *Trudenfuß* (protective pentagram) made of consecrated wax
lying on the breast, so that the *Trud* (as the creature is also called) does
not steal the child's milk.

– See also *El Broosha*, the Spanish version of a Vampire cat in *Spirit Beings
  in European Folklore, Compendium 4*.

Dachsteinweibl

The *Dachsteinweibl* (Woman of Dachstein) is a spirit that appears as a
small wrinkled witch, covered with warts. She belongs to the folklore
of the Dachstein mountain range (Dachsteingebirge, Dachsteinmassiv
or simply Dachstein) of the northeastern Alps, located in the Austrian
provinces Styria, Salzburg and Upper Austria. When the *Dachsteinweibl*
appears, it is an omen of bad weather or a disaster that is about to occur.
According to legend she was once a high-hearted, wicked cowherd
who was transformed into a hideous phantom-witch and condemned
to wander until Judgment Day. She is mentioned in *Alte Sagen aus dem
Salzburger Land* (1948) by Karl Adrian.

Dialen

In Swiss folklore *Dialen* (sing.: *Diala*; also *Waldfänken*) are a kind
of female Satyrs who live in caves where they sleep on beds of moss.
Despite their goat feet, they are described as very beautiful. They are also
portrayed as friendly and helpful to people.

Donanadl

In the Hochfilzen (Tyrol, Austria) on high Alpine pastures, shepherds report of the *Donanadl* (pl. & sing.), a kind of Alpine spirit. He was generally considered to be good-hearted. He was small in stature, looked like an old man and always wore bad, ragged clothes. Often he appeared alone, but sometimes there were several of them together. If a Donanadl appeared anywhere on the mountain pasture, one could be sure that the cattle were protected from all accidents and that the milk yield was considerably higher than on other mountain pastures that did not enjoy the protection of such a good and benevolent spirit. If snow fell during the summer, it certainly drove the cattle down, from the steep and slippery slopes to safe grassy places. It is for these reasons the owners of such mountain pastures, where Donanadl stayed, were envied by others. These guardian spirits often stayed in the Alpine huts and "ate" with the shepherds, milk farmers and milkmaids, when they were offered food. Sometimes, however, they would suddenly disappear. In the winter time the Donanadl lived in the cribs of the stables. If the fodder lady came late to the stable, she could be sure that these little spirits had already taken care of the cattle and provided them with plenty of fodder. On the slopes in the Salzach valley there used to be many feeding stables, in which one could often see such small creatures. The last Donanadl, however, disappeared when a compassionate milkmaid, who thought she was doing a good deed, wanted to give him a good skirt instead of the miserable smock he was wearing. *"Au weh!"*, he cried, *"jetzt muß auch ich gehen!"* (Oh dear! Now I have to go too!) With that he disappeared and was never seen again. But three days later, in a remote corner of the stable, he is said to have been heard complaining and weeping bitterly. But no one saw him again. The data on the Donanadl were preserved by Adrian Karl in *Alte Sagen aus dem Salzburger Land, Wien, Zell am See*, St. Gallen, 1948.

Donaumandl

According to a legend of Niederösterreich, the *Donaumandl* was a *Wassermann* who dared to go to the shore three times in ancient times. Because the boats-men, who slept directly next to the Danube next to their Zillen (boats), but always pulled the blankets over their heads out of fear, the water-spirit thought that people are beings who only have feet and never dared to land again. The wood artist Ernst Adlsberger carved a life-size Donaumandl out of wood with a chainsaw. It can be admired on the shore of the Wallsee.

Doppelgänger

Doppelgänger is a German word that can best be translated more freely as "your walking copy". The word crossed the borders of German speaking countries, but did not integrate in 'universal English' as the term poltergeist did. It has a less spectacular connotation, but nevertheless raises questions about something that is perhaps even more more mysterious than a stone throwing or furniture moving entity. This is illustrated by the story below (translated from German into English), that took place in Breslau (now Polish Wrocław) and was recorded by Oskar Kobel (1868-1944) in *Legends from Silesia*:

"A Breslauer doctor once had a strange experience. Late in the evening he came home from visiting his patients. There he saw a man walking across the street who looked exactly like him; he wore the same hat and coat and always kept the same pace with him. Whatever he did, he imitated him. Thus they reached the doctor's apartment. The figure approached the front door, unlocked it and closed it again, and, judging by the sound, climbed the stairs. When it reached the top, it turned on the light. The doctor, however, did not enter his house, but instead climbed a tree that stood opposite his window and saw his landlady enter the room, chat unselfconsciously with the figure, set out the supper, and how the latter (his Doppelgänger) finally went to bed and turned out the light. Now the doctor ran to a nearby friend, told him everything and stayed with him overnight. The following morning someone knocked at the door of his friend's house. The doctor's landlady appeared and wailed, "For God's sake, think the doctor is dead. The ceiling broke off during the night and fell on the bed!" She did not believe all the friend's assurances and said, "But I spoke to him just last night!" At last the man believed dead appeared, and now all three of them went to his apartment to solve the case. In particular, they investigated who the man might have been who was the spitting image of the doctor and who had gone to sleep last night. The debris of the ceiling was removed and an empty bed was found…"

Der Mann mit dem Sack.

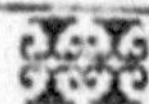

Ich heisse der Mann mit dem Sack/	Die stettigs schreyen/ greinen/ zannen/
Darein ich denn die Kinder zwack/	Mit denen lauff ich dalb von dannen.

Hör Mann komb einher in mein Hauß/
Trag mir das wainend Kind darauß/
Thu es in deinen Sack einschieben/
Ich kan es gewißlich nie mehr lieben/
Trinck ich es daß es nie mehr dürst/
So ich ihm strele oder bürst/
Ich bade es mit allem fleiß
Ich geb ihm Muß vnd ander Speiß/
Ich zieh es auß/ ich leg es nider/
Ich heb es von sein Beth auff wider/
So will es eben schweigen nit/
Drumb nimb es nur fahr hin darmit.

Ibo her/ es ist mir eben recht/
In meinen Sack ichs schiebe schlecht/
Die Kinder alle/ die stets greinen/
Vnd immerzu nur schreyen/ beinen/
Ich hab schon darein vil gesteckt/
Sihe wie manchs den Kopff außher reckt/
Die Füß der gleichen vnd die Händ/
Ich will sein losen an der Wänd/
Wo ich dann hör ein zannend Kind/
Das schieb ich in mein Sack geschwind/
Drumb sey ein jedes Kind fein frumb/
Daß es in meinen Sack nie kumb.

Zu Augspurg/ bey Abraham Bach Brieffmaler/ auffm Creuz.

Doppelsauger

In eastern Germany, the Wends, who occupied the land between the Elbe and Oder rivers, used the word *Doppelsauger, Dubblesüger* or *Dubbelsuger* (all meaning: "double sucker") to describe a creature that could manifest itself as either a vampiric Revenant or etheric energy-Vampire. A Doppelsauger is created when a mother allows her child to breast- feed long after it should have been weaned. Eventually the time would come when that person would one day be near death. When that happened, a gold coin had to be placed in his or her mouth – before dying – to prevent him/her from rising as a Revenant. If the person died before the coin could be placed, some sort of propping device had to be employed to keep the chin from resting against the chest. This preventative measure had to be taken to see to it that the deceased did not rise up after dying. In either event, after the body has been removed from the home, the threshold of the front door had to be removed and replaced. This would prevent the Doppelsauger from being able to find and return to its old home. But despite these precautions the Doppelsauger was still able to drain the life-energy from its victims, starting first with its own family before moving on to others, and without ever leaving its grave. The only way to destroy a Doppelsauger was by striking it in the back of the neck with a spade.

Drak

The *Drak* (also called *Fürdrak, Drakel, Alf, Stöpke* and *Glüswanz*) is a flying house spirit. Although it looks like a dragon, it has nothing in common with it. Probably the name is not derived from Drakon, but from the English *mandrake* or *mandragora*. He is native to northern and central Germany, as well as to neighboring Slavic regions, and brings grain, corn, butter, bacon, ham and gold to the farmer through the chimney. Therefore, many wealthy farmers were also said to have a Drak in their service. Most of these spirits have proper names, such as *Steppchen, Alf, Langschwanz, Kortwämsken, Glüsteert* (glowing tail), *Tragerl, Federhänschen* and the like. The names are mostly similar to those given to *Goblins*, but the Drak is not a Goblin, even though it shares many characteristics with them. The appearance of a Drak is that of a small dragon with a glowing tail, with which it travels through the air. In eastern Pomerania he is known as *Alf* and in some places as a fiery snake with a duck's head or as a glowing cauldron with a tail. He can also change his shape and appear as a fiery meadow tree with a broad

Bussebella or Der Mann mit dem Sack (17th century) by Abraham Bach, Sr.

head, a fiery sack of grain or other things of this kind, but he can also change into animals, for example into a gray goose or a wet chicken. With the help of certain formulas, you can force him to discard some of his treasures. Examples of such formulas are *"Halb Part"* or *"lat fallen, wat nich dien hört"* (drop what does not belong to you). The second formula also explains where the Drak gets his treasures from; by simply stealing them from elsewhere. He always demands good rations from his "owner". It is probable that the belief in the Drak arose from observations of meteorites, shooting stars, northern lights, or the firelight of a fireplace.

Drud

A *Drud* or *Drude* (masculine form: *Druderer*) is a special kind of – usually female – Alp in Bavarian folklore. It was not regarded as a nature-spirit, but as an etheric projection of the double of someone at whose baptism a mistake was made. The name derives from the ancient word *trudan* (to tread, or press). She sits on the chest of sleeping people at night and causes nightmares as well as anxiety and shortness of breath. A Drud is doomed to have to find a victim to squeeze every night. Adults, children and pets are haunted by her. For this purpose, her double detaches from the body and can enter a room as a spirit through the smallest crevices and keyholes and subsequently appear in different forms; as a cat, or a feather, for example. A Drud is a normal human being, e.g. a servant or a landlady. A woman who has to practice this Drud curse knows about it, but hides it from the people around her. She can be freed from this curse only if someone provides her with a tame pet, which she then squeezes to death. To ward off and unmask Drudes there are several means and methods:
• The *Drudenkreuz* or *Drudenfuß* is a pentagonal star placed at the foot of the bedstead or above the door to ward off the Drud. So-called *Drudensteine* (drud-stones), also called *Hühnergötter* (chicken gods) are also said to have a repelling effect. These are pebbles with a natural hole in it. They were hung in the roof truss of the house for defense.
• The *Drudenkraut* was a wreath of *lycopodium* (ground pine or creeping cedar), which had to be twisted from a single vine and nailed above the stable door to keep the Drud out of the stable. Also a broom, leaning upside down against the stable door, does not let the Drud in.
• If you slept on your right side or got into bed with the right foot first, the Drud could not harm you.

• You could unmask a Drud if you ordered her to come back the next
  day to borrow something. She would then be forced to do so and be
  the first person to knock on the door the next morning. The Drud thus
  unmasked must then be convinced to desist from attacking the victim
  in the future. Walpurgis Night was also called Drudennacht, when
  witches and Drudes danced on the crossroads. A poem about the Drud,
  in local dialect, pressing the air out of its victim, reads as follows:

"D'Drud hout mi druckt,
af da Brust is ma gsessn,
hout mi druckt wöi niat gscheit.
D'Luft is ma wegbliebn,
druckt hot's di ganz Zeit.
Wenns druckt höit nu weida,
höit i brauchat bal an Sarg."

E

Ebajalg

In Estonian folklore the *Ebajalg* or *Tuulispask* (also: *Tuulispea, Tuulepööris, Tuulevood*) is a malicious spirit which acts as a destructive whirlwind. The term Ebajalg (pl.: *Ebajalaks*) is especially common in the southern part of Estonia. These wind-spirits are described as having great strength, often leading to destruction. In Estonian folklore, it was a common belief that a meteorological phenomenon like a whirlwind could be caused by the soul of a person – usually a witch – who had temporarily left the body, or less often by the soul of a dead person. The Ebajalg could also be a creature made or sent by a witch, or the Devil. Strong whirlwinds could damage the grain, hay, etc., but they could also bring bad luck, illness and other evil. They were warded off by magic spells. A common spell was to throw a bladed weapon at the whirlwind, in the hope that its body would be injured by the blow. The Ebajalg or Tuulispask is often believed to be a female. In a few cases they are regarded as male, though. In Virus, such a *Wirlwind-woman* is often called *old Finnish woman*. It is believed that such a witch can turn people into a wind vane as well, thus trapping them. Although throwing a blade at an Ebajalg will cause wounds in the etheric and remote physical body of the witch, it could also save the bewitched person. When the soulless body of a person who has become a whirlwind is found and turned over, the soul cannot enter until the body is in its former state. The motive of the Ebajalg is to plunder crops from the field, plundering piles of hay, stealing dried laundry, etc.; in short, she plunders whatever she likes. If people try to hinder her, she fetches the clothes and hair of the hinderers, or pushes them the ground, *"so that their bones rattle"*. The Ebajalg is usually invisible to the viewer. It is known, however, that the figure of a witch appears when someone scolds or angers the Wind-spirit. In such a case, the ugly figure of the Ebajalg is seen to stare back at the angry person.

Eismanndl(e)

The *Eismanndl(e)* (Ice man) or *Eismännlein* (Little ice man) is a *Kobold* that lives on the snow-covered peaks and glaciers of the Tyrolean Alps. The spirit is described in detail in *Mythen und Sagen Tirols* (1857) by

Johann Nepomuk Ritter von Alpenburg. The text below is compiled from Ritter von Alpenburg's translated notes on the Eismanndle:

These mountain spirits are also known as *Eismanndl, Ferner – Norggen* (Glacier men), *Fernerzwergl* (Glacier dwarfs), *Kösmanndln* (Glacier men; *Kös* or *Käs* is also glacier), and finally *Wettertermacher* (Weather makers) and *die Alten* (the Old Ones). The Eismanndl looks aged, with snow-white hair and a white beard, both of which fall long, even the beard still touches the ground. The weather-beaten face is serious and wrinkled, the blue eyes look over the eagle nose calm, sure and firm. The robe is gray-green, like old tree lichens, from afar also playing in the yellow-green; a *Wetterhut* (a hat that protects against the weather) with bent brim shades over the face. The normal shape of the Eismanndle is dwarfish, but its strength is enormous. He is capable of assuming the body of a giant, and of transforming itself into whatever it wants. It are the Eismanndl who push the glaciers forwards and backwards, who, for their own amusement, draw shingle-like figures and huge arabesques on the snow in the midst of the most horrible snowstorms over long stretches of snow on broad slopes; they cause the so-called *Schneegrugeln* (snow-ruining), in which, in the hottest summer days, snow and hail suddenly cover green alpine valleys over a wide area, thundering without preceding lightning. They, the ice men, cause the frightening *Fernerbillen* (barking of the glacier), and excite the rolling noise in the interior of the glacier.

The abodes of the ice men are ice crevasses that are connected to each other over long distances under the glaciers. The little ice men like to sit on remote peaks and rocky outcrops of the high alpine region, and look with sensible seriousness at the surrounding infinite world of ice needles and ice pyramids staring upwards, let themselves be danced around by misty figures and – as *Wettertermacher* – form clouds into solid balls. They build and heap cloud from cloud, compress them, tear them apart, blow them into flakes, weave them into veils and blankets of fog, send them as high-altitude smoke over all distances, brew weather, hurl hail, send avalanches down into the depths. They build glistening snow bridges over abysses, lead the good safely over them, cause bad people to fall abruptly. That ethical element, which is inherent in the *Saligen* (female Alpine spirits), to be helpful to all good and fearful and frightful to all loose, also pervades the ice-men. They protect innocence and punish and avenge wickedness and crime. They do not grant the fugitive villain a free place, they chase him through weather and wind, and plunge him down into the cold ice night of horrible distant crevasses in death and damnation. But the lost ones, who are not evil-doers, they point to the right path.

Ekerken

According to J. Vallick in his work *Von Zauberern, Hexen und Unholden*, *Ekerken* (Squirrel) is a strange hybrid of an *Incubus* with a pubic hair fetish and a *Goblin* who helps out on a farm in Herzogtum Kleve (the Duchy of Cleves) in Germany. His duties include feeding the horses as well as punishing negligent fellows. At night, however, he lies with the maids to pluck their *"secret and hidden hair"*, but since he is mostly invisible, one usually sees only a small hand. Due to the later witch trials, the Ekerken is called *Incubus of the serfs*, which is probably due to his nocturnal habits and it is said that he could only be driven out if the respective woman was burned as a witch. The Brothers Grimm wrote of him:

"Bei dem Dorf Elten, eine halbe Meile von Emmerich im Herzogtum Kleve, war ein Geist, den die gemeinen Leute Ekerken zu nennen pflegten. Er sprang auf der Landstraße umher und neckte und plagte die Reisenden auf alle Weise. Etliche schlug er, andere warf er von den Pferden ab, anderen kehrte er Karrn und Wagen unterst zuoberst. Man sah aber mit Augen von ihm nichts als eine menschlich gestaltete Hand."

(Near the village of Elten, half a mile from Emmerich in the Duchy of Cleves, there was a ghost whom the common people used to call Ekerken. He jumped around on the road and teased and tormented the travelers in all kinds of ways. He beat some of them up, threw others off their horses, and turned their carts and wagons upside down. But with one's eyes one saw nothing of him but the shape of a human hand.)

Elbst

The *Elbst* is a coiling serpent-like creature in a mountain lake near Seelisberg (Switzerland). It sometimes appears in the form of a moss-covered log or a drifting island, luring careless people into the depths. At night it comes ashore and kills livestock. It is also known to take on the form of a dragon or black sow. Its appearance is a herald of bad weather.

Elementals or Elementalgeister

According to Paracelsus, human beings live in the *exterior* elements and
the *Elementals* live in the *interior* elements. The latter have dwellings
and clothing, manners and customs, languages and governments of
their own, in the same sense as the bees have their queens, and herds
of animals their leaders. Elementals are beings described in occult and
alchemical works from around the time of the European Renaissance,
and particularly elaborated in the 16th century works of Paracelsus, who
wrote the following about them:

> *"They live in the four elements: the Nymphæ in the element of water, the
> Sylphes in that of the air, the Pigmies in the earth, and the Salamanders in
> fire. They are also called Undinæ, Sylvestres, Gnomi, Vulcani, &etc. Each
> species moves only in the element to which it belongs, and neither of them
> can go out of its appropriate element, which is to them as the air is to us,
> or the water to fishes; and none of them can live in the element belonging
> to another class. To each Elemental being the element in which it lives is
> transparent, invisible and respirable, as the atmosphere is to ourselves."*
> (– *Philosophia Occulta*, translated by Franz Hartmann)

In modern times the names of the Elementals got standardized as
Gnomes, Undines, Sylphs, and *Salamanders*, corresponding to the
four Empedoclean elements of antiquity: Earth, Water, Air, and Fire,
respectively. According to Paracelsus, the Elemental spirits are very
similar in nature to humans; like humans, they possess a physical body
and an astral body. Their body, however, consists of "subtle flesh", which
enables them to exist both in their Element and in the human world:

> *"The Elementals are not spirits, because they have flesh, blood and bones;
> they live and propagate offspring; they cant and talk, act and sleep, &etc.,
> and consequently they cannot be properly called 'spirits.'. They are beings
> occupying a place between men and spirits, resembling men and as well as
> spirits, resembling men and women in their organization and form, and
> resembling spirits in the rapidity of their locomotion."*
> (– *Philosophia Occulta*, translated by Franz Hartmann)

Unlike Agrippa von Nettesheim, Paracelsus thinks the body of Elemental
spirits do not consist of the respective element, but is more subtle, so that
the spirits can move through their element. Moreover, the Elemental

spirits are not only similar to humans in appearance and diet, but also live in an orderly society and pursue work. The main difference between humans and elemental spirits, according to Paracelsus, is that spirits do not possess a soul and thus, despite their longevity, have no share in Eternal Life. However, they can receive a soul if they enter into marriage with humans, understood by Paracelsus as a sacrament, and beget children. Therefore the Elemental spirits are eager to seduce humans. Especially in his description of the female water-spirits he connects here to the folkloric narrative motif of the marriages of *Fairies*, especially where it concerns female spirits or Nymphs, or certain East-European water-spirits, or Spanish Nymph-like creatures.

Elwetritsch

The *Elwetritsch* (also *Elwetrittche, Elwedritsch, Ilwedritsch*; pl. *Elwetritsche(n)*; in Latin *bestia palatinensis*) is a bird-like mythical creature, reported in southwestern Germany and especially in the Palatinate. The Elwetritsch is to be regarded as the local equivalent of mythical creatures from other regions, such as the Bavarian *Wolpertinger* or the Thuringian *Rasselbock*. Elwetritsch are described as being chicken-like in the broadest sense. However, it is said that they can hardly use their wings, which is why they have to stay mainly in the undergrowth or under the vines. Sometimes Elwetritsche are depicted with deer antlers, and their beaks are often depicted as very long. Elwetritche are believed to have originated from crossbreeds of chickens, ducks, and geese with *Goblins* and *Elves* living in the forest. As poultry descendants, they naturally lay eggs, but because of their forest-spirit origins, their eggs grow during the incubation period. Eggs in different sizes and stages of maturation are artistically represented at the Elwetritschenbrunnen in Neustadt an der Weinstraße.

Elves

Elves are humanoid mythical nature-spirits from Germanic and Nordic mythology and folklore. In medieval Germanic-speaking cultures, Elves seem to have been generally regarded as beings with magical powers and supernatural beauty, ambivalent/shy toward ordinary people and capable of helping or hindering them. However, the details of these beliefs have varied considerably across time and space and flourished in both pre-

Christian and Christian cultures. Literature from the English Renaissance brought Elves together with the *Fairies* of Romanesque culture, making these terms somewhat interchangeable today.

The word *Elf* comes from the Proto-Germanic *albaz*, next to *albiz* or *alboz*, and Old Norse *alfr*. For the relationship of the root *alb* two approaches are considered reasonable: like Old High German *elbiʒ*, Old Norse *elptr*, Russian *lébed* (лебедь) "swan" and Latin *albus* "white", to the Indo-European *albh* (to shine, to be white), in the sense of "light figure, white misty figure", from which also comes the Latin *albus* "white". Corresponding terms in the Germanic languages are:

Old Norse: *Alfr,* pl. *Alfar, Ahd, Alb*
Gothic: *Albs,* pl. *Albeis*
Icelandic: *Álfar, Álfafólk* and *Huldufólk* (hidden people), *Högfolk.*
Danish: *Elver, Elverfolk* or *Alfer*
Norwegian: *Alv, Alven, Alver, Alvene, Alvefolket*
Swedish: *Alfer, Alver* or *Älvor*
English: *Elf, Elfen, Elven* (from Old English: *Ælf*); English feminine is "*Elfina/Elfa*", "*Elfinas/Alfas*" (pl.)
Dutch: *Elf, Elfen, Elfjes, Elven, Alven* (from Middle Dutch: *Alf*)
German: from English: *Elf* (m), *Elfe* (f), *Elfen* (pl.). The masculine *Elb* is reconstructed by Jacob Grimm, *Deutsches Wörterbuch*, who rejects Elfe as a recent Anglicism (in 1830). *Elb* (m, pl. *Elbe* or *Elben)* is a reconstructed term, while *Elbe* (f) is attested in Middle High German. *Alb, Alp* (m), pl. *Alpe* has the meaning of "*Incubus*" (Old High German *Alp,* pl. *Alpî* or *Elpî)*

The Old Indo-European *rbhúh* gives us a clue about the original nature of the Elves as the rbhúh was a class of mythical craftsmen, with a basic meaning of "skillful, industrious" (related to Latin *labor* = work), with a motivation of *albaz* as "craftsman, magical helper," since Elves, along with *dwarves*, are also considered skilled blacksmiths. The German word *Elfen* goes back to Old German *Alb* or *Elb* in the singular or *Elbe* or *Elber* in the plural. From the feminine form "Elbe" the plural "Elben" was additionally formed in the 16th century. In the 18th century the word forms were displaced by the English form "Elves". In the Icelandic *Snorra Edda* of 1220, Elves are linked to the *Aesir,* especially to the fertility god *Freyr,* and a distinction is made between light Elves (*Ljósálfar*) and dark Elves (*Dökkálfar),* names that strongly reflect their disposition:

*"Sá er einn staðr þar, er kallaðr er Álfheimr. Þar byggvir fólk
þat, er Ljósálfar heita, en Dökkálfar búa niðri í jörðu, ok eru
þeir ólíkir þeim sýnum ok miklu ólíkari reyndum. Ljósálfar
eru fegri en sól sýnum, en Dökkálfar eru svartari en bik."*

(There is a place called Álfheim. There dwells the people called the Light
Alves. But the Dark Alves dwell down in the earth, and are unequal
in face, and still more unequal in their pursuits. The Light Alves are
fairer than the sun in face; but the Dark Alves are blacker than pitch.)

Other authors mention a hierarchy in which the *Aesir* come in the first
place, the *Elves* in the second and the *dwarves* in the last. Still others place
the Elves close to the dwarves, since *Álfr* is in fact a word part of some
dwarven names, e.g. *Álfr, Gandálfr, Vindálfr,* etc. The dwarf *Alberich* from
the *Nibelungenlied* is a good example. Only one author places Elves near the
giants. A demonic side of the Elves lies in the German word *Hexenschuss,*
which is a transfer of the older expression *Albenschuss,* as well as the word
Albtraum (Nightmare), which is still in use today. However, there are many
more positive portrayals of the Elves than negative ones. In the heroic saga
of *Wieland the Blacksmith,* Wieland is described as a leader and compatriot
of the *Alben,* which had to do with his skill as a blacksmith. In the ancestral
line of King Harald Schönhaar, names derived from the term *Alben* also
appear (Álfr, Álfgeirr, Gandálfr, Álfhild). *Álf* was for a long time common
as part of a name in Norse names. Old English poetry uses *ælfsciene* as well
as *albenschön* for beautiful.

Emuu

Emuu, a variant of the ancient word *Emo* (mother), is an Eastern Finnish
and Karelian *nature-spirit* that "gives birth" to or creates a certain plant
or animal species and is responsible for the functioning and care of the
species. Hunters often used spells to ask these "ancestral parents" of
animal species for hunting luck. It was thought that the ancestor would
decide to whom it would give its offspring as prey. Scholars from the
Finnish folklorist Christfried Ganander (1741-1790) onward have used
the word Emuu for these creatures, and the word also appears in recorded
spells. But other variations of the word "mother" and other words
meaning "mother" or "parent" were also used to designate these spirits.
Some ancestors of plants and animals are known by name:

Hillervo	– Mother of otters
Hongatar/Hongotar	– Mother of bears, protector of honey
Höyheneukko	– Mother of game birds
Juoletar	– also Mother of Otters
Juonetar	– Mother of deer
Kati	– Mother of trees
Kytöläinen	– Mother of worms
Käreitär	– Mother of foxes
Käres	– Mother of snakes
Käärämöinen	– Mother of lizards
Lemmes	– Mother of alders
Laus	– Mother of reindeer and elk
Lovetar	– Mother of wolves
Lukutar	– Mother of the black fox
Mammotar	– Mother of worms and the Mother of snakes
Nokeainen	– possibly Mother of a sable, weasel or beaver
Tapiotar	– Mother of birds
Tuheroinen	– Mother of waterfowl, who also helped to catch wolverines and otters
Tyytikki	– Mother of squirrels
Ulappala	– Mother of dogs
Äimätär	– Mother of wolves

Erdhenne

The *Erdhenne* (earth hen), also called *Coluber domesticus*, *Erdhühnlein*, *Erdglucke*, *Erdglutsch* and *Herdhendl*, is a domestic spirit from the Alpine region, the Oberpfalz and Bavaria. The voice of this spirit is said to come from the ground or from a dark corner of the parlor, and to sound like the gurgle or peep of a hen leading her chicken hens, which gave it its name. The Erdhenne, like the *Unke* (toad spirit) or the *Hausotter* (home otter), is said to be a benign guardian spirit that warns the inhabitants of the house of impending misfortune. It was once said that whoever saw the Erdhenne would have to die within the same year. Johann Andreas (1785-1852) wrote in his *Bayerischen Wörterbuch* (Bavarian dictionary):

"Das Erdhuenlein, Phänomen, das sich nach der Theorie alter Weiber des Nachts gern in den Kinderstuben wie ein runder, heller Schein sehen läßt, in dessen Mitte etwas dunkleres zu seyn scheint. Vermutlich von dem

durch sogenannte Buzenscheiben einfallenden Mondlichte erzeugt."

(The little Erdhenne, phenomenon, which, according to the theory of old women, can be seen at night in the children's rooms like a round, bright glow, in the middle of which something darker seems to be. Probably produced by the moonlight falling through so-called crown glasses.)

An old folktale of Tirol is less skeptical about the creature: A long time ago, an Erdhenne stayed at a Baumgarten (orchard) in the Gerlostal. It happened several times a year that when people sat together in the parlor in the evening, they heard a clucking sound coming from the floor. They knew that the spirit was announcing itself in order to warn of a danger. But what was even more important was that it always answered questions readily. Once, the spirit clucked particularly long and hard, and the people were already afraid, because they thought a great disaster was imminent. Then the farmer asked the ghost what was wrong. *"Look in the old kitchen!"*, was the answer, and at the same time the clucking stopped. When the people looked in the old kitchen, they noticed *gschmödete* (hay fire) in the hay barrel and the smell of burning hay was already spreading throughout the room. The damp hay had ignited itself. Thanks to the warning of the Erdhenne, the developing fire was discovered in time and the farm was saved from a conflagration.

*"In Das Große Deutsche Sagenbuch the Erdhühnchen is portrait
as a herald of disease or death, depending on its peculiar behavior:
In Osterland, there is a lot of talk about the Erdhühnchen. As
Lachtäubchen (Eurasian collared doves) or even as big starlings, they
run through the sick rooms and announce an approaching death
with their cluck, cluck! According to other legends, the Erdhühnchen
appears eight to fourteen days before a death and looks like an
old ash-gray, shaggy hen with a short neck. At midnight it makes
an opening in the floorboards of the living room. If it only gurgles
and flutters nine times, a member of the house becomes fatally ill;
but if it throws up a mound of earth, someone must soon die."*

F

Fänggen

In the folklore of Tyrol and Graubünden (Switserland) the *Fänggen* (Sing. *Fangg*; also *Fangga, Fanggin, Wildfangg, böses Waldweib*) are female forest and tree demons and *Urriesen* (primeval giants). They have dirty long black hair in which bits of bark dangle, black eyes that sometimes glow like embers and emit flashes of lightning; their voices are harsh and blaring and sound like men's voices. Their clothes consist of skirts made of wild cat fur, tree bark and the skins of foxes and other animals. The Fangg is gruesome, huge, hairy all over the body, the face distorted, the mouth stretched from one ear to the other. This demon is always hungry and prefers to eat children's meat. Therefore the children are not allowed to go outside in the evening. Fanggen were thought to live in isolated communities and those who shared the same forest were bound to this forest, which reminds of the Greek Hamadryads. If the forest was felled, they disappeared; if a tree died, or was cut down, of which a Fangga bore the name, her existence was also gone.

The Fänggen mainly inhabited a large primeval forest in the Urgthal, between Landeck and Ladis and another forest, called the "Bannwald", at the Pillerberg in the Oberinnthal. There were few male Fänggen. The children these fathered, usually daughters, were placed by their mothers with peasant families to protect them from their hideous fathers. These daughters worked hard but never integrated because they did not want to convert to Christianity.

Fenixmännlein

Fenixmännlein (*Fenixmännel, Fenskemännel, Fenisleute*) is the name given to a group of Silesian dwarf-like demons, who are said to be related to the earth-spirits and dwarves, as they pursue the same occupations. Like most nature-spirits, they live near humans and try to exchange the children of humans with their changelings. Rarely are they malicious. Fenixmännlein are described as being on average larger than a dwarf but smaller than a human, suggesting a kinship with *Walen*. They are said to live in groups and make their homes inside hills and bushes.

Feurige Hund

In Tyrol at some locations a ghostly *Feurige Hund* (Fiery Dog) is seen
and feared by the locals. In the district Außerfern at the Fuchsmühle "auf
der Kög", there is a fiery dog that always jumps back and forth across
the brook at night (recorded in: *Der Feurige Hund I: aus Reutte. Metzler,
Sagen aus dem Außerfern: Zeitschrift für Österreichische Volkskunde 23,
1917*). If you go from the Plansee towards Reutte, you have to descend
down a rather steep slope; this part of the road is called the "Roßrügge".
The carters don't like to drive up there during the day, and even less at
night! For more than one person has seen a fiery dog lying on the road
there in the deep dark of night, which did not let them pass until the bell
rang (recorded by Will-Erich Peuckert in *Ostalpensagen,* Berlin 1963).

Feurige Männer

In Bavarian folklore the *Feurige Männer* (Fiery Men), also called
Landsknechte, are ghostly beings. They look like people and are dressed
like them. Fire comes out of their mouths. Their back is hollowed out like
a cavity, from which the fire breaks out. With it they light the way for the
people going home. The Feurige Männer are poor souls who have to suffer
because they have moved *Grenzsteine* ("boundary stones", indicating the
border between the fields of two landowners) in life. As a punishment,
they often have to carry these boundary stones around, always shouting,
"Wou dou i den hi?" (Where do I put it?) If a person answers, *"Dahin, wo
du ihn genommen hast"* (To where you took it) then they are redeemed. In
the past, Feurige Männer were often seen, and every peasant had certainly
seen one of them once in his or her lifetime. One did not need to be afraid
of them, if one did not offend them. They would light up your home and
escort you to your front door for a small fee. But if one does not give them
what they were promised, they lead the person away through the air or
set fire to his house. If a Fiery Man approaches, one must not run away,
otherwise they will sit on one's back and lead one astray. But if one offends
the spirit with the bad word *"Geltenscheisser"*, then he avenges himself by
Aufhugeln (lifting up) and seducing.

An Austrian story

In former times it often happened that fiery figures appeared to fishermen
who were fishing on the river Salzach near Laufen, below Salzburg,
on so-called "Lässel" or "Losnächte". At first they were as small as

candlelight, like *Will-o'-the-wisps*, but gradually they grew larger and
larger, finally growing into giants. Just as they grew, they gradually would
become smaller and smaller after that, until they disappeared from view
altogether. This last narrative was preserved in: *Salzburger Volkssagen, Bd.
2*, Wien/Pest/Leipzig, 1880, by R. von Freisauff.

Feuerputz or Feuermann

The *Feuerputz*, also called *Brünnling, Feurputz, Glühender, Züsler*,
but most commonly *Feuermann*, is a fiery Phantom. Although this
figure can appear in many guises, it is described as predominantly
anthropomorphic. The most common guises are a burning, glowing
skeleton, a black man in a pillar of fire, a fiery horseman, a burning
plowman, or a fireball (very bright meteor). In the *Sächsischen
Weltchronik* it is mentioned that the guards of two neighboring castles
saw such a fireball, which is said to have shone like a torch, as it went
from the wall of one castle across a field to the other. This is said to have
happened in the year 1120. Renward Cysat, a Lucerne historian, is said
to have once encountered a Fire Man and writes that he, in the company
of some others, saw four *Züslern* moving at a location where no houses
stood, nor people would walk, carrying lights. Cysat describes the
Züsler, as they are called in Switzerland, as skeletons, with flames leaking
through their bones, eye sockets etc.:

> *"Füwr durch den Lyb, durch die Sytten, Rippen,*
> *Augen, Mund, Nasen und Ohren usschlahe"*

> (Fire raging through the body, through the
> bones, ribs, eyes, mouth, nose and ears)

Feuermänner (pl.) are souls that have sinned in life and have to atone
for it after death. Their fiery appearance is therefore their purgatory. The
nature of the guilt these souls have incurred can vary greatly. According
to researcher Herbert Freudenthal (in *Das Feuer im Deutschen Glauben
und Brauch*, Berlin und Leipzig 1931) They could have been shopkeepers
with false weights and measures, fraudulent orphans' guardians,
dishonest administrators, forgers of documents, perjurers, violent bailiffs
and officials, unjust judges, unscrupulous merchants, highwaymen,
arsonists, quarrelsome people, thieves, church desecrators, suicide

committers and murderers, unrepentantly executed people, all of whom
are followed by a curse into the grave. Cysat, on the other hand, mentions
as the primary sin that of taking advantage of one's neighbor by plowing
away or moving the *Grenzstein* (boundary stone), which separated one's
property from one's neighbors. Feuermänner try to achieve redemption,
which leads to the fact that they behave friendly towards people and even
illuminate the way for them with the glow of their burning body. Already
a simple *"Vergelt's Gott"* (God's retribution) is to be sufficient in order to
redeem the Feuermann.

Flodder

The *Flodder*, also called *Flodderduivel* (Flodder devil) is a tormenting
spirit from West-Brabant folklore. The creature resides in ditches,
ponds and along dikes. From the water it lurks at the shore, looking for
nocturnal walkers, in order to jump on their back and then lets itself be
carried along like a leaden burden. As soon as the victim reaches the
inhabited world, the demon suddenly disappears. Flodder gets its name
from the sound it makes when it emerges from the water. The creature
is related to *Lange Wapper* and *Kludde* from Flanders, *Blauwe Gerrit*
from the Dutch Veluwe-region, the *Ossaert* from Zeeland and Flanders,
and the *Stoep* from the Dutch province of Gelderland. The German
Aufhocker and the *Bahkauv* from Aachen also show similarities. Flodder's
appearance manifests itself somewhere between a spirit and a beast. Not
material, but visible. So the Flodder is untouchable, but nevertheless
weighs enormously on the back of the victim. In some Brabant legends
the tease appears in the form of a large, black dog. Sometimes this
tormentor would try to get its victim to fall into the water in order to
drown him or her. Sometimes it would end a ride on the back of its victim
by giving this person a lick across the face.

Föhrweibele

Föhrweibele is the name of a local spirit who pretended to be a *Weibele*
(little woman), and who inhabited the Föhr, close to the Wenterhofe in
Unterinu (Tyrol), for a long time. Especially on Christmas night and on
Three Kings (Epiphany), she caused a hellish spectacle and startled people
and cattle out of their sleep. At first, the witch went haunting a stable,
but when she was successfully chased out of there, she settled on the dill

above it and continued to haunt there. Finally, a devout Franciscan priest succeeded in banishing her for good. Her story was collected by Johann Adolf Heyl in *Volkssagen, Bräuche und Meinungen aus Tirol*, Brixen, 1897.

Frau Gauden

Frau Gauden, also known as *Frau Gode, Frau Gaur, Fru Goden, Frau Wohl*, and *Mutter Gauerken*, is a being from the folkloric tradition of Mecklenburg. She is said to be cursed, because she expressed to prefer to eternally hunt rather than go to Heaven, and her daughters, who expressed the same desire, were transformed into small dogs who either pull her wagon or sled, or serve as hunting dogs. She visits the homes of humans during the Twelve Nights of Christmas and punishes the lazy while sometimes rewarding the virtuous or those who help her.

Frau Holle

Frau Holle, *Holda* or *Hulda* is one of many supernatural female beings in folk belief, who is in contact with the underworld from which she originates. The nature of these types of beings ranges from helpful and kind to punitive and harsh. Holda is called *The White Lady* but also *The Black Grandmother*, this has similarities to the fairy tale about Frau Holle (*Vrouw Holle* in Dutch). Holle is a death goddess. There are other names, such as *Vrou-Elde, Eastre, Fri, Fria, Fricka, Friga, Frige, Frigg, Gode, Ostara, Fri(a), Frig, Bertha, (Frau) Gode, (Frau) Wode, Frija, Holda, Huda, Huld(r)a, Nerthus, Frea, Eastre, Bertha, Brechta, Frau Venus, Harfer, Herke, Hold(e), Holl(e), Hulle* or *Frigga*.

The name *Holle* is thought to originate from the German *huld* (gracious, friendly, sympathetic, grateful), Middle High German *hulde*, Old High German *huldī* (friendliness). Quite similar to the Danish and Swedish *huld* (fair, kindly, gracious) or *hyld* (secret, hidden), Icelandic *hollur* (faithful, dedicated, loyal), Middle English *hold, holde*, Old English *hold* (gracious, friendly, kind, favorable, true, faithful, loyal, devout, acceptable, pleasant), to Proto-Germanic *hulþaz* (favourable, gracious, loyal), proto-Indo-European *kel-* (to tend, incline, bend, tip). The name *Hludana* is found in five Latin inscriptions: three from the lower Rhine (Corpus Inscriptionum Latinarum XIII 8611, 8723, 8661), one from Münstereifel (CIL XIII, 7944) and one from Beetgum, Frisia (CIL XIII, 8830), all dating from 197 AD - 235 AD. Many attempts have been made to interpret this name. Marija Gimbutas names *Hulda* (or *Holda*, *Holla*, *Holle*) as having originally been an ancient Germanic supreme goddess who predates most of the Germanic pantheon, including deities such as Odin, Thor, Freya, and Loki, continuing traditions of pre-Indo-European Neolithic Europe. As Christianity slowly replaced Scandinavian paganism during the Early Middle Ages, many of the old customs were gradually lost, or assimilated into Christian tradition. By the end of the High Middle Ages, Scandinavian paganism was almost completely marginalized and blended into rural folklore, in which the character of *Frau Hulda* eventually survived.

Like Perchta, Frau Holle was seen as the leader of the *Wild Hunt*. Between December 23 and January 5, she checks whether people were industrious or lazy during the previous year. She is associated with the Nerthus described by Tacitus, and she is considered to be the most important person in the world. Frau Holle makes it snow by patting out her pillow; compare this to Frigg from Nordic mythology: she spins the clouds. When it snows, people in Hesse say: *"Frau Holle shakes up her bed"*. In the Netherlands this Holle association with snowflakes is also used. Germanist Erika Timm assumes that Frau Holle was a nickname for Frigg, used as an independent name during and after Christianization, as it was dangerous to invoke the names of pagan deities.

Holda's connection to the spirit world through the magic of spinning and weaving has associated her with witchcraft in Catholic German folklore. She was considered to ride with witches on thistles, which closely resembled the brooms that witches are usually thought to ride. Holda was often identified with Diana in old church documents. As early as the beginning of the 11th century she appears to have been known as the leader of women, and of female nocturnal-spirits, which *"in common parlance are called Hulden, from Holda"*. These women would leave their houses in spirit, going *"out through closed doors in the silence of the night, leaving their sleeping husbands behind"*. They would travel vast distances through the sky, to enjoy great feasts, or to fight battles amongst the clouds. The 9th century *Canon Episcopi* censures women who claim to have ridden with a "crowd of demons". Burchard von Worm's later recension of the same text expands on this, in a section titled: "De arte magica":

Later canonical and church documents make her synonymous with
Diana, Herodias, Bertha, Richella, and *Abundia.* Carlo Ginzburg (1990)
has identified similar beliefs existing throughout Europe for over 1,000
years, whereby men and women were thought to leave their bodies in
spirit and follow a goddess variously called *Holda, Diana, Herodias,
Signora Oriente, Richella, Arada,* and *Perchta.* He also identifies strong
morphological similarities with the earlier goddesses *Hecate/Artemis,
Artio,* the *Matres of Engyon,* the *Matronae* and *Epona,* as well as figures
from fairy tales such as *Cinderella* for instance. A 16th century fable,
recorded by Erasmus Alberus, speaks of *"an army of women"* with sickles
in hand, sent by *Frau Hulda.* Thomas Reinesius in the 17th century
speaks of *Werra of the Voigtland* and her *"crowd of Maenads".*

Frau Holle has been regarded as a goddess of life, death and the Earth
and she also gave her name to the underworld. *Hel, Perchta, Cailleach* and
Nehalennia are all associated with Frau Holle. Like Perchta and Spillaholle
she is the patroness of spinsters and weavers, and there are parallels with
the *Völva, Nornen* and *White Ladies*-variabels like *Weiße Frauen/Dames
blanches/Witte wieven* etc. Frau Holle is sometimes mentioned as queen
of the *Gnomes* or *Elves.* Is was believed that she lived inside a mountain,
the Hohe Meißner (between Kassel and Eschwege), the Hörselberge near
Eisenach (especially Hörselberg) and also Hollerich (the realm of Holle)
are mentioned as places where she lives. In the nineteenth century, girls
still danced at the Hollelochs near Schlitz. Only the first stanza of the
song that was sung is still known:

*"Miameide – steht auf der Heide –
Hat ein grün's Röcklein an.
Sitzen drei schöne Jungfern daran.*

Die eine schaut nach vorne,
die andre in den Wind.
Das Weibsbild an dem Borne
hat viele, viele Kind."

Young girls used to take a bath in the Frau-Holle-Teich on the Hohe Meißner in the hope to become fertile. The water from this pond was said to be medicinal. According to traditional tales, the pond is bottomless. Excavations around the pond also point to a possible sacrificial site, Stone Age flints have been found. Also coins from the Roman Imperial period (from the time of Titus Flavius Domitian) and ceramic shards from the Middle Ages (and older) have also been found.

Freil

In the folklore of Brixental (Tyrol, Austria), *Freil* is a local term for a *Wilde Frau* (Wild Woman) or *Fangg*. In legends she often appears along with the Kasermanndl, another Alpine spirit, who takes possession of the Alpine meadows once the cattle and people have returned to the valleys.

G

Gabwartus

Gabwartus or *Gabartus* was sometimes used by the Nadrawen as a synonym for the *Kaukarus* or *Kaukas* (plu.: *Kaukai, kaukuczei*), a Baltic household-goblin with chthonic (underworld) features. They are believed to be the former *Kaukuczei* or earth-gods, who used to bring them many goods and blessings in their barns and stables.

Genius cucullatus

The *Genius cucullatus* (pl. *Genii cucullati*) is a dwarfish Celtic hooded demon and guardian spirit. The worship of the genius cucullatus can be proven by inscriptions and pictorial evidence in Germania and Noricum, Gaul and Britain. The name of the genius cucullatus is derived from the cloak *(Celtic sagum)* with hood (Celtic *cucullus, cuculla,* also *bardocucullus* – "Bard's Hood"), the classical travel clothing of the Gauls. The Genii cucullati are depicted both singly and in groups of three, sometimes together with a seated goddess. The term Genius cucullatus is found on two dedicatory inscriptions from a sanctuary in Wabelsdorf near Klagenfurt in Carinthia (Roman province Noricum), on some votive stones in Augusta Treverorum (Trier, Roman province Gallia Belgica), but also in Britain, e.g. in Corinium Dobunnorum (Cirencester, Roman province Britannia prima – here together with a mother deity). The reliefs show them partly as bearded dwarfs (Trier), partly as adults the size of children (Cirencester). They sometimes hold swords or scrolls, but more often they hold eggs as fertility symbols and are found near healing springs as cone-shaped stone statuettes. In the garrisons along Hadrian's Wall they were apparently worshipped as protective spirits in battle, their votive stones having been donated by legionaries. Their function as emergency helpers can be seen from their clothing – they are always ready to travel in order to help. A more serene scene shows flying Genii cucullati as hunting helpers on pottery fragments from Camulodunum (Colchester, Roman province of Britannia). The Genius cucullatus is probably related to the Asia Minor healing god *Telesphoros* (Completer), also wearing a hooded cloak, a companion of Asclepius and Hygieia. The connection is possibly made by the Celtic Galatians, in whose world of gods taken from the Gaulish homeland to Asia Minor he held a place. The ancient Genii cucullati may have served as the blueprint for popular notions of dwarf-like daemons and helpers with pointed-ears – ultimately embodied in our garden Gnomes.

German field demons

In Germany, numerous kinds of demons are recognized as dwelling in trees; and, according to Prof. Mannhardt, whole troops of emissaries of the Devil (here better read: Pan, or the fertility gods and goddesses instead of Devil) are thought to haunt the fields, and lurk among the crops of wheat and vegetables. Among the most noticeable of this legion are the *Aprilochse*, a demon dwelling in the fields in April; *Auesau*, or *Sow of the Wheatsheaf*, a spirit which lies concealed among the corn; *Baumesel*, a Goblin of the trees; *Erntebock*, a demon which steals part of the corn during harvest; *Farre* or the *Little Bull*, one of a number of spirits dwelling in the corn-fields; *Gerstenwolf* or *Barley-wolf*, a demon which devours the barley; *Graswolf*, a spirit haunting pastures; *Habergeiss* or *Haferbock*, Goat of the Oats; *Halmbock*, a Goblin whose hiding-place is among straw or the stems of plants; *Heukatze* and *Heupudel*, *Hay Cat* and *Pup*, demons dwelling in hay; *Kartoffelwolf* or *Potato-wolf*; *Katzenmann* or *Catman*, a monster dwelling amidst the wheat; *Kleesau* or *Sow of the Clover*; *Krautesel* or *Ass of the Grass*, a spirit especially inimical to lettuces; *Kornwolf, Kornsau, Kornstier, Kornkuh, Kornmutter, Kornkind*, and *Kornmaid*, all demons, spirits who protect the harvest, fertility of the land and crops.

Gierach

In northern Poland *Gierach* (also: *Gierrach, Girrach, Givach*) was a Vampire-Revenant related to the German *Nachzehrer, Dodelecker* (Licker of the Dead) or *Totenküsser* (Kisser of the Dead). The word Gierrach is of German origin (the former dominating local language) and he is also called *Gierhals*, which has the same meaning (Ravenous throat). The term is hardly used anymore, but is often mentioned in German folklore from the sixteenth to the eighteenth century, although certainly known earlier. Recent researches have shown he was not just known in parts of Germany, in contact with Slavic people, but also in western parts, such as the Eifel.

Gierfraß

The *Gierfraß* or *Gierfrass* is a vampiric Revenant figure in the folklore of Pomerania Germany. Gierfraß translates as "voraciousness" and the name suggests the creature as the local Pommerian version of similar beings like the *Gierach* or *Nachzehrer*.

Glöckler

Glöckler are people representing figures from the *Rauhnachts*-traditions in the Salzkammergut and neighboring regions. The embodied figures are *Schönperchten, good spirits of light,* who are supposed to drive away the *Rauhnachtsgeister*, the *Wilde Jagd (Wild Hunt)*, once and for all. The *Glöcklerlauf* (Walk of the Glöcklers) therefore takes place during the last *Rauhnacht*, on January 5th, the night before Epiphany. The name Glöckler is derived from the Middle High German *klocken (to knock)*, so it does not originally refer to bells (a noise that is common in Krampus, Perchten and other carnival customs), but rather to a tradition of going from door to door on Knocking Nights.

It is assumed that the Glöcklerlauf in its present form developed from several customary elements at the southern tip of Lake Traunsee and spread from there in the course of the last century. The Glöcklerlauf is often depicted as a pagan custom. In earlier times, people would have used the nightly spectacle to drive away the winter spirits (and thus winter itself) and awaken the forces of nature in the soil. Or also that it was a custom in honor of the light and fire deities. However, the folklorists Grieshofer and Gillesberger are of the opinion that the Glöcklerlauf was invented in the 19th century out of an economic emergency. In the middle of the 19th century, in the Ebensee salt works, *Braunkohle* (lignite) was suddenly collected as a cheap fuel for heating the breweries. This had fatal consequences for about 900 men who were employed in the local wood industry, who had always provided wood as fuel for the brewers, as they lost their jobs and income. In order not to have to beg for support, they offered, among other things, a spectacle: the "Glöckeln". The bell-ringing is thus probably *Heischens,* a special kind of ritual begging.

The first written mention of bell-ringing in Ebensee dates from around 1850. In a chronicle from 1873, the Ebensee peoples are described performing dances with cowbells and transparent paper lanterns, or with cardboard boxes into which patterns had been punched and which they lit with candles. Around 1900, the masked *Glöckelngeher* (bell-ringers) were displaced by *Glöcklern*, bell-ringers who had paper fringes glued to the underside of their caps instead of face masks and white clothes (the work clothes of the brewery workers).

Gnomes

Where *Salamanders* rule the Fire-Element, *Undines* Water, and *Sylphs* the Air, the *Gnomes* are the Elementals of the Earth. Paracelsus uses *Gnomi* as a synonym of *Pygmæi*. Of all Elemental spirits – who do primordially belong to the occult tradition – the Undines and the Gnomes have the strongest overlap with folkloric creatures. Due to their appearance as dwarfs or dwarfish humanoid looking creatures, they resemble all kind of *Kobold*-like spirits, and in more than one case these spirits, who are often distinguished by certain features, qualities or their locality, belong to the generic class of the earth-spirits or Gnomes. This chthonic or earth-dwelling spirit has precedents in numerous ancient and medieval mythologies, often guarding mines and precious underground treasures, notably in the Greek *Telchines* or *Dactyls*, Germanic dwarfs and for example the Welsch *Coblynau*. The Gnomes are of various sizes, most of them much smaller than human beings, though some of them have the power of changing their stature at will. This is the result of the extreme mobility of the element in which they function. Concerning them, Abbé de Villars wrote: "*The earth is filled well-nigh to its center with Gnomes, people of slight stature, who are the guardians of treasures, minerals and precious stones. They are ingenious, friends of man, and easy to govern.*" Not all authorities agree on the amiable disposition of the Gnomes. Many state that they are of a tricky and malicious nature, difficult to manage, and treacherous. All writers agree, however, that when their confidence is won, they are faithful and true. The Gnomes marry and have families, and the female Gnomes are called *Gnomides*. Some wear clothing woven of the element in which they live. In other instances their garments are part of themselves and grow with them, like the fur of animals. The Gnomes are said to have an insatiable appetite, and to spend a great part of their time eating.

The word *Gnome* comes from the Renaissance Latin *gnomus*, which first appears in *Ex Libro de Nymphis, Sylvanis, Pygmaeis, Salamandris et*

Gigantibus, etc (A Book on Nymphs, Sylphs, Pygmies, and Salamanders, and Giants, etc) by Paracelsus, published posthumously in Nysa in 1566 (and again in the Johannes Huser edition of 1589-1591, from an autograph by Paracelsus). The term Gnome may be an original invention of Paracelsus, possibly deriving the term from Latin *gēnomos* (or Greek γη-νομος, literally "earth-dweller"). In this case, the omission of the ē is referred to as a blunder by the *Oxford English Dictionary*. Paracelsus classifies them as Earth-Elementals. He describes them as two spans high, very reluctant to interact with humans and able to move through solid earth as easily as humans move through air. Because of their link with the Earth-Element some writers also recon the spirits of trees and plants to the class of the Gnomes. Manly Palmer Hall, for example, writes:

"Just as there are many types of human beings evolving through the objective physical elements of Nature, so there are many types of Gnomes evolving through the subjective ethereal body of Nature. These earth-spirits work in an element so close in vibratory rate to the material earth that they have immense power over its rocks and flora, and also over the mineral elements in the animal and human kingdoms. Some, like the Pygmies, work with the stones, gems, and metals, and are supposed to be the guardians of hidden treasures. They live in caves, far down in what the Scandinavians called the Land of the Nibelungen. In Wagner's wonderful opera cycle, The Ring of the Nibelungen, Alberich makes himself King of the Pygmies and forces these little creatures to gather for him the treasures concealed beneath the surface of the earth. Besides the Pygmies there are other Gnomes, who are called tree and forest sprites. To this group belong the Sylvestres, Satyrs, Pans, Dryads, Hamadryads, Durdalis, Elves, Brownies, and little old men of the woods."

Each species of plant or tree was served by a different but appropriate type of nature-spirit. Those working with poisonous shrubs, for example, were offensive in their appearance. It is said the nature-spirits of poison hemlock resemble closely tiny human skeletons, thinly covered with a semi-transparent flesh. Great trees also have their nature-spirits, but these are much larger than the Elementals of smaller plants.

Gongers

In the folk belief of northern Germany and Dutch Friesland *Revenants* are called *Gongers* (sing. *der Gonger,* "he who goes"; also *Gänger*). Claude Lecouteux writes of Gongers that they cannot find peace, either because they are missing a certain object or because they have not atoned for a misdeed committed while they were still alive, such as moving a boundary marker, committing suicide, etc. (*Encyclopedia of Norse and Germanic Folklore, Mythology, and Magic,* 2016). Their hand should not be shaken as it will then burn up and come off the arm. Friedrich Nork in *Die Sitten und Gebräuche der Deutschen und ihre Nachbarvolker,* Stuttgard 1849 mentions Gongers as drowning victims in Friesland who do not appear to their direct relatives but to their immediate descendants ("*...aber nicht dem nächsten Blutverwandten, sondern denen im dritten oder vierten Gliede.*"). They appear to them at dusk or at night as long as it takes for the descendants to believe their relative did actually return from the realm of the dead.

Graumännchen

The *Graumännchen* (Little Gray Man) is a small, gray spooky figure that appears in legends of Lower Saxony and central Germany. One of its features is guarding a treasure.

Greiss

Greiss is a cattle-killing *demon* from the legends of the Alpine region. He is a personification of cattle diseases, especially of the so called *Rauschbrandseuche*. According to tradition, the Greiss can appear in the form of a black cat, a squirrel or a stranger, or be evoked by the baptism of a lamb. It can destroy the livestock of entire alps. To prevent this, sacrifices could be made, preferably a calf; to defeat the Greiss, a silver-white bull must be led to the alp by a virgin. This will render him powerless.

H

Habergeiß

The Habergeiß or *Habergoaß* is a demonic figure in the folklore of German speaking areas, in the form of a goat with horse hooves, or a bird that either has the voice of a goat or is disfigured in some way. Mythologically, it finds its equivalent in Scandinavia in the *Julbock*, and in Romania in the *Capra*. The *Goat of Thor* associated with it is also called *Hafar* in Old Icelandic. There is also a legend in Switzerland of the thunder-causing *Rollibock*. The Habergeiß is firmly anchored in various local customs, especially in carnival and in Maypole customs and in the *Perchtenlauf* (Walk of the Perchten).

The Habergeiß as a billy goat

During the Perchten(-*lauf*) at the end of December, the so-called Habergeiß is on the move, accompanying the *Perchten*. The Perchten(-*lauf*) is not to be confused with the *Krampus*(-*lauf*) which takes place at the beginning of December (especially 5/6 December, St. Nicholas. The Habergeiß always carries a *Zistl* on its back; a carrying basket that used to be common among farmers. The children like to be told that the Habergeiß takes the children away in this Zistl. Sometimes a distinction is made between a white and a black goat (meaning the color of the coat). The costumes are often taller than 80 inch/2 meters and correspondingly frightening. This form of the Habergeiß is found mainly in Carinthia, Salzburg and Styria. In folk legend, the Habergeiß is usually described as a three-legged billy goat with glowing eyes and a long beard. In some legends this billy goat does not have fur but plumage. Seeing the goat is considered a bad omen. According to an old legend, the Habergeiß is the pet of the Perchten (a kind of goat daemons) and surpasses them in strength.

The Habergeiß as a bird figure

As a local *Alb* or *Mahr* the Habergeiß or *Nachtschwalbe* of Steiermark (Austria), often enters through a keyhole in owl-quiet flight despite its huge head, which it lays down heavily on the sleeper's chest. Here the Habergeiß is described as an ugly, demonic bird, sometimes with three legs. The fur (sometimes plumage) is red like blood, or yellow, depending on the area. The bleating always sounds frightening and terrifying. It is said to suck the blood from the veins of farmers and cattle.

The Habergeiß in other guises
- Sometimes (more common in Swabian) the word Habergeiß is used to describe very thin or very ugly women.
- Regionally (Swabian, Franconian) Habergeiß is the common expression for the weaver's goat.
- Sometimes a messenger of death, or an unspecified animal that heralds disaster.
- In Tyrolean dialect, *Waldkauz* or *Steinkauz* (tawny owl or little owl) is called *Hobrgoaß*.
- The *Bekassine*, a species of bird of the snipe-family, is called the *Haberbock* or *Haberziege*, because the sounds it makes resemble bleating goats.

Origin of the name
The compound *haber* means billy goat (cf. dialectally *Häberling* = a one year-old billy goat), *Geiß*, *Ziege, Zicke* (goat). This name, as well as the synonym *Bockgeiß*, are tautological composites, and the often-heard account according to which the homonym *Haber* means *oat* does not hold up etymologically. In Old Norse as well as in Celtic, *hafr* means *buck*. It is assumed that the Habergeiß was formerly a fertility-daemon whose meaning changed in the course of time. Thus, through folk etymology, the name has often been misunderstood as *Haferziege* (oat-goat).

Haltija or Haltia
In Finish folklore and shamanism *Haltijas* or *Haltias* are local animistic spirits, often depicted as a Gnome, or Elf-like creature that guards, helps, or protects something or somebody. The word is possibly derived from the Gothic *haltijar*, which referred to the original settler of a homestead – although this is not the only possible etymology. It can also be derived from the Finnish verb *hallita*, which means "to rule", "to command", "to master". These Haltijas could be male or female, and could take a human as well as an animal's form. Haltijas could be found everywhere in nature, both in the biological and abiotic parts. Every human has a Haltija, usually called *Haltijasielu* (haltija-soul) or *Luontohaltija* (nature-haltija), which is one of the three parts of a person's soul. The tradition

blends with the Swedish *Tomte* or the Finnish *Tonttu*, a being analogous
to Haltija, but which lives in a building, like a home *Kotitonttu* or a sauna
Saunatonttu. The *Maan-Haltija* (tutelary of land), guarded the property
of an individual, including their house and livestock. Votive offerings
would be given to these Haltijas at a shrine, as thanks for the help given
and also to prevent the Haltija from causing harm. Sometimes Haltijas of
certain families and farms acted against other families and their farms by
stealing their wealth or making the animals infertile, for instance. Many
local Haltijas were believed to have originally been the sacred spirits of
ancestors. In some cases a Haltija was the first inhabitant of the house.
Sometimes, while building a new house, a local nature-spirit could be
"employed" to work as a Maan-Haltija. Some say Haltijas are divided into
races, or folks, which are called *Väki*. The concept of Haltija and Väki
is rather complex, as sometimes the Haltija acts like a nature-spirit, or
sometimes more like a genius loci or Deva, a houshold-spirit, or even like
the personal genius from antiquity.

There are many different kinds of Haltijas. There are, for example, Water-
Haltijas (or *Veden Väki*) and Forest-Haltijas (or *Metsän Väki*). Even
graveyards have their own Haltijas; *Kalman Käki* (Death Folk). As stated
earlier, human settlements also have Haltijas. Later, such local spirits are
also referred to as a *Tomtegubbe* ("old man of the homestead" in Swedish).
The *Kotihaltija* (home-Elf, home-Gnome) is the *Tonttu* who lives in every
home. He takes care of the house, and it is important to treat him with
respect. The *Saunatonttu* lives in the sauna and protects it, but also makes
sure that people do not behave improperly in it. *Joulutonttu* is Finnish for
Christmas Elf. Unlike the Christmas Elves in some countries, the Finnish
Joulutonttu doesn't have pointy ears. There are also personal *Haltijas*,
which are protective spirits, similar to angels in Christianity. One of them
is called *Luonto*, which means "nature". In Estonian mythology a similar
being is called *Haldjas*, whereas the term used for a holder, master, or
owner-occupier is *Haldaja*.

Väki means either "power" or "group", of which the meaning of "power"
is etymologically older. The meaning of väki meaning "folk" is the result
of the anthropomorphication of abstract concepts like Kalman Väki, the
power of dead spirits. It does not constitute a separate supernatural force
like mana, but is a generic concept for "potency" or "power", including –
but not separately distinguished as – magical potency. There are different

kind of Väkis or Haltijas. In the case of Veden Väki (Water Folk) or Metsän Väki (Forest Folk), the word "Väki" can refer to them as a folk or as their magical powers, but usually both at the same time. For example, if someone gets sick while swimming, this could be caused by the Väki of water, that becomes attached to a person. In this sense "Väki" is seen as a magical power emanating from water, that can make people ill, but it can also mean that Haltijas (spirits) are attached to a person. In comparison, if someone goes fishing, they can ask the Water Väki to bring fish by calling individual Haltijas belonging to that Väki by their names. Here, Väki is understood more as a folk. Some Väki and Haltijas are:

- *Kalman Väki* (Väki of Death) means ghosts and spirits, but also the magical power that can be found in a graveyard. This power can make people ill and it can also be used against other people.
- *Metsän Väki* (Väki of Forests) means Haltijas of forests. Their leader is Tapio, the king of the forest. It also means magical powers of the forest.
- *Naisen Väki* (Väki of Woman) is usually understood as special magical powers of women.
- *Puun Väki* (Väki of Wood) means the race of Haltijas of trees, and also the power of wooden material, which can cause pain if you are hit by a wooden object.
- *Raudan Väki* (Väki of Iron) means Haltijas of iron. They can hurt people who are hit by bladed weapons. Väki of iron can also be commanded to heal the wounds they have given.
- *Tulen Väki* (Väki of Fire) means spirits of fire, but also the destructive forces of fire and healing power of warm air, for example in a sauna.
- *Veden Väki* (Väki of Water) means Haltijas of water. Their leader is Ahti, the king of the sea. Veden väki is also the magical power of water that can make people sick or heal them.
- *Vuoren Väki* (Väki of Mountain) usually means the haltijas of hills and large stones.

Haltija Väkis of different environments and materials were thought to be in conflict with each other. For example, when wood is burned, it is an assault in which Väki of Fire is beating Väki of Wood. Väki of Fire can be used to scare other Väki away. For example, if you were made ill by Väki of water, that attached to you while you were swimming, this Väki, and the illness, could be removed in a sauna, which had many Väki of fire.

Haselwurm

Semi-mythical worms play an important role in the Tyrolean legends,
and of these the *Haselwurm*, which is also sometimes called *Weißer
Wurm* (White Worm, Snake), *Wurbl or Wurmb, Murbl, Paradeiswurm,
Paradeisschlange* (Snake of Paradise) or *Wurm der Erkenntnis* (Wurm/
Snake of Acknowledgement). It is clear that like the Swedish *Vitorm*, the
Haselwurm was believed to have – or store in its body – great magical
powers. Johann Nepomuk Ritter von Alpenburg provides curious data
about the creature, and a magical ritual to obtain it in his *Deutsche
Alpensagen*, Vienna 1861. He writes that in *"Auf der Schön"*, a farm above
the Higna (Higenau) on the Reiterberge, a very carefully preserved *house
record* from 1661 is preserved, which is said to have been written by
Wolfgang Hechenblaikner. In addition to various remedies and spells
that were in use at that time, the record, according to the author, contains
so much information about the Haselwurm, that it can be considered as
the most complete source. Johann Nepomuk Ritter von Alpenburg uses
Weisse Natter as a synonym for Haselwurm. *Natter* is the German term
for *grass snake*. So *Weisse Natter* means: "white grass snake." Perhaps,
in some folkoric tales, the Haselwurm was the albino version of this
common European snake species. However in other stories the size of the
Haselwurm far exceeds the size of the grass snake, which is usually about
40 inches long/1 meter, up to a rare maximum of 70 inch/1.80 meter.
According to Heinrich Eckstorm in *Chronicon Walkenredense* (1617):

> *"In July 1597, a woman from Holbach in the Harz Mountains is said to
> have collected blueberries and encountered a gigantic hazel worm. She fled
> to the nearby village of Zorge, where she found shelter with a woodcutter.
> Eight days later, the woodcutter himself encountered the worm, which lay
> across the road and was so large that he first mistook it for a fallen tree.
> The creature was greenish-yellow and had feet on its snakelike body."*

Below I quote Johann Nepomuk Ritter von Alpenburg on the Haselwurm
in a fragment from:

> *Eine Schöne Wissenschaft vom Haselwurm
> oder Weisse Natter unter der Haselstaude*

> *"[...] Where you find hazel bushes that have mistletoe, dig them up
> completely along with the trees, and before you dig them up and want the*

"

Tatzelwurm seen in Sarganserland in 1660 (1723) by Johann Jakob Scheuchzer (1672-1733)

worm, which must be done on a Friday in the full moon before the sun rises, say the incantation:

> *I adjure thee, pure worm, by God the Father, by God the Son, and by God the Holy Ghost, Amen; that thou depart not from this place, till I carry thee hence.*

Then make three † over it. Then you make three circles around the perennials and start digging without saying a word. As soon as you see the hazel worm, take powdered "Artoimoissia" ("wormwood" or "Artemisia absinthium") and throw a lot into it, if it wanted to escape, but then you will find a beautiful white adder, it is not poisonous nor evil and does not squirm like another adder, just attack it comfortingly without any fear. As soon as you have it in your hand, say the following 13 words aloud:

> *Stuiz hote : Hodivie : Evna : Ferlier : Kher : Khenlina : with a high : Allerues : Eurmite : Segma : Shen Malita : Eeml : Eso malitu Mür.*

As soon as you have spoken this, the worm will patiently submit to everything, and he will immediately be submissive to you. Now peel off its skin and take out its tongue, but put the tongue into the peeled off skin and tie everything in a white cloth. This serves to make it invisible. If you hold it in your right hand, no one will see you, whether on horseback or on foot. If you then breathe on a door or a lock, it opens by itself and closes again; if you take the skin with the tongue from the right hand into the left hand, you are also visible again.

After the skin is peeled off, the tongue torn out, then cut the viper into pieces, boil it in a new pan and eat from it as much as you can: immediately you will recognize the nature of all herbs and certain richness and memory. All the world is yours, no one can be your enemy, all rights you win, all wealth falls asleep to you: you may not be caught, all evil spirits must flee or be subservient to you. The eating of the adder does not harm thee.

No art is easier to accomplish; and what a man reads, whether Christian or secular, he knows all by heart, and never forgets, likewise what he has never heard, and what he begins ends happily: it is about the black art."

Hausschmiedlein

In Bohemia, Moravia, and Austria, people believed in the *knocker*-kind of
Goblins – known in Germany as *Wichtlein*. This underground creature was
called the *Hausschmiedlein* (little house-smiths). Bohemia's mythological
Knockers were associated with the sound of a smith working hard at his
anvil, or with a miner. People believed that whenever a miner's death is
imminent, they would knock three times upon the wall; when an accident
was about to occur they could imitate the sounds of miners at work.

Hehmann

The *Hehmann* is descibed by P. Hillebald Ludwig Seeb in *Sagen
Niederösterreichs* (1892) as an evil bird, who lures travelers into the
deepest part of the forest, using his peculiar cal: *heh heh heh*.

Heidenfräulein

In Austrian folklore the *Heidenfräulein* is a beautiful female nature-spirit,
related to the *Salige Frauen*. In *Sagen aus Tirol*, collected and edited by
Ignaz V. Zingerle, Innsbruck 1891, a short story about a Heidenfräulein is
preserved, which contains her typical features:

> *"In ancient times, a shepherd boy saw a beautiful maiden sitting
> on a high rocky ledge in the rich fields, combing her golden hair.
> She called down to him, as he looked up in wonder, turning up the
> brim of his hat. She beckoned him and the boy obeyed. Then he
> suddenly saw – as if the mountain were of the clearest glass – how
> deep inside the mountain gold was stored in brightly shimmering
> veins and masses. When he turned down his hat, everything had
> disappeared. The maiden was a Heidenfraulein (Heather Maiden)."*

Heinzelmännchen

According to legend, the *Heinzelmännchen* were Cologne's household-
spirits. They did the work of the citizens at night when they were asleep.
However, because they were being watched, they disappeared forever.
In addition to their small size, typical attributes, such as the pointed
hat and their diligence, show that the Heinzelmännchen belong to the
group of *Goblins, Pixies* and *dwarfs*. The folklorist Marianne Rumpf

(1921-1998) gives two explanations for the origin of the name in these folk tales in an article in the journal for narrative research *Fabula* from 1976: Firstly, *Heinzelmännlein* was a name for the *Alraune* (Mandrake), which was used as a household-spirit. Secondly, *Heinz* or *Heinzenkunst* were names of devices used in mining to drain water. Therefore, according to Rumpf, the operators of such helpful devices may have been called Heinzelmänner. The Heinzelmännchen are among the models of the garden Gnomes invented at the end of the 19th century.

Hiisi

Hiisi is a term in Finnisch mythology, originally denoting sacred localities and later on various types of mythological entities. In later Christian-influenced folklore, the Hiisi are depicted as demonic or trickster-like entities, often seen as the native, pagan inhabitants of the land, similar in this respect to mythological giants. They are nature-spirits, found near salient promontories, ominous gorges, large boulders, pits, forests, hills, and areas with other outstanding geographical features or rugged terrain. According to John Abercromby (in *The pre-and proto-historic Finns: both eastern and Western, with the magic songs of the West Finns*, 1898), Hiisi was originally a spirit of hilly forests. In Estonian *hiis* or *his* means "sacred grove", usually on elevated ground. In the spells (magic songs) of the Finns the term Hiisi is often used in association with a hill or mountain, and Hiisi as a person is also associated with the hills and mountains, often seen as the owner or ruler of them. His name is commonly associated with forests, and some forest animals. Mauno Koski associates the Finnish Hiisi and the Estonian *Hiis* primarily with burial sites, or sacred areas associated with burial sites; with a secondary meaning of *hiisi* as a (noun) term applied to dominant, exceptional, or anomalous geographical features. After Christianization its semantic meaning may have been lost, or became unclear – this may have led to the 'anthropomorphism' of Hiisi-sites, where they are called "giants", for instance, or the change from Hiisi being used as a common noun to being used as a proper noun, indicating the name of a deity or spirit. In today's Estonian *hiis* still means "sacred grove".

It is likely that Hiisi's "evil nature" has been magnified over time, with the Christianization of Finland in the 12th and 13th centuries being the start of the change in portrayal. In more recent times his nature is nearly synonymous with that of a Christian devil. In Bishop Mikael Agricola's list of Finnish pagan gods, Hiisi is given as a god of forest game (or fur), together with a similar god Tapio. Oral folklore concerning Hiisi mostly describes the creatures that dwelled in the Hiisi-sites as Trolls or giants. Many of the stories describe how a certain place (such as an odd rock formation, etc.) was created by the actions of these mythological creatures. Later, the original aspect of nature's awesomeness inherent in the *Hiidet* (pl.) was diminished, and they passed into folklore as purely evil spirits, vaguely analogous to Trolls. According to this later view, Hiidet were often small in size, but also in some occasions gigantic. Hiidet could travel together in a noisy procession, and attack people who did not give way to them. If somebody left their door open, a *Hiisi* could come inside and steal something. If you were chased by a Hiisi you should seek safety in a cultivated area. In folklore, it was the cultivated areas which were blessed, in contrast to the pagan holiness residing in the awesome and forbidding features of raw nature, and evil Hiisi could not step inside areas sanctified by human cultivation.

Hinzelmann

Hinzelmann (also *Heinzelmann* or *Lüring*) is the name for a legendary *Kobold*. He is said to have done good things, like doing housework. However, he could become angry if he was provoked. Hinzelmann appeared without form and had the voice of a child. Ludwig Bechstein also mentions appearances in the form of a dead child. His home is said to have been in the Bohemian Mountains. He entered the world of legends mainly because of his goings-on in Hudemühlen Castle in Hodenhagen in 1584-1588. In 1588 he left Hudemühlen voluntarily and then settled in Eystrup. According to the legend, Hinzelmann will return if three conditions are fulfilled at the same time; if the cook fills a broken water bucket with a broken ladle, if the dachshund throws young under a willow tree, and if a child is born with only one eye. The Brothers Grimm also wrote down the legend of Hinzelmann, which they took from a book published in 1704 by a priest named Feldmann at Eickelohe.

Hödeken

The *Hödeken* (also *Hödekin*, *Hüdekin*, *Hütchen*, after the felt hat he is said to always wear) is a legendary figure from the Leinebergland, Lower Saxony, Germany. Hödeken is a *Kobold*, who also transmitted news as a messenger between Hildesheim and Winzenburg. The path between Winzenburg and Hildesheim, called cathedral yard, which Hödeken is said to have hurried along after the death of the last count of Winzenburg to deliver the death message, is called "Rennstieg" (Raceway). The Brothers Grimm describe the legend in their *Deutsche Sagen* from 1816-1818 like this:

"The Hödekin was a helpful house-spirit of the bishop of Hildesheim. He prevented the night guards from falling asleep, gave the bishop military advice and warned him of coming dangers. Occasionally he also helped other Hildesheimers. Once someone asked the Hödekin to protect his wife during his absence. The woman was visited by several lovers. The Hödekin jumped between them, summoning horrible figures or throwing them to the ground before the woman could be unfaithful. When the man returned, the Hödekin complained that he would rather herd all the pigs of Saxony than such a woman again. The Hödekin was not to be trifled with: he strangled a kitchen boy who had irritated him, cut him into pieces, and cooked the meat over the fire."

Hommelstommel

Hommelstommel is a creature from the Lower Saxon folklore of the province of Groningen, the Netherlands, bordering East Frisia. It usually appears at night or during gray windless weather with a soft drizzle. In one story, told in the Oldambt (eastern part of the province), Hommelstommel is horse from above and human from below. In more stories the creature is a headless horse that keeps trudging after terrified walkers. In the west of the province Groningen he is also called *Hompelstompel* and in some places there were stories of a calf without a head. There are different views on the essence of Hommelstommel. In the Oldambt he was probably originally seen as a form of *d'Ole* (the Old One), which at first meant a pagan deity or field-spirit, and later the Devil. It could also be the ghostly appearance of a headless animal or the ethereal form of an astral traveling witch.

Hoymann

A *Hoymann* is a ghostly creature of the region Waldthurn, Bavaria, that walks alone in certain places and makes its presence known by shouting loudly. He gets his name from his call *"hoy, hoy, hoy"*, which he occasionally utters several times in succession, and so loud that it can be heard from afar. His figure is that of a tall man. He usually wears a hat with a large brim and has a long white beard. His abode is the forest. He always walks the same paths. Since he is an enchanted figure, he is not allowed to go beyond the corridor created by his walks. He is always seen walking above the forest on the tops of the trees, calling out. The call is a warning, because the Hoymann punishes crimes committed to the forest. When he calls, one must not answer him, because he feels mocked by it. He sits on the back of such a caller, who then has to carry him to his home. His appearance is not bound to a certain time. The Hoymann is still alive today in the saying: *"Der schreit ja wöi a Hoimo!"* (That one shouts like a hoyman!).

I

Irrlicht

Irrlicht (also called *Sumpflicht*, and *Ignis fatuus*) is the name given to a particular luminous phenomenon that is ostensibly sighted from time to time in swamps or bogs, or in particularly dense, dark forests, and (more rarely) in cemeteries. The Latin *ignis fatuus* – documented no earlier than the 16th century in Germany, where it was coined by a German humanist – appears to be a free translation of the long-existing German name *Irrlicht* ("wandering light" or more context-correct "light that makes you make a mistake or light that lures you away from the right direction"). The *Irrlight* – also *Sumpflicht* (swamp-light) – was conceived of in German folklore as a mischievous nature-spirit and the Latin translation was made to lend the German name intellectual credibility. Besides Irrlicht and Sumpflicht, the spooky light aka lamp ghost has also been called *Irrwisch* (where wisch translates to "wisp" as in the English *Will-o'-the-wisp*), as found in e.g. Martin Luther's writings of the same 16th century. In the German-speaking world, the terms *Irrlicht* and *Irrwisch* are the most common. From old German writings *Spuklicht* (Ghost light) and *Totenlicht* (Light of the Dead) are handed down. The name *d'Raulicht* originates from Luxembourgish usage, which found its way into German as early as the Middle Ages and contributed to the (albeit obsolete) designation *Traulicht*, or *Trauerlicht* (Mourning light).

In folklore *Irrlichter* (pl.) are usually considered either the malicious work of supernatural beings, or the souls of the unfortunate deceased. According to popular belief, following Irrlichter or even trying to catch them brings bad luck. In the natural sciences, their existence as independent beings is fundamentally rejected. Reports about alleged sightings are nevertheless investigated, because in nature there are living beings as well as gases, which can produce lights, which are again quite similar to Irrlicht descriptions. The descriptions of Irrlichter vary; mostly they are described as small flames, more rarely they are said to be fist- or even head-sized fireballs. Their color is usually described as bluish, greenish or reddish. There are also different statements about the movement of the Irrlichter. They are said to either remain motionless on the spot or to light up wildly flickering and immediately go out again. Less credible reports tell of Irrlichter that move away from the observer or, on the other hand, literally chase him, as if they were externally controlled by intelligent beings with a will of their own.

Irrwurzeln

At Götzens (Tyrol, Innsbruck region), which is said to have received its name from idols worshiped there, is a so called *Irrweg*, a road where for some strange unexplained reason people get lost, or do not find an acquaintance they made an appointment with on a specified location along the road. The German verb *irren* means "to err" or "to be mistaken" and it can also be used in the connotation of "taking the wrong direction, or road". On the Irrweg at Götzens – quoting Ignaz V. Zingerle from his work: *Sagen aus Tirol*, Innsbruck 1891:

> *"It has often happened that two acquaintances pass each other there without noticing each other. The summer before last, two ladies had arranged to meet on this path. Although both were on the same path at the appointed time, they did not find each other, and each had to return home alone. (Innsbruck.) In the Mußegger forest near Wörgl (Kirchbbühel), there are Irrwurzeln (err-roots). If you step on one, you get lost until someone else comes along.*

Ignaz V. Zingerle collected another story from the Ritten-region:

*"The old Rißer-Schuster once walked to his home in Lengmoos, late in the
evening, from Kematen, where he had worked for a farmer. While walking
in the forest he heard beautiful music from afar and saw, when he looked,
a large illuminated house. He became curious and walked in the direction
of where the music seemed to be coming from, but it always remained
the same distance away. Suddenly he heard a ringinging sound and in an
instant everything disappeared, but he was standing far away from the
path, down at the Unterinner-Eck. When asked how it happened, he said:
"Ich bin auf eine Irrwurzel getreten." (I stepped on a Irrwurzel.)"*

The Irrweg and Irrwurzel-phenomenon is quit unique, but ghostly houses,
even those that can look and feel real, as if one steps back in time, do
happen, and are not restricted to this weird 'Bermuda Triangle-like' road
and forest near the town of Götzens, Austria. Some examples are recorded
in *Modern Mysteries of Britain*, London 1987, by Janet and Colin Bord.

J

Jievaras

In Lithuanian folklore the *Jievaras* is a field-spirit depicted as a *Tree of
Life*, worshiped for a fertile season and a good harvest. The Jievaras is a
manifestation of vitality and the dynamic forces of nature and the earth
and a symbol of the continuously generative, feminine element. In some
cases, Jievaras is the spirit of the cereal to which sacrifices are made after
the rye harvest. Rites for Jievaras were performed at the end of the rye
harvest. An important part of the ceremony, to prevent the land from
becoming barren, was the offering of bread, sometimes cheese, which
was buried in the ground where the last rye had been cut, with the words:
"Davei man, žemele, duodam ir tau" (You gave to me, O earth, we give to
you). During these offerings, the so-called Jievaras-songs were sung. The
Tree of Life in Lithuanian mythology, as well as in other Indo-European
mythologies, was associated with the dynamic driving force, the Sun, or
light, which had extraordinary significance for the earth's crops and for all
vegetation.

K

Kabouter

A *Kabouter* is a mythological creature, appearing in countless fairy tales (and other folk tales) scattered around the world. Kabouter is the Dutch and Flemish word for *Leprechaun*. In folklore, they are akin to the French *Lutin*, Scandinavian *Tomte* or *Nisse*, the English *Hob*, the Scottish *Brownie* and the German *Kobold*. There are numerous other designations for these, usually depicted as dwarfish humanoid creatures. *Kabouter* is probably derived from the Germanic word *kuþa-walda* (house keeper) or *kuþa-hulþa* ("the house well-wisher" – as the German *Kobold* "haughty, good or evil house-spirit"), which is probably a compound, the first member of which is related to Middle Dutch *cove* (East Middle Dutch *cave* 'hut, cottage'; German *Koben* "stable, barn"; English *cove*, Swedish *kofve* – compare the Old English *cofgodu*, *cofgodas*). Kabouters are often confused with *Gnomes*, not only in Dutch but also in other languages and cultures. However, strictly speaking, a kabouter is a *house-* or *forest-spirit* while a Gnome is an *Elemental* and *earth-spirit*. Depending on the region where they occur and according to folklore, they differ in appearance and behavior. However, certain things they all have in common:

- Their (default) small stature and their ability to make themselves invisible from people.
- They choose to be around people and, so it is told, are willing to faithfully do all kinds of chores for a small fee.
- If treated badly, they can act as tormentors, or leave the place, after which the prosperity they brought soon vanishes.

According to the folklore of the Low Countries, kabouters are a very old race of beings. As a result, they also expect to be treated with respect. Other beliefs held that these little people were the spirits of deceased ancestors. However, it is more commonly believed that they are supernatural creatures, completely separate from humans. They are described as dressed in brown or red, often with a red hat and usually imagined with white beards although there are also female kabouters. Kabouters are immensely strong despite their small bodies and they possess a certain magic. There are good and bad kabouters. Sometimes they help humans, but they can also work against them. This can consist of minor harassment, such as making noises and moving things around like a *poltergeist*, or more malicious behavior.

In the Netherlands, Kabouters are also called *Klaboutermannetje* (West Flemish), *Alf, Alverman(neke), Auvelmannetje, Auvelemenke, Auverman, Eviemannetje, gnoom, Havermannetje, Hetsemannetje* (Limburg), *Kabaatermanneke, Kobold, Nachtwerkertje, Til* (De Peel), *Blauwe Gerrit* (Veluwe), *Witje* (female kabouter), *De Zwarten en Witten* (denoting evil and good intended Kabouters), *Estermantsjes* (Groningen), *Ierdmantsjes* (Friesland), *Owermennekes* or *Outermannetjes*. *Mare* is also used, which we also encounter in Nightmare and which credits the Kabouter with *Alp*-like features.

Kaolmenke or Kaspar

As in many countries, a mining spirit is also known in Limburg in the southern Netherlands, where this creature is called *Kaolmenke* (Little coal man) or *Kaspar*. The creature protects coal supplies and sometimes its red eyes can be seen in the dark. Whistling underground it could cause disasters. The Kaolmenke could cause collapses of mine shafts and tunnels, just like the British and Welsh Blue Cap, Knocker and Coblynau. Kaolmenkes were suspected of grabbing unguarded food or mining tools. The creature wears miner's clothing and can make itself invisible.

Kasertörggelen

Kasertörggelen are child-ghosts in the folklore of Tyrol. They are described in *Folk legends, customs and opinions from Tyrol,* collected and edited by Johann Adolf Heyl, Brixen 1897. All summer long the Kasertörggelen live invisibly on the Stubai mountain pastures. They are ghostly children, quite harmless in general, except that they can't stand rude jokes or curiosity. Around St. Martin's Day (11 November) they leave the alpine pastures, and people bless their houses before the ghosts pass through the village in the evening between eight and nine o'clock. They then close the shutters as tightly as possible.

Once there was a curious servant who secretly looked out. Just then they passed by, an uncounted crowd of children. The last ones were already approaching; suddenly a child's voice sounded:

Geh, thu dö Balklan zu!
(Go, close the shutters!)

At that moment the servant went blind. He tried all possible means of healing, he also asked pious clergymen for advice; all in vain. Finally an old farmer's wife advised him: Next year watch more (again)! He did it. The ghostly children passed by again, and the servant already thought they were over, when a voice sounded:

Go, thu dö Baltlau au!
(Go, open the shutters!)

Then he was able to see again. Another time a farmhand, who was living carelessly, met the departing Kasertörggelen on the road between Fulpmes and Mieders. At the very end, a small child limped after the procession. It was in a shirt, but it was too long, so that it was dragged along by the child. The overconfident man started to laugh, but immediately stiffened in horror when the little one said: *"Vater, derfst nit z'lachen, weil mir kein besseres Leichentuch geben hast."* (Father, you must not laugh, because you have not given me a better shroud.)

Kaukas or Kaukutis

In East Prussia, Latvia, but especially in the Lithuanian language area, the *Kaukas* (pl.: *Kaukai*) is a lower mythical being. *Kauk(k)uczei* and similar plurals denotes: "earth peoples" or "earth gods". *Kaukutis* means *little Goblin. Kaukas* comes closest to the German *Kobold.* They are also called *Kaukarei* and they emerge as distinctly chthonic beings, associated with small bumps on the ground and the ghosts of the dead and the unborn, and sometimes people regarded them as the souls of deceased children, especially of unbaptized infants. However, there is much more similarity with other traditional European household-spirits, which attract prosperity as long as certain customs or small offerings are maintained, and leave the house or run amok when they feel neglected.

As deities or daemons of fortune the *Kaukuczei* are compared or equaled to the *Bardzukkai* (*Barstukks*) and *Markopete.* The *Kita vertus (IV.9.20)* describes the similarities and differences between the Bardzukkai (Bezdukkus) and the Kaukkuczei:

Kobolds "Flok, Mik and Puk" in the poem Liliana (1905) by Apel·les Mestres (1854-1936)

*"Einige Nadrawen haben auch einen unterscheid unter den Kaukuczijs
und Bezdukkus diese wohnen eigentlich in den Wäldern, unter dem
Bäumen, die Kaukkuczei aber in den Scheunen, Speichern, auch
Wohnhäusern. Beyde aber nennen sie doch Barzdukkus, weil sie
auff eine Art, zumahlen was der Barth betrifft, gestalt seyn."*

(Some Nadrawen also have a distinction among the Kaukuczijs
and Bezdukkus, the latter actually live in the woods, under the
trees, but the Kaukkuczei in the barns, storehouses, and also
dwellings. Both, however, are called Barzdukkus, because they are
shaped in one way, especially as far as the beard is concerned.)

The oldest evidence comes from the *Elbingen vocabulary*: Old Prussian
cawx – Middle Low German *tufel*. This is also associated with a toponym
documented from 1251 onward as *Kuke, Chucunbrasth, Cucenbrast*,
translated as '*desz Teufels durchfahrt*' (the Devil's passage). The creature is
also mentioned in Lithuania, as early as 1547 in the first book written in
the Lithuanian language (transl. *The Catechism of Martynas Mažvydas*)
where it says: "*Kaukus, Szemepatis ir laukasargus pameskiet...*" (desist
from the Kaukas, Zemepats and Lauksargas).

In 1613 Lasicki writes: *"Kaukie sunt Lemures"* (Kaukie are lemures).
Lemures are shades or spirits of the restless or malignant dead. The
term Kaukas appears frequently in Lithuanian sagas. In Latvian, *Kauks*
is more rarely attested and then translated as *Heinzelmännchen*. In
addition, other names occur occasionally in Lithuanian and Latvian,
like *Pūkas* or *Pūks* from the German *Puck*. In Latvian Kaukas is also a
nickname for a *screamer*.

Etymology
There are several interpretations of the etymology, which linguistically
assume an Indo-European root *keuk* (to bend), but semantically argue
differently. According to Mažiulis, Kaukas is a hunchbacked dwarf.
Vladimir Toporov sees Kaukas as a *genius loci* specifically of hills, which
would mean that the creature inherited its name from designations for
hills. Šeškaukaitė and Gliwa see connections with Lithuanian *kukalis*
(Claviceps purpurea), which would make Kaukas a vegetation demon,
embodied by ripe seed pods and the ergot. In fact, the Kaukas-etymology
remains rather complex:

- Prussian:
  kaukas, kauks, kuks, kukis, cux, cawx, cawsk, barstukai = subterranean, dwarf, Troll, Goblin, devil, small man
  kauk = howl
  kaukas, kuke, cawks, cux = ghost, devil
  caymis = village, place
- Prussian-Lithuanian:
  kaukas, kaukelis, kaukytis, kaukutis, kaukoružis = dwarf, ghost, Goblin, Brownie, mandrake, wealth-bringing household god
  kaukarna = elevation, actually clods of earth lifted up by the frost, small hills on the meadows, "Frosthölsterlein".
  kaukis = mandrake (bot. mandragora officinalis), clinging umbel, carrot clinging umbel, field burdock
  kauke, kaukas = Goblin, subterranean spirit
- Latvian:
  kaukona = howling
  kaukt = howl, roar
  kaukis = black-headed (bird), a screamer
  kaukona, kaukt = howling, moaning
  kukainis = insect
- Lithuanian:
  kaimas = village, place

Function and properties

The multitude of different characteristics and functions is partly contradictory. The Kaukai, when described, are usually depicted as small males or as infants. Kaukai are benign beings who bring wealth, blessings and good harvests to their hosts, and also do chores themselves. Only when they are offended or not properly fed can they tend to take revenge or leave the farm. Kaukai can be acquired by hatching a testicle from a boar or a rooster. In addition, they may settle on a farm of their own accord, or be forced or persuaded to do so by gifts. Close relations, up to and including possible identity, exist with the *Barstukks*, who are also depicted as dwarves, but are servants of the *Puškaitis* and live under elder trees. More overlap lies in the fact that the term Kaukai is also used as a reference to a pagan cult-place or to a dwelling place with elder trees, and the habit in every household to place food scraps on the elderberry bushes in the evening, to make the Kaukai favor the household.

A German text *Toliau (IV.9.22)* reports on a ritual condition imposed by a Kaukas that has a particular location in mind, on an unsuspecting innkeeper:

"Wenn diese Kaukucźei einen Ort belieben, sollen sie des Nachts einen hauffen Späne an einen Ort deß Hauses zusammen tragen, denn auch allerhand Mist von Vieh und Pferde, in die Milch-Töpfe werffen. Da nun der Wirth die Spähne unberühret und unverstöret, daneben auch von der bemisteten Milch getruncken, siehe, denn sollen sie sich ihme zeigen, und auch bey ihm bleiben."

(If these Kaukucźei favor a place, they must carry a heap of wood shavings to a place in the house and throw all kinds of dung from cattle and horses into the milk pots. When the innkeeper leaves the shavings untouched and undisturbed, and also drunk of the manured milk, then he will see the Kaukas which will remain with him.)

The *Aitvaras* or *Aitwars*, another class of spirits, are regarded as an opposite partner of the Kaukas – both are compared to the *Dioscuri*. The *Toliau (IV.9.19)* states however that Aitwars are regarded als *Alf* (Elves).

Jetziger Zeit nennen die Nadrawer diese Barźdukkas, auch Kaukucźus, […] und halten davor, daß sie den Leuten Getreydigt und Reichthumb zuschleppen, jedoch, daß sie diese vom Aitwars, den man hie sonsten Alf heist, unterscheiden.

(Nowadays the Nadrawer call these Barźdukkas, also Kaukucźus, […] and they consider them as bringing grain and wealth to the people, but that they distinguish them from the Aitwars, which are here called Alf.)

Kautek

In Prussian folklore the *Kautek* is a very small and friendly household-spirit, looking like a little man of only a few centimeters in size. Some say it was dressed in red clothes, or wearing a red hat. The name allegedly derives from the Old Prussian language, where *kauks* means "devil", but other linguists think the word kautek was simply a medieval term for "small man". Yet despite its "devilish association", the Kautek is actually quite benevolent once it picks a house to live in – it will do many small household chores overnight while the owners of the residence are asleep. However, it would not be a household-spirit if it didn't have some darker features. It liked to play pranks on neighbors, and could cause illnesses among the family members. It might even swap one of its own children with the babies of the host, leaving a changeling to grow up as a human child.

Kiddelhund

The *Kiddelhunde* (tickle-dogs) are related to dog or wolf shaped German field-daemons like the *Kornhund* and *Roggenwolf*. It was said they would look for children in order to tickle them to death. Most likely the function was a scarecrow effect, to scare children into obedience and keep them out of the fields.

Kielkropp

In the folk-belief of the Elbe-region, Germany, a *Kielkropp* resembled a *changeling*-baby but was born naturally. The Kielkropp was born all right and proper as to its body and limbs, but its head was larger than that of the largest man. Of such children the people at that time believed that this child had to be some sort of *Cambion*, with the devil himself – or one of his associates – as their father, and that they brought only misfortune into a house. The Kielkropp was described in the 19th century by folklorist Benjamin Thorpe.

Klaboutermann

The *Klabautermann*, *Kalfatermann* or *Klabattermann* (from Low German *klabastern* "to rumble", "to go about noisily" or from likewise Low German *kalfatern* "to seal with pitch and tow") is, in nautical superstition, a ship's spirit, or Goblin, who – usually invisibly – warns the captain of danger and likes to play practical jokes. The figure of the Klabautermann is connected with sailing. He lives in the hold, where he hammers, stows and throws boards; only sometimes he lives under the windlass. He also comes on deck, climbs the mast, climbs in the rigging, and sits on the bowsprit or jib boom of sailing ships. If he shows his face on the ship, it is said to be a bad sign and to indicate the imminent danger of the ship's sinking.

In shipbuilding, the Klabautermann helps to seal the ship's deck. On board, he makes himself heard by banging and other noises. It is said, *"Wenn er klopft, bleibt er, wenn er hobelt, geht er"* (When he knocks, he stays; when he flies, he goes). His appearance resembles that of a sailor – with a hammer and pipe, sometimes with a sailor's chest, with red hair and green teeth. Some sailors claim he leaves the ship only when it sinks; others, however, that he occasionally disembarks to announce the ship's arrival at the captain's house. According to an old sailor custom, a chicken belongs on every ship to scare off the Klabautermann.

Kludde

In Flanders *Kludde* is a nocturnal demon that can take on different guises and harasses passersby. Kludde is associated with the Schelde-region; Dendermonde and other villages in East Flanders, but stories also exist in the vicinity of Antwerp, such as Hemiksem and Schelle. In the municipality of Wichelen there is even a *Kluddepad* (Kludde-path). Kludde is also known in the areas around Dilbeek, Zemst and Zemst-Laar in Flemish Brabant, where it resides in the former swamps, forests, meadows and the river Zenne. He is a tormentor who often hides under bridges or in hollow trees. Hikers can only deduce his arrival by the sound he makes. This is because Kludde rattles a chain that he is obliged to wear on his left ankle. Once he has signaled their arrival, he jumps on the unsuspecting passerby, who is then obliged to carry him on his or her back for the rest of the night. When daybreak comes, or the passerby reaches his destination, Kludde disappears again. A local variant (from Breendonk) says that Kludde, after having jumped on the backs of nocturnal hikers, gets heavier and heavier. Until the poor hiker, who cannot get rid of the tormentor, drops dead. In some tales, Kludde is described as a monstrous black dog that walks on its hind legs. He can also take on the guise of a large black cat or giant black bird as well. The faster the passersby run away, the faster the creature follows them closely. In addition, he can enlarge and shrink himself. In other stories, he is more likely to be a man wrapped in a hairy dog skin, reminiscent of the legend of the *Werewolf*. Kludde lets his appearances depend on the situation. For example, he can transform himself into a normal cat that is approached by an endeared passerby, with horrifying consequences. As a big black bird he flies at night over farms and wakes up everyone with his cry: *"Kludde, Kludde, Kludde"*. Kludde resembles similar creatures like *Flodder*, *Ossaert* and the German *Aufhocker*-like spirits and in most cases appears to be belonging to a class of nocturnal shapeshifters that love to play pranks on passerby. However, there is a legend in Wichelen that describes how a woman stuffed a piece of cloth in Kluddes mouth to shake him off. The next day, one of the servants in the village was found to have fibers from that same cloth between his teeth, so the villagers could immediately identify this servant as Kludde.

Kobold

Kobold is a German term for usually humanoid looking house and nature-spirits, with often a certain adaptation to human activities. In many regions, Kobolds are known by local names, such as the *Heinzelmännchen* of Cologne. Other names are *Chimmeken, King Goldemar, Heinzchen, Heinze, Himschen, Heinzelmann, Hödekin, Kurd Chimgen, Walther, Wolterken, Allerünken, Alraune, Galgenmännlein* (in southern Germany), *Glucksmännchen, Hütchen,* and *Oaraunle*. Kobolds that live in human homes, for example, wear the clothing of peasants, while Kobolds that live on ships (*Klaubautermännlein*) smoke pipes and wear sailors clothing. The belief in Kobolds dates from at least the 13th century, when German peasants carved Kobold effigies for their homes. These practices hypothetically may have derived from an ancient belief in the mischievous Greek *Kobaloi,* spreading out further into Europe. Other similar sprites include the household *Lares* and *Penates* of ancient Rome, or native German beliefs in a similar room-spirit called *Kofewalt* (whose name is a possible root word of the modern Kobold, or a German dialectal variant). It is a very plausible theory that the Lares and Penates, that were "kept" by their Roman worshipers in small statues, are at the base of the carved wooden Kobold, the later garden Gnome. According to 13th-century German poet Conrad of Würzburg, medieval Germans carved Kobolds from boxwood and wax and put them *"up in the room for fun"*. Mandrake root was another material used. People believed that the wild Kobold remained in the material that was used to carve the figure. These Kobold effigies were 12 to 24 inch / (30 to 60 cm) high and had colorful clothing and large mouths. The German mythologist Jacob Grimm has also traced the custom to Roman times and has argued that religious authorities tolerated it even after the Germans had been Christianized. The Middle High German *Kóbolt* or *Kobólt* could be a compound, the first part of which is etymologically derived from *kobe* (hut, stable, hovel), while the second component may belong to *hold* (sublime, good, as in "Unhold" or "Frau Holle") or to *walten* (in *Kofewalt*: to rule, possess). In the latter case the name actually means "caretaker of the house, guardian of the house". In 1908, Otto Schrader traced the word to *kuba-walda*, meaning "the one that rules the house". Linguist Paul Wexler has proposed yet another etymology, tracing Kobold to the roots *koben* (pigsty) and *hold* which in his interpretation as part of the word "Kobold" does not mean "good or sublime" but " stable spirit".

The Kobold as a house-spirit protects the house, but likes to tease its inhabitants, though without causing harm. For example, he may appear in the form of a feather that falls on one's nose while sleeping, causing a sneeze. In the Erzgebirge (Ore Mountains), he appears as a reclusive black cat living in the house during the day, while at night he emerges from the chimney as a dragon-like creature to carry money to his owner. Beneficiaries of Kobolds therefore often become wealthy, but cannot die until they have passed on the Kobold to another person. According to popular belief, they were given a bowl of milk or some food overnight, which to the household-spirit represented an act of sacrifice. Although usually invisible, a Kobold can materialize in the form of an animal, a fire, a human being, and a candle. The most common depictions of Kobolds show them as human-like figures, the size of small children. There are also Kobolds that live in mines. These are usually depicted as hunched and ugly. Sometimes mythical mergers between the house-spirit and the spirit of the builder of the farm also occur in folkloric sources. Therefore, the concept of the Kobold often does not precisely distinguish between a spirit of nature and a spirit of the ancestors (which is another thing they have in common with the Lares and Penates). Closely related to the mythological concept of the Kobold are the Irish *Leprechauns*. There are also strong similarities with the house spirit *Cofgod* (pl.: *Cofgodas*; English: cove gods) from Anglo-Saxon religion. The name of the element *cobalt* comes from the creature's name, because medieval miners blamed the sprite for the poisonous and troublesome nature of the typical arsenical ores of this metal *(cobaltite and smaltite)* which polluted other mined elements.

Appearances
Kobolds may manifest as animals, fire, human beings and objects. Fiery Kobolds are also called *Drakes*, *Draches*, or *Puks*. A tale from the Altmark,

recorded by Anglo-Saxon scholar Benjamin Thorpe in 1852, describes the Kobold as *"a fiery stripe with a broad head, which he usually shakes from one side to the other..."* A legend from the same period taken from Pechüle, near Luckenwald, decribes the Kobold as flying through the air as a blue stripe and carrying grain. *"If a knife or a fire-steel be cast at him, he will burst, and must let fall what which he is carrying."* Some legends say the fiery Kobold enters and exits a house through the chimney. Legends dating back to 1852, from western Uckermark, ascribe both human and fiery features to the Kobold; he wears a red jacket and cap and moves through the air as a fiery stripe. Such fire associations, along with the name Drake, may point to a connection between the Kobold and the Latvian and Lithuanian *Aitvaras*. Kobolds that live in human homes are generally depicted as humanlike, dressed as peasants, and standing about as tall as a four-year-old child. A legend recorded by folklorist Joseph Snowe from a place called Alte Burg, in 1839, tells of a creature *"in the shape of a short, thick-set being, neither boy nor man, but akin to the condition of both, garbed in a partly-colored loose overcoat, and wearing a high-crowned hat with a broad brim on his diminutive head"*. The Kobold *Hüdekin* or *Hödekin* (little hat) of Hildesheim wore a little hat down over his face. Another type of Kobold, known as the *Hütchen*, is said to be 1 to 3.25 feet / 0.3–1 meter tall, with red hair and beard, clad in red or green clothing, a red hat and may even be blind. Yet other tales describe Kobolds appearing as herdsmen looking for work as little, wrinkled old men wearing pointed hoods.

As said before, some Kobolds resemble small children. According to dramatist and novelist X.B. Saintine, Kobolds are the spirits of dead children and often appear with a knife that represents the means by which they were put to death. *Heinzelmann*, a Kobold from the folklore of Hudermühlen Castle in the region of Lüneburg, appeared as a beautiful boy with blond, curly hair reaching to his shoulders and dressed in a red silk coat. His voice was *"soft and tender like that of a boy or maiden"*. Legends variously describe mine Kobolds as 2 feet / 0.6 metre tall old men, dressed like miners, to short, bent creatures with ugly features, including, in some tales, black skin. Folklorist D.L. Ashliman has reported Kobolds appearing as wet cats and hens, and Nancy Arrowsmith and George Moorse (in *A Field Guide to the Little People*, London, 1977) mention Kobolds in the shape of bats, cats, roosters, snakes, and worms. The people of Altmark believed that Kobolds appeared as black cats while walking the earth. The Kobold *Heinzelmann* could appear as a black marten and a large snake. Most often, Kobolds remain completely invisible. Although *King Goldemar* (or *Goldmar*), a famous Kobold from Castle Hardenstein, had hands *"thin like those of a frog, cold and soft to the feel"*, but seldom showed himself. The master of Hundermühlen Castle, where Heinzelmann lived, convinced a Kobold to let him touch him one night. The Kobold's fingers were childlike, and his face was like a skull, without body heat.

Kodukäija

A *Kodukäija*, *Külmking* or *Nook* in Estonian folklore is a Revenant (German: *Wiederganger*), someone who has to walk around as a demonic dead person, for having committed some crime, or for some other reason. Mostly, he or she haunts his or her former place of origin.

Koolhoas

The *Koolhoas* was a hare made of straw that was hidden in a field of rapeseed before harvesting, that functioned as a home for the field-spirit of the same name. The name Koolhoas comes from the Lower Saxon *kool* (here: rapeseed) and *hoas* (hare). This folkloric custom was practiced in the northeastern part of the Netherlands. The custom disappeared after the onset of large-scale mechanization of agriculture, in the early 20th century. If the Koolhoas was found when threshing, it was laid up. Finally, the hare was laid on the last load, with everyone uncovering their heads in respect. Only when the farmer had gone around with the jenever (a gin-like alcoholic beverage) could this cargo be taken away. Sometimes there was no doll, but the last sheaf of grain (called the hare) underwent the same honor. This sheaf was often cut by the *arenlezer* (ear reader), the farmhand who walked behind the mowers to collect the fallen ears. The custom stems from the belief that a spirit resides in the field, ensuring a good yield and protecting the field.

Kornmann

The *Kornmann* (corn man) is a male corn demon and *Kinderschreck* (child scare) of German legend, that resides in the fields and acres and sometimes throws an iron rod. The Kornmann has various names.

Some of them have to do with field crops, such as *Hafermann* (oat man), *Roggenmann* (rye man), *Weizenmann* (wheat man), *Gerstenmann* (barley man), *Weizenalter* (wheat elder), *Barstenalter* (probably: boulder man), *Kornvater* (corn father), *Erdäpfelmann* (potato man) and *Fruchtmann* (fruit man). Other names refer to other field plants or to the harvest itself, such as *Grummetkerl*, *Grasteufel*, *Feldmann*, *Erntemann* and *Schewekerl*. The Kornmann is also named in the diminutive, referring to his sometimes dwarfish figure. Corresponding names include *Kornmännchen, Kornmännlein, Kornmannl* (all meaning little corn man), *Getreidemännchen* (little grain man), *Troadmannl, Hafermännchen* (little oat man), *Holmmandl, Feldmännlein* (little field man), *Kleemännchen* and *Graamannl.*

Appearance and habits

The Kornmann wears a large black hat and a huge big stick. He has red eyes and a fiery mouth. The Kornmann is also thought of as bright white. He has a black face, hence he is also called *Schwarzer Mann* (black man). The Kornmann is also seen as a black or grey male resembling a dwarf who wears a red cap. His song is the chirping of crickets. When not appearing as a dwarfish figure the corn-man may show himself as an old man. This is referred to by names such as the *der Alte* (the Old one), *Großvater* (Grandfather) and *alter Mann* (Old man). Sometimes the Kornmann also takes on the nature of a *Will-o'-the-wisp.* The Kornmann even appears as an *Aufhocker* or *Druckgeist,* a phantom figure that jumps on the back of its victim and wants to be carried around, becoming heavier with every step its victim takes. The Corn Man lives in an underground cave. He transforms the heaps of grain in the field. Where he sits, the grain lies smoothed on all four sides. The corn-man lures and teases the wanderers, and also leads those who meet him away through the air, just as the wild hunter does. It fits in with this, that as a Schwarzer Mann he is also connected to the weather. If a thunderstorm comes up during the harvest, then *"bald kommt der schwarzer Mann"* (soon the black man comes).

Saathahn

The *Saathahn* (seed rooster) is a feast to celebrate the completion of sowing, originally consisting of a rooster: when one has sown the grain, corn and forage, then one gives the Saathahn to the farmhands and handmaids, followed by a festive drinking of wine or sometimes the last beer, as it was custom in Munich. (*"So man gesäet hat den traid, korn und fesen, so gibt man den knechten und diernen den sathan, ye vieren ain gans und yedem ain trincken wein kelhamer aus gnaden."* – 1500 Schmeller II 334). It is said that the Kornmann, also called the *Säemann*, *"habe den Saathahn"*, i.e, the Kornmann keeps this special rooster called Saathahn under his custody. For this reason, children in Salzwedel were sent out into the fields during the sowing season with a piece of green shrubbery to fetch the *Saathahn*. Elsewhere, on the first day of Fastenzeit (Lent), the children drive the *bösen Sämann* (evil seedman) out of the field with burning straw wipes.

The connection to the Heidmann

In his *German Mythology*, Jacob Grimm mentions the *Heidmann*, a phantom that sneaks around houses and looks through the windows at night. Whomever he looks at in the process, will die within a year and a day. The name Heidmann is strongly reminiscent of *Heidemann* and *Heidemänneken*, two names of the Kornmann.

The Kornmann as a *Kinderschreck* (child scare)

The Kornmann catches children and takes them away. He puts children in his sack and takes them to his underground cave. Sometimes the Kornmann takes the children only for a limited time, for example, he takes them into the forest and brings them back to the field after a year. More often he takes them permanently. Sometimes the Kornmann takes away the children's caps. He also knocks about or pummels the children and this is said to cause freckles. In some places the Kornmann often also takes over the function of frightening children from other daemons, like the *Roggenmuhme* (corn aunt) or the *Kornhexe* (corn witch). For example, the Kornmann beats children's heads off, strangles them, or squeezes them to death on his iron chest. He sticks children in the butter churn or hits them on the seat of their trousers. The Kornmann also blinds children or beats them with lameness. The Kornmann also resembles the Roggenmuhme in that he appears with sickles, scythes or knives. Hence he is called *Sichelmann* (sickle man), *Sensenmann* oder *Sesselmann*. Like the Roggenmuhme, he cuts off the children's legs or other body parts, or even slaughters the children and eats them, or sucks their blood.

Krampus

Krampus, also *Kramperl* or *Bartl*, is in Advent-customs a frightening figure, in the company of *Nikolaus* (St. Nicholas). He is widespread in the eastern Alps, in southern Bavaria and the Upper Palatinate, in Austria, Liechtenstein, Hungary, Croatia, Slovenia, Slovakia, the Czech Republic, South Tyrol, Welsh Tyrol (Trentino) and parts of northern Italy outside the Alps. While Nikolaus gives presents to the good children, the naughty ones are punished by the Krampus. The figure of Krampus originated – like many other demonic figures of the Alpine region – from pre-Christian times. The group of Nikolaus, Krampus and other companions is called *Bass* or *Pass* in Bavarian dialects. The name Krampus derives from Middle High German *Krampen* (claw), or Bavarian *Krampn* (something lifeless, or withered). In many regions the figure of the Krampus has mixed with Perchten-customs like the *Schiachperchten*. In the Bavarian Alpine foothills and in the Austrian Salzkammergut, Styria and Salzburg, the Krampus is more commonly known as *Kramperl*. In Styria and Carinthia, in addition to Kramperl, the term *Bartl* is also used, a short form of *Bartholomew*. Due to the centuries-long Slovenian-German bilingualism of Carinthia and Styria, it can be assumed that the Slovenian term *Parkelj* is also derived from Bartl. In Salzkammergut, the term *Miglo* also occurs. In the Tyrolean region, one speaks more frequently of *Tuifl*, *Tuifltåg*, or *Tuifltratzen*, derived from the term *Teufel* (Devil). Also the term *Ganggerl* is used.

Historical evolution

The Krampus custom was originally widespread throughout the Habsburg Empire and neighboring areas, and was then banned during the time of the Inquisition, as no one was allowed to dress up as a devilish figure – on the penalty of death. However, this winter-custom continued in some hard-to-reach places. There are no sources before the end of the 16th century. Starting from the monastery schools (children's bishop's feast), it seems that it was not until the middle of the 17th century that the custom (re)developed: accompanied by frightening figures, devils and animal masks *(Habergeiß)*. In the Counter-Reformation period, parlor games were created, which still exist in Bad Mitterndorf, Tauplitz and Pichl-Kainisch (Salzkammergut), in the Salzburgerland and in Tyrol. Since this time the *Krampuspassen* formed, parallel to the *Perchtenlauf*, wherein only the able-bodied, unmarried men of the village are allowed to participate, and with this the event became public again since the middle of the 19th century. Outside the Counter-Reformation areas, the Krampuses remained displaced by the North German Protestant-influenced *Knecht Ruprecht*. In the Alemannic-Protestant area, the two forms mixed, probably having a common origin in an Italian figure of the 16th century; Italians nurtured the idea that the Devil devoured the souls of sinners. Evil is especially strong in the harsh winter season and therefore manifests itself in this figure, which was depicted accordingly.

Krampus parades
In many villages and towns in the eastern Alps, southern Bavaria and the Upper Palatinate, Austria, parts of the Principality of Liechtenstein, Hungary, Slovenia, Slovakia, the Czech Republic, Italy (limited to South Tyrol, Welsh Tyrol (Trentino) and especially in the Vinschgau and Pustertal valleys) and parts of Croatia, there are still Krampus parades, in which people dressed up as Krampus parade through the streets with the loud noise of their bells to scare passersby. They also make use of their long rods, threatening people. The *Tuifltratzen* (Tyrol) or *Kramperltratzn* in parts of Austria *Kramperlstauben* (*stauben* = to chase away), is in some places a test of courage for the children of the area, who try to tease the Krampuses without being caught or beaten. Krampus Day is on December 5th, the eve of the feast of Nikolaus on December 6th. Usually both figures appear together on the evening of December 5th, but sometimes on December 6th. Among the largest parades with over one thousand Krampuses (2008) is the Krampuslauf in St. Johann im Pongau, which takes place annually on December 6th, as well as the largest Krampuslauf in Austria in Klagenfurt. The latter stretching over a distance of 1.5 kilometers.

Kratt

Kratt (also *Pisuhänd, Puuk, Tulihänd* – Fire hand) is a creature in Estonian folklore, that flies around as a fire or sparking yoke and collects all kinds of goods (grain, clothes, money, etc.). According to earlier Estonian beliefs, the human soul itself could become a Kratt under the influence of witchcraft. More recently, the notion of a Kratt as a kind of ghost in a machine – a man-made creature lacking human characteristics, made from various objects – became widespread. It has been commonly believed that in order to revive such a Kratt made by human hands, it is necessary to give three drops of blood to the Devil and sell one's soul to him.

There are quite detailed instructions on how to make a Kratt. The most common of these is that a Kratt is made from three pieces of old, tattered bath tow, tied around a broomstick, a glowing charcoal placed in the heart, and on the darkest and cloudiest night of the full moon, a covenant is made with the Devil at the crossing of three paths. To make the contract, three drops of your own blood must be poured into the glowing heart of the Kratt. The teachings vary however from text to text, some of which state that the most appropriate time to perform the Kratt-ritual is on the third Thursday night of each month, and that instead on a crossing of three paths, the ritual should be performed at the crossing of five paths. The finished Kratt looks half-man, half-animal, half machine. It usually has a red beard and must be given work to do at all times, so that it does not attack its master and take him underground with it to the old dragon (Devil). To get rid of the Kratt, the creature must be given a job it cannot do, such as making a rope out of sand.

Red fire-walkers

Estonian folklore also distinguishes this constructed Kratt from people capable of turning themselves into so called *Red fire-walkers* in order to steal from neighboring villages. Similar to the mechanical Kratt they fly around as sparking fires. To transform themselves into a flame, these thieving people use a stone in the corner of the room at which they sniff. Thus in this case, the Kratt is associated more with a human being than a supernatural being, and the family, to which this kind of "human Kratt" belongs, feeds it porridge. A fire-walker is usually a darkly dressed man with a beard and a pointed black hat.

Kuhwampen

The *Kuhwampen* of the Pinzgau regio (Austria), is a female *Alp* or *Trud*. It was described by Marie Andree-Eysn in *Volkskundliches aus dem bayrisch-österreichischen Alpengebiet,* Braunschweig 1910, not as a unique creature, as some Alps are, but as the projected double of the wife of a farmer who at night visited a cobbler, who was staying in her home, and who stabbed the Kuhwampen in the eye with his awl. The next morning it turned out that the farmer's wife had a stitch in her eye.

Kupolė

In Lithuanian lore *Kupolė* is the spirit of springtime vegetation and flowers. A pole with branches, decorated with flowers and plants is also called a Kupolė, and is a symbol of the Tree of Life, the flourishing and maturation of plants. The *Festival of Kupolė* (*Kupolinės*) was associated with the *Feast of St. John the Baptist (Joninės)* but in fact used to be dedicated to the goddess *Lada* or *Lado*. During this festival, women pick sacral herbs, dance and sing special songs. Kupolinės is also known as *Rasos*. Compare this with *Ziedu māte* in Latvian folklore, *Kupala* in Poland and *Ivan Kupala* in Russia. The Festival of Kupolė is celebrated at the moment when the sun and nature itself are at their peak. It is the moment of transformation, when all the flora shifts from the blooming stage to that of maturing seeds and fruit, thus giving rise to new life. It is therefore also the period of weddings: young girls willing to get married play a game in which they stand with their backs turned towards the Kupolė and throw their flower wreaths over their heads. The number of tries needed until the wreath stays on a branch indicates the number of years left until the girl's marriage. In the period of the Summer solstice, herbs and plants are believed to be particularly full of vital and magical force. These plants are also called *kupolės*, since, just as with crops, this is the time they thrive and flourish (Lithuanian: *kupa*). However, when picked after the Day of St. John's feast, the powers of the herbs fade, so people try to pick all medicinal herbs before or during the feast. On the day of the feast itself it was the considered the right time for picking the so called *magical kupolė*, a special bouquet of flowers, herbs, and plants, which was used both as a divination tool to predict the future and for protection against evil forces. For the future/fortune-telling, one has to pick a separate bouquet of 9 herbs, which had to be picked in bunches of three from three different spots, by walking three steps in ever different direction to go from one spot to another. The plants had to be collected in silence. The ancient Lithuanians believed that the act of wading in new grass and picking medicinal herbs strengthened a person in all aspects and offered protection from evil spirits.

Kurbur the Klabauf

Klaubauf is a Bavarian variant of the Krampus, who baked children into pies! This traditional *Bogey*-story is of course part of the Klaubauf festivities. The Bavarian village of Hötting however is haunted by a

Klaubauf-figure, called *Kurbur* by the people there. He lives in the "Höttinger Klamm", which is a terrible rock crevice. At one point, the rocks bend over the path between them in an arc, like a gothic vault, so that the path becomes completely dark. This bottleneck has the strange name *die Hundskirche* (the dog church). Kurbur is extraordinarily feared there, especially by children, who have a rhyme for him that describes his nature and work in striking brevity. This rhyme reads:

"Kurbur aus der Klamm
Frißt d'Bub'n und d'Madl z'samm."

(Kurbur from the ravine
Eats the boys and girls together.)

In this Höttinger ravine sat in the Otternloch a demonic spider, which once entrapped seventeen victims at once, and sucked their blood. The story of Kurbur was published in *Mythen und Sagen Tirols*. Collected and edited by Johann Nepomuk Ritter von Alpenburg, Zurich, 1857.

L

Lange Wapper

Lange Wapper figures in several Flemish folk-myths. It is a tit sucking *giant*, *shapeshifter*, *water-sprite* and trickster, with a statue in the City of Antwerp. His folk tales were told especially in the city of Antwerp, but there are also legends about him in Blankenberge, Bevel, Kessel, Nijlen and Wilrijk. In fact, one legend about him started in Wilrijk in the 16th century. A farmer found an enormous amount of garden parsley and a red cabbage in his bed. When he touched the vegetables, they turned into a cute baby. As he was unable to take care of the child, it was adopted by a family living in Antwerp. Many years later the boy helped people in need. One day he saved an old woman who was thrown into the river Schelde by a youth gang. The old woman thanked the young man by giving him some gifts, such as the ability to shape-shift and to make himself so tall he could move from one town to another with a single giant leap. As he preferred to be in his tall size, he got the nickname Lange Wapper (tall

Wapper). The man turned into a water-sprite that liked to live near the sea, near rivers or canals. He appears at night and chases the drunkards. At first as a small man, but he is able to make himself bigger and bigger, until he towers over the houses. When the drunk comes home, panting and sweating, Lange Wapper looks in through the window and laughs like the Devil. Sometimes he disguises himself as a small child, to drink mother's milk. When a mother takes this child to nurse and put it in a crib, Lange Wapper lets himself grow so big that he no longer fits in the room.

Langtüttin

The *Langtüttin* (long teat, long tit)is a female demon figure, so called because of her long, pendulous breasts. Old High German *Tutte* stands for *Zitze* (teat). The name Langtüttin comes from Tyrolean legend. In East Central German lore, one speaks of the *Tittenwief* or *Zitzenweib* (teat wife) and in East Prussia of the Roggenmöhn. In Scandinavian folklore, the *Slattenpatte* is a comparable demonic figure. The Langtüttin is one of the corn demons and today only functions as a child fright figure. As such, she runs after children and offers them her breasts. Milk flows from one breast and pus from the other, sometimes also blood and tar. The breasts can also be black or even made of iron. So they say in northern Germany "*Frau Anna Marlene Ittchen mit ihren eisernen Tittchen*" (Madam Anna Marlene Ittchen with her iron titties). For children, an encounter with the Langtüttin often ends fatally. In order not to be hindered by the long breasts when being pursued, the Langtüttin throws her breasts over her shoulders.

Laukų dvasios

Laukų dvasios are Lithuanian field-demons, spirits, that are running through the fields. Quite similar to the field demons or field-spirits in German-speaking Europe, which have been described extensively by the folklorist and Germanist Wilhelm Mannhardt, as the *Roggenwulf*, *Sauzagel*, etc., we find the same kind of field daemons in the Baltic region. With the great similarity that small whirling winds, which made a trail through the fields, were seen as the presence of the field-demons, that – like the German spirits – often had specific animal forms. These demons had the task of protecting the crops and ensuring a good harvest, and

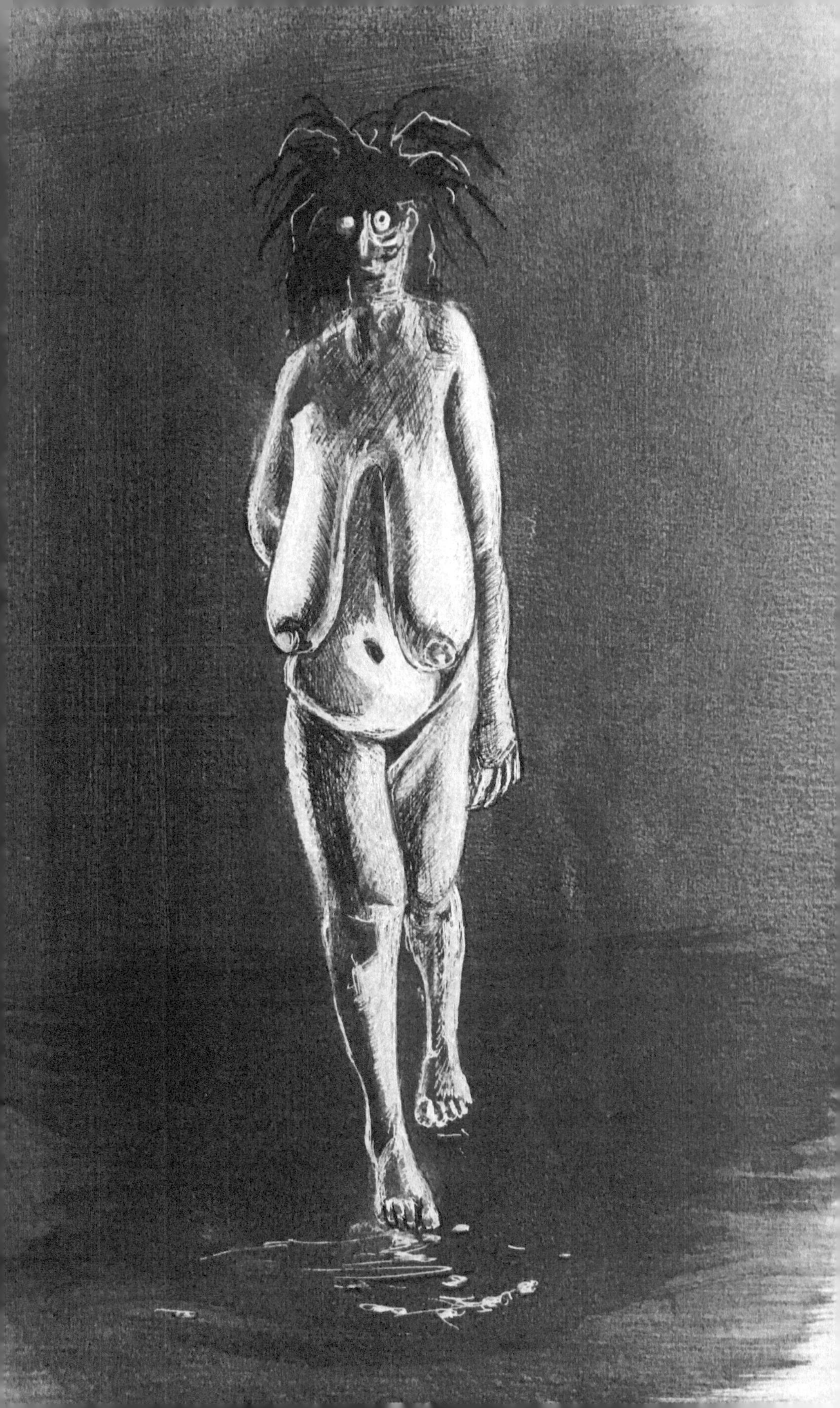

were therefore kept under control with annual rituals. When crops in the fields waved in the wind, people saw this as being the actions of spirits. Laukų dvasios include *Nuogalis*, *Kiškis* (hare), *Meška* (bear), *Lapė* (fox), *Katinas* (tomcat), *Bubis, Bubas, Bubė, Baubas, Babaužis, Bobas, Maumas, Raudongalvis* (red-headed), *Raudongerklis* (red-throated), *Žaliaakis* (green-eyed), *Papléštakis, Guda, Dizikas, Smauglys* (boa), *Ruginis* (spirit of rye), *Papioké, Pypalas, Žebris, Arklys* (horse), *Vilkas* (wolf).

Lauma

In Latvian mythology the *Lauma* (pl. *Laumas*) is a birth helper, she looks after the health and well-being of both mother and baby. If the mother does not survive childbirth or doesn't accept her child, the Lauma assumes the role of the child's surrogate spiritual mother. She spins the web of life for the child, and weeps for the fate of some children. The fact that the cloth of life can, to some extent, weave itself, indicates the existence of a power above that of the Lauma. A Lauma could be a good worker, but if you made her angry, she would immediately destroy what was done. They showed themselves helpful to good people, while evil and lazy women were punished by them. The Lauma also appeared as a dark omen when a woman violated the ban on women's work (laundry and spinning, less often weaving) on the night of Thursday to Friday. If a Lauma saw a woman spinning at that time, she would help, but as soon as the Lauma finished her work, she would kill the woman. If they were angry, they sheared the wool from the sheep, tangled the mane of the horses or milked the cows empty. According to some lore they even killed the children of lazy mothers and ate them. They could also substitute an unbaptized child, left unattended, for a sheaf of hay for the parents, which would then turn into a living child. The parents would raise the child as if it were their own, but one day it would leave them and run off to the Laumas. That was how the Laumas bred. They were also believed to kidnap children, sheerly out of maternal feelings. Thus over the years, her image has been degraded. Associated with baby-stealing (since she is incapable of mothering and raising children of her own), the Lauma lost her looks and her sweetness, transforming into an old and malignant hag. She weeps over the fate of her destiny, hoping one day to regain her beauty.

Laumė

Originally the Lithuanian *Laumės* (singular: *Laumė*) are very ancient atmospheric goddesses of Lithuanian mythology. It is possible that the image of these goddesses was formed during the Mesolithic period, just after the end of the Ice Age. The Laumės were depicted in the form of animals, such as mares or female goats, bears and dogs. Later, Laumės had an anthropomorphic appearance: usually with bird claws instead of feet and resembling females with the head or lower body of female goats. Other forms comprised half human/half dog or half mare, similar to centaurs. Similar to a Cyclops, Laumės often had one eye. They also had large breasts with stone nipples; in this regard pieces of belemnite found on the ground are referred to as "Laumės nipples". Laumės were dangerous, they could kill a man by tickling or pinching and eat their bodies, behavior similar to that of the *Lamia* of Greek folk belief. Lithuanian myth also claimed that the Laumės had huge cows, that could be milked by all people. However, after very cold winters, the cows died; belemnite fossils were said to be the remains of their udders. The Laumės were afraid of iron tools. In Lithuanian, *Laumės juosta* (Laume's bow) means the rainbow, *Laumės žirgas* (Laume's horse) means the blue dragonfly, and *Laumės šluota* (Laume's broom) means mistletoe, which is also called Hexenbesen (witches' broom) in German.

The Laumės are supposed to have descended from heaven to Earth. They lived near lakes, abandoned bathhouses, on lake islands or in dense forests. That is why numerous water-bodies in Lithuania have names associated with the word Laumė. Laumės like to gather near rivers, lakes, marshes, in meadows, where the dew falls during the night at new or full moon. They dance and have fun, leaving marks in the form of circles (similar to fairy rings) in the meadows. Usually the power of the Laumės was the greatest on Friday of the New Moon, during the rainiest days of the month in Lithuania. Laumės could cause hail, storm or rain by singing, dancing or curses. In Lithuania a traditional Laumės-song was sung during the celebration of marriages, up until the 19th century. The song was sung while the young women danced in a circle, with one of them in the center. It was claimed that the dance and the song could make rain. In later times, the Laumės were depicted as extremely beautiful women, who appeared naked or were wearing very fine clothing. Laumės usually manifested in groups of three. They had the ability to perform women's tasks like washing or communicating with children perfectly, and they were especially skilled at spinning. Laumes loved boys, respected those who worked and helped those who were in need. They punished those who ridiculed them, and those who were lazy. Men who try to fool the Laumas are rushed to their deaths. When they married a human, they were a good wife and mother. But these marriages lasted only a short time.

Lauterfresser

The *Lauterfresser* (just want to eat) or *Lautfresser* is a famous Tyrolean spirit – originally the historical figure Mathias Perger (1587–1645), who was executed after being accused of witchcraft. Perger allegedly took part in a witches' Sabbat where Belial, gave him a bearskin that allowed him to change his shape. Lauterfresser was capable of almost everything. He could assume any shape, change the weather, talk with rats, mice and horses and had a superhuman strength. He was allergic to children and made them disappear. Most legends about the spirit were collected by Johann Adolf Heyl in *Volkssagen, Bräuche und Meinungen aus Tirol*, Brixen 1897. The spirit owned his name Lauterfresser to something Mathias Perger said while still alive: "...*der Brixner Hexenmeister Lauterfresser – so genannt weil er am liebsten "lauter" gegessen hatte, vielleicht also magenkrank war...*" The German *lauter* translates as "just" or "only". Eating was all Perger wanted to do while still alive, and the German quote above suggests that he could have been suffering from a stomach illness.

Leckfräulein

In Tyrol, the *Leckfräulein* (pl. & sing.) lived in caves near the Locherer in the Lecklahn. Sometimes, when they came to a lonely farm, the owners shared a meal with them. This guaranteed good luck and thus the farmers liked to see them, in the stable, in the barn, in the room. Everywhere they prevented misfortune. So one day they appeared again and ate some of the food. However, the baker's wife was in a bad mood and hit a Leckfräulein with a ladle on her hand. Embittered by this ingratitude, she shouted, "*Auf und davon und nimmer her, Und kein reicher Locherer mehr!*", informing the baker's wife that her happiness was gone forever. The Leckfräulein left the house through the chimney. The curse happened; happiness and blessing flew out of the chimney with her. That the curses of the Saligen, here called Leckfräulein, came true is repeatedly mentioned in Tyrolean folk tales. Main source: Johann Adolf Heyl – *Volkssagen, Bräuche und Meinungen aus Tirol*, Brixen 1897.

Leeton

In Latvian folklore, there is an *Alp*-type of nocturnal visitor, known as the *Leeton*. The Leeton jumps on horses and can literally ride them to their deaths during the night, draining them of their life energy as the creature makes them race around the field.

Lietuvēns

Lietuvēns (Russian: *Lietuonis*; in Latvian also *Lītūņš*) is an *Alp*-like entity of Latvian mythology. It is the same creature as the Slavic *Mara,* the Russian: *Mapa,* German *Mare* or *Moor.* The creature tortures people, cattle and horses during the night and is connected to sleep paralysis, being a spirit that sends nightmares to people and pets at night. In Latvian folk culture, Lietuvēns is usually described as a labored wretched child. It is small in height, moves fast and comes at noon or night. Sometimes, but rarely, it turns into an ugly vicious woman, reminiscent of a witch. It always leaves through the same place: where it entered. Commonly it's some hole or crack in the wall; it can also be a keyhole or slot in the door. Sometimes the weakened victim is able to see just a bit of the Lietuvēns and feel that it is lying on top with all its weight while not giving the victim any opportunity to move or run away. It becomes harder to breathe and eventually the Lietuvēns leaves, in rare cases leaving its victim on the verge of death. Folklore however offers two remedies against these nocturnal beings, when under attack. The first is to move the pinky or big toe of the left foot to get rid of the Lietuvēns. It instantly runs away. The second is using either the Latvian cross or the classic pentagram for protection. The Latvian cross was even carved in the hoofs of animals to ward of the Lietuvēns. The best protection against the Lietuvēns is using this cross, but farm animals can also be protected from attacks by attaching a knife, comb, or scythe to their back.

The hole, crack or keyhole, which forms an entrance for Lietuvēns, has to be fixed with a piece of mottled wood. It should be cut with left hand and brought to the house with a thick part first. Everything has to be done at night when a Lietuvēns has already come in. Without finding an exit, the creature often turns into a beautiful young woman and stays in the house while the exit is closed and escapes as soon as the door is unlocked.

Lindwurm

Lindwurm is the name for a dragon or snake-like mythical creature
– the Old High German *lint* translates as "snake." The Lindwurm is
usually bipedal, but four or more legs are also possible. It resembles a
dragon and is sometimes referred to as a subspecies. The creature has
no wings or only a short pair of wings, and is mentioned mainly in old
Germanic sagas. Usually, a Lindwurm has a long tail and short legs
and the creature is sometimes described as a man-eater. The dragon
Fafnir from the Nibelungen saga is a Lindwurm. The Lindwurm is the
emblem of numerous Central European cities, including the Austrian
city of Klagenfurt am Wörthersee and the Slovenian capital Ljubljana
(Laibach). Places that have *Limb-* or *Lind-* in their names often have a
dragon legend as their central myth, such as Limburg an der Lahn among
many other towns. Lindwurms are said to live in the underground lake
in the Spißbrand (a mountain near Lilienfeld), the underground lake
of the Untersberg (Ramsau) and a very noisy specimen was believed to
inhabit the Golm, a mountain also near Lilienfeld. In total there are over
a hundred different Lindwurm legends. Most of them are found in the
southern part of Germany (especially Bavaria), Austria (especially Styria),
Tyrol and Switzerland.

Loreley

The *Loreley* (also *Lorelei, Loreleï, Lore Lay, Lore-Ley, Lurley, Lurelei,
Lurlei*) is a slate rock in the Upper Middle Rhine Valley near Sankt
Goarshausen, which is located on the eastern, right bank of the Rhine,
132 m./145 yards high (193.14 m./212 yards above sea level) rising
steeply on the inside of a Rhine bend. It is also the name of a mythical
Undine, who was supposed to live on this rock since the fairy tale *Lore
Lay*, which Clemens Brentano told in ballad form in his novel *Godwi*
(1801). Brentano's invention had such a strong reception on the spot that
even before the middle of the 19th century his tale was stylized as an old
legend (as a "fairy tale of old times") by Heinrich Heine and many others.
So, in contrast to what is generally believed, Loreley was indeed based on
the "*Undine*-concept", but a literary invention instead of a local *water-
spirit*, which in later days of course may have received Tulpa or thought
form-like qualities due to its immense popularity over two centuries of
attention by writers, artists, musicians and people who love the myth.

Ludki or Luttchen

Ludki (Lusatian: *Ludki* or *Lutki*, German: *Luttchen* "little ones", *Lutchen*
in Mark Brandenburg – compare the Low Saxon *leutje* "little") in the
folk-beliefs of Lusatia (Lausitz, Łużyce), are dwarfish *earth-spirits*, who
are identified with the souls of ancestors. They were imagined as tiny
creatures with beards, dressed in red or white, living in caves under
mountains and hills, who fled from the sound of church bells. They were
considered friendly, sometimes visiting people's homes to borrow dishes,
which they always returned with a small gift in gratitude.
– See also the Sorbian *Lutken* in *Spirit Beings in European Folklore,
    Compendium 3.*

Luupainaja

In Estonian mythology, the *Luupainaja* (Bone-presser or Bone-wrestler)
is an *Alp*-type nocturnal spirit that oppresses sleepers. Other names for
the Luupainaja include *Painaja, Painak, Panijas, Paanjas, Painakane,
Luupaanija, Luupaine, Luupatak, Tallaja.* The Luupainaja is named after
the way it harms people, as well as animals. These demons are known as
pressers or *wrestlers*, because they wrestle with their victims, oppressing
the human body so that it cannot move. This oppression and torture
causes the victims to sweat profusely and, when they wake up, their limbs
tremble and their heart is pounding. A prolonged oppression can even
lead to the victims death. The Luupainaja not only tortures people, but
also tries to weaken the strength of farm animals. Like so often in the case
of nocturnal Alp-like creatures, stories exist that suggest the Luupainaja is
not always a non-human entity, but can also be the projected double of a
living person. In most stories the Luupainaja appears as a young woman,
but they can also appear as old women and old men. In animal form they
may take the shapes of black cats, horses, dogs, etc., and they also sit on
the back of other animals, mostly cattle. There's a story about a horse in
the stable being attacked by a Luupainaja in the guise of a black cat that
suddenly disappears – as if dissolving into thin air – after the farmer
starts beating the cat with a whip. The creatures can also take the shape of
an object, most notably a goose feather.

Getting rid of a Luupainaja

There are several ways of getting rid of a Luupainaja. The simplest way
is to move your big toe. It was believed that if you felt a Luupainaja

oppressing you, you had to move your big toe and the Luupainaja would escape. Another common way was to light a fire, as light was thought to frighten the Luupainaja. In Järvamaa, it is customary, after the arrival of the Luupainaja, to block all holes from which the air escapes from the room with wooden sticks. In this way the creature gets trapped in the room. Of course, somebody else has to put the sticks in, because the one who is being trampled by the Luupainaja can't use the sticks during the trampling, and afterwards it would be too late. If it is impossible to make the room airtight, then the person that is tormented by the Luupainaja must find out who is trampling him. If the Luupainaja places itself upon them, all they have to do is call out the name of the person who is suspected of being the attacker. As one cannot get a word out of one's mouth when the Bone-wrestler is trampling, it was probably understood that the name was called out when the person woke up and recognized its attacker. That the Luupainaja could very well be an attacker projecting his/her double, is also underlined by a remedy which uses a whip and tar:

"Make a whip of three strings three Thursday evenings, dip the whip in tar, and then hide and wait for the Luupainaja to enter. If the Luupainaja appears on the back of a person or an animal, strike this person or animal three times on the back with the tarred whip. Immediately the Bone-wrestler will disappear and never return. After that, you can still recognize the Luupainaja the next day as he or she will have stripes on his or her face."

In some areas of Finland owls were shot and nailed on the barn or stable door to protect the farm animals from the Luupainaja, that seems to be afraid of these birds. It also appears to have an allergy for copper coins and cypress wood.

M

Mare

– See under *Alp, Nachtalb; Moor*

Marluzine

In the folklore of Henegauwen/Hainaut, a province in the southwest
of Flanders, Belgium, *Marluzine* is a *Fairy* specialized in air currents.
She was believed to be the whistle in the locks, the slammer of doors
and was fond of tickling legs with her breeze. However she is also a
vegetation-spirit, a guardian of gardens and vegetable gardens. When she
felt mistreated, she became the little local storm-wind that flattened the
wheat field of her offender. She was also blamed for carrying away violent
children, together with animals or plants, in a gust of wind.

Mātes

Originally the Latvian *Mātes* (Mothers) are personified maternal forces
that represent a certain aspect of nature. Later in history many new Mātes
appeared, who for example represented household activities or items like
food. The Mātes are mentioned in Latvian folklore and their number is
about seventy. These Mātes, with a few exceptions, rarely play a role in
Latvian mythology. They are often mentioned only once, without being
described in more detail. Some of them are probably spontaneous poetic
formations. Types of mātes are:
- nature: *Dabas māte* (Mother nature); *Meža māte* (Forest mother);
  Āru māte (Field mother); *Lauku māte* (Meadow mother); *Dārzu māte*
  (Mother of the garden)
- plants: *Ceru māte* (Mother of perennial plants); *Krūma māte* (Bush
  mother); *Lazdu māte* (Hazel mother); *Mieža māte* (Barley mother);
  Linu māte (Linseed mother); *Ogu māte* (Berry mother); *Rožu māte*
  (Rose mother); *Sēņu māte* (Mushroom mother); *Ziedu māte* (Blossom
  mother); *Lapu māte* (Leaf mother)
- animals: *Bišu māte* (Mother of bees); *Briežu māte* (Deer mother); *Govu
  māte* (Cow mother); *Lopu māte* (Mother of livestock); *Zirgu māmulīte*
  (Horse mother)

- weather: *Laika māte* (Weather mother); *Vēja māte* (Wind mother) *Miglas māte* (Mother of nebulae); *Lietus māte* (Rain mother); *Sniega māte* (Snow mother)
- water: *Ūdens māte* Water mother; *Upes māte* (River mother); *Jūras māte* (Sea mother); *Bangu māte* (Water spring mother)
- food: *Piena māte* (Milk mother); *Sviesta māte* (Butter mother); *Rauga māte* (Yeast mother)
- night & death: *Nakts māte* (Night mother); *Pieguļas māte* (Mother of the night shelter); *Miega māte* (Mother of sleep); *Mēra māte* (Plague mother); *Veļu māte* (Mother of the dead); *Nāves māte* (Death mother); *Kapu māte* (Mother of the cemetery); *Smilšu māte* (Sand mother); *Kara māte* (War mother); *Skauģa māte* (Mother of envy)
- geographic places: *Rīgas māte* (Mother Riga); *Daugavas māte* (Mother Daugava); *Gaujas māte* (Mother Gauja)
- household: *Rīšu māte* (Spinning mother); *Dzīpariņa māmuliņa* (Little yarn mother); *Žagaru māte* (Mother of brushwood); *Abras māte* (Baking trough mother); *Tabaciņa māte* (Mother of the tobacco horn); *Naudas māte* (Money mother); *Pirts māte* (Bathroom mother); *Rūšu māte* (Grube mother)
- miscellaneous: *Uguns māte* (Fire mother); *Mūža māte* (Mother of Life); *Gausa māte* (Mother of thriving or Flourishing); *Mēslu māte* (Fertiliser mother); *Ceļa māte* (Road mother); *Tirgus māte* (Market mother); *Sāta māte* (Mother of Temperance); *Jāņu māte* (Johannis mother / Mother of (St.) John); *Ziemeļa māte* (Mother of the North)

Comparisons with other mother cults

The Latvian religion with its large number of *Mothers* stands alone. Only the neighboring Estonians know a similar form of Mother-cult. Among the Germanic and Celtic peoples there is a *Matron*-cult, but these Matrons always occur in threes and usually form local place Mothers or clan-Mothers. Parallels are often drawn between the Latvian Mother-cult and other prehistoric matriarchal religions; however, Haralds Biezais disputes this assumption, arguing that the other Balts do not know of a similar Mother-cult. In Lithuanian mythology, the male demigod: *Patis* (Lord) sometimes stands in opposition to the Latvian *Māte*, such as *Žemepatis* (Earth lord), *Laukpatis* (General), *Vėjopatis* (Wind lord) or *Dimstipatis* (Household lord).

Menninkäinen

The Finnish *Menninkäinen* (pl.: *Menninkäiset*) or *Maahinen* (earth-Elf) is
a short, shy, *Goblin*-like nature-spirit, often described as hairy, who lives
underground, or in the woods, far away from civilization, but it sometimes
wanders into human habitation out of curiosity, and can be friendly if
coaxed gently. Some are said to be mischievous and trick children into
wandering deep into the forest, or they riot in the church at night as little
devils. The creature likes shiny objects. Menninkäiset were probably
originally thought to be spirits of dead people, but folk lore about them has
changed during time, and they gradually changed into something else.

Mermaid

A *Mermaid* (*Zeemeermin* or *Meermin* in Dutch; *Sirène* in French) is a
legendary half-female, half-fish creature of medieval folklore, which later
developed in a worldwide used generic term for water or sea-creatures
whose upper half is a human female body and whose lower half is a
fishtail. The first mention of Mermaids is in the *Book of Enoch*, where
the fallen angels, because of *Satan*, the devil, openly rebel against their
creator, God, and made love to the daughters of the Earth, who begot
Sirenes (Mermaids):

> *"Then Uriel said to me: 'Here the angels, who have joined themselves*
> *to the women, will stand. Their spirits, taking many forms, have*
> *defiled men, and they will make them wander to sacrifice to demons*
> *as to gods, until the day of the great judgment, – the day when they*
> *will be judged to be lost. As for their wives, who have seduced the*
> *angels, they will become Sirens. And I, Enoch, I alone have seen*
> *the vision, the end of all; and no man shall see as I have seen.'"*
> (– Book of Enoch 19:1-3)

The Mermaid of Northern European folklore, should not be confused with
the Mermaid of Greek mythology, half-woman, half-bird, even though
both of these female sea creatures have in common the bewitchment
of sailors. (See under *Sirens*). For the Scandinavians, the Mermaid is
a fearsome monster called *Margygr* (sea giant). The Norwegian work
Konungs skuggsjá ("Royal Mirror" in Old Norse) describes her as a
creature resembling *"a woman above the waist, for this monster had large
nipples on its chest, like a woman, long arms and hair, and its neck and head*

were in all shaped like a human being. This monster appeared tall, with a terrible face, a pointed forehead, wide eyes, a large mouth and wrinkled cheeks". In the sixth century, the English monk Aldhelm de Sherborne described them as *"virgins with scaly fish tails"*. These two representations coexisted until the 15th century, when the flying Mermaids were replaced by a pretty woman with long hair and a fish tail. At that time, the German naturalist Johannes de Cuba made them live in chasms at the bottom of the sea. *"They are often found in the sea and sometimes in rivers"*, said the Flemish writer Jacob Van Maerlant. Note that the English originally used the term *Siren* for an ancient Mermaid (half woman, half bird) and *Mermaid* for a Scandinavian Mermaid (with a fish tail).

Encounters

Illustrious navigators have said they have encountered Mermaids. Christopher Columbus, in 1493, would have seen three of them near the coast of Santo Domingo, *"but they were not as beautiful as they were described..."*. An opinion that is not shared by the sailors of an American ship, who observed, around 1850, near the Sandwich Islands (Hawaii), a Mermaid *"of great beauty that gave way in nothing to the most beautiful women"*. These Mermaids are certainly marine mammals, such as manatees and dugongs, which live in the shallow waters of archipelagos, lagoons and estuaries. In 1403, near Edam in Holland, a specimen was captured by two young girls. It was a woman, found naked in the water and speaking no known language, who was nicknamed the *Meermin van Edam* (Mermaid of Edam). She lived with humans for several years and was buried according to the rites of the Christian religion.

Medieval bestiaries describe Mermaids as women *"from head to thigh"* and fish *"from there to the bottom, with claws and wings"* in a syncretism that ties together the fabulous traditions of Greek and Germanic mythologies. They left to posterity their image engraved in the stone of steles, tombs or Romanesque churches where they personify the soul of the dead. During the Romanesque period the creature was often associated with the image of lust. In many stories, Mermaids are represented with a mirror and a comb. According to Edouard Brasey, these ocean-creatures look into a mirror, which symbolizes the planet Venus in the astrological tradition. Aphrodite, Venus for the Romans, can be compared to Mermaids for several reasons. On the one hand her link to the sea; she would have arrived on Earth by the sea in a shell. On the other hand Aphrodite is a goddess of beauty, having for attribute a mirror, a feature found with Mermaids, correlated to their beauty. The Mermaids as well as Aphrodite personify beauty, they are those who are always chosen and whose charm makes victims. Even if she does not have a fish tail, Aphrodite would be *"the ancestor of Mermaids and the protector of sailors"*.

Fresh water Mermaids
Many European legends mention Mermaids, living not only in the sea, but also in rivers and small streams. They are called Mermaids or by vernacular names such as *Ondines, Nixes* in the Germanic domain, *Dragas* or *Donas d'aiga* (Water ladies) in Occitania, etc., but their description generally conforms to traditional imagery: beings half woman and half fish. According to some stories, they are immortal. The first two centuries of their life they enjoy themselves and discover the ocean, but then they get lonely and want to love and be loved by a human. They are usually represented with a fish tail, either in one piece or divided in two. In the 19th and 20th century, in occult circles, depictions of Mermaids were mostly regarded to represent the *Water-Elementals* or *Undines*.

Metsaema

Metsaema is the mother-spirit of the forest in Estonian mythology. The name Metsaema translates to "forest mother" in Estonian – from *metsa* (forest) and *ema* (mother). For this reason, the word Metsaema can also be used as a descriptor of other similar deities in Eastern European mythology, for example *Vir'ava*. As mother of the forest, Metsaema acts as a ruler and a guardian. In some sources she is acting as a midwife and is connected with fertility. Forest-spirits are said to be found in each forest, ruling over the animals, birds, trees, and berries. Wild animals such as bears, snakes and wolves are commonly connected with them, across many European mythologies. The shared elements of Finnic, Slavic, Baltic and Turkic mythology can be seen in similarities between other forest mother spirits. Metsaema has strong similarities with *Vir'ava*, from Mordven mythology, and *Meža mate*, from Latvian mythology. Other related deities are the Lithuanian goddess of the forest and animals, *Medeina*, and the Finnish goddess of the forest, *Mielikki*.

Mother deities are prevalent in early Estonian and Latvian mythology (called *Mātes* in Latvian). Forest-spirits in Estonian mythology are most often female, as can be seen with the similar *Metsaneitsi*, *Metsapiiga* and *Metsapreili*, all translating to "Forest-Maiden". Estonian mythology has male and female forest-spirits. *Metsavana* is the old man of the forest and forest father. These kinds of deities are normally seen as solitary, but are linked in some Russian and Karelian texts as husband and wife. According to the Estonian writer Friedrich Reinhold Kreutzwald (1803-1883), straw puppets dressed alternately as *Metsaema* (forest mother) and *Metsaisa* (forest father) were used in *Metsiku Tegemine Festivals* in the 17th and 18th centuries.

Metshaldjas

In Estonian folklore, a *Metshaldjas* (forest-fairy; pl.: *Metshaldjad*) is a forest-spirit, able to appear in human, animal or bird-form. Metshaldjad were not always clearly distinguishable, but their walking, whistling or laughter could sometimes be heard. Metshaldjad encompass the *Metsavana* (Forest-godmother), *Metsataat* (Forest-godfather), *Metsaisa* (Forest-father), etc. Male Metshaldjad are usually depicted as old men with a birch-roofed hat on their heads, mossy beards and furry coats, or as wild animals, but mostly they remain invisible and are only sensed by their tricks, or they manipulate a person's eyes so that he can walk around their home without getting recognized. They sometimes enforce a human girl to marry them. If she refuses, they will disfigure the girl's eyes or forcibly take her as his wife. The children or *Cambions* born of such a "marriage" become people superior in strength and intelligence. Despite these primitive actions, Metshaldjad in general were regarded as divine creatures, more beautiful and wiser than humans, punishing people for their evil deeds. Metshaldjad can deceive walkers in the forest, leading them astray, but only those who have somehow offended them. Wanderers in the woods can then only find their way back home by listening to their dogs barking or to a rooster calling.

There are various rules of behavior, commands and prohibitions that one had to remember when going into the woods. For example, in order to obtain a safe passage, straw, twigs, skins, belts, flowers, fruit and other objects containing 'power' were used to make a bandage which was tied around a tree to show the Metshaldjas that a sacrifice was offered. Sacrifices were also made by leaving berries or feathers near a hornet's nest or an ant's nest in the forest, or placing a basket with freshly harvested food. Once

angered, there was little hope to escape these *forest-fairies*. A hunter that
violated the rules, could be attacked by a Metshaldjas, who had turned
itself into a beast, and no bullet, not even a silver one, could kill him. When
a Metshaldjas came to punish someone, it was heard from far away. The
ground rumbled, the trees moved and the branches trembled. Sometimes
a Metshaldjas invited a wanderer into his home, fed and nourished him.
Finally, he would send his guest on his way, who then realized that what
seemed only a few hours, had cost him years of his human life-time.

Metsavana

Metsavana, also known as *Metsataat* or *Metsaisa*, is the old man or
the ancient one of the forest, a forest deity in Estonian mythology.
Metsavana is a compound of *metsa* (forest) and *vana* (old, ancient). The
names Metsataat and Metsaisa translate to "forest-father" or "old forest
man". Metsavana is one of the many types of forest-spirits found in
Estonian mythology. Others are for example *Metsaema* (forest-mother)
and *Metsahaldjas* (forest-fairy). Finnic folklore has links with Slavic
mythology, which is shown in Metsavana's similarities with the *Leshy*
and corresponding Komi forest-spirit, *Vörsa*. Female forest-spirits are
generally more common in Estonian and Latvian mythology, while male
forest-spirits are found more often in Russian folklore. Estonian forest-
spirits are often seen as tricksters, generally benevolent but posing some
danger to humans who stray from the path or act against them. In Komi
folk religion, he is referred to in pseudonyms to avoid catching his notice,
using names such as *Djadja* (uncle) and "old man". Each forest has its own
Metsavana. Metsavana is usually described as a tall elderly man with an
unkempt beard, overgrown with moss. Metsavana rules over the forest,
deciding how plentiful the hunters' harvest will be, and he can also speak
with the birds and animals. In addition, a Metsavana acts as the protector
of wild animals like bears, wolves, snakes and foxes.

Mittagsfrau

The *Mittagsfrau* (Lady Midday) or *Přezpołnica in Polish,* is a nature-
spirit in female form in German and Slavic folk-mythology (see also
Poludnitsa and *Roggenmuhme*). She appears on hot days at noon,
especially at harvest time, and confuses people's minds, paralyses their
limbs, questions them to death, or kills them by cutting off their heads

with a sickle. Those haunted by the Mittagsfrau can only save themselves by telling her about peasant work, especially flax processing, until one o'clock. After the hour of rest between twelve and one has passed, the Mittagsfrau loses her power. In *Wendisches Volksthum in Sage, Brauch und Sitte*, Berlin Nicolai, 1882 by Willibald von Schulenburg we read:

"Die přezpołnica hatte den serp (Sichel) in der Hand, und sagte, wenn jemand mittags auf dem Felde war: "Serp a šyju, Sichel und Hals". Und wer nicht eine Stunde lang erzählen konnte, dem hat sie den Kopf abgehauen"

(The přezpołnica (Mittagsfrau) had the serp (sickle) in her hand, and said, if someone was in the field at noon: "Serp a šyju, sickle and neck". And whoever couldn't tell the story for an hour, she cut off their head.)

The Mittagsfrau appears in different forms: either as a black-haired woman with horses hooves for feet or as a whirlwind. The whirlwind has another personification as the *Wichor* (Lower Sorbian). In descriptions, for example made by the Lower Sorbian priest Bogumił Šwjela, she is described as pale as death, hollow-eyed and with sunken facial features. In many illustrations she is seen wrapped in a white robe or shawl. This also gives an indication of her connection to the mythical realm of the dead; traditionally, according to Lower Sorbian customs, women in deep mourning would wrap themselves in a large white mourning shroud. She shares common traits with the Slavic *Wila*. Both like to steal children and swap them for *Wechselbälge* (changelings). In the imagination of the Sorbs and Czechs, a woman should therefore not leave the house at midday. As a whirlwind, the midday woman is also related to the sisters of the Bulgarian storm spirits *Vichri*. Lady Midday-legends are widespread in rural Europe and probably partly originated in hot summer days, during the harvest times, when many farmhands and maidservants were also sent to the fields in the midday heat and occasionally suffered from sun stroke.

Other names

In Upper Sorbian her name occurs in the two variants *Přezpoł(d)nica* and *Připoł(d)nica*, in Lower Sorbian she has many names, one is the *Pśezpołdnica* with phonetically changed ś to ř. Other Lower Sorbian names are *Serpownica* or *Serpašyja*. In Poland, it is known as Południca. In the Czech Republic, it is called Polednice, which is also the original title of the symphonic poem *"The Noonday Witch"* by composer Antonín Dvořák.

Mermaid (De Meermin, of het 'Groenne Wijf of 1403) etching (1786) after burned painting

AFBEELDING, van de Meermin, (Groenne Wyf), in de
Purmer-meer Gevangen Aº 1403, na de SCHILDERY
Daar van hangende, in het Prinſenhof tot EDAM.

Moort or Mahr(t)

The *Mahrt* or *Mahr*, *Maar* or *Nachtmahr*, in Niederdeutsch (Low German) and in the dialect of Mecklenburg *Moor*, *Moort* or *Moortrieder*, refers to a legendary figure who usually appears as a female personification of a *Nightmare* that causes nightmares or sleep disturbances. The verbs *morriden* or *morrieden* (the riding of the Moor) are also derived from her name, which express a restless sleep, sometimes interspersed with shortness of breath, a feeling of pressure on the chest and experiencing nightmares. In Low German, the term *Mahr* or *Mahrt* prevails for the *Alb* or *Alp* (compare Old High German, Old Norse, Swedish *Mara* or Frisian *Nachtmerje*, Ost-Frisian *Nachtmähr*, Danish *Mare*, English *Nightmare*, French *Cauchemar*); outside Germanic, it corresponds to Old Slavic, Russian *Mora*, which also stands for *Alp*, but predominantly a female one. The gender of the Moor is, just like that of the *Incubus/Succubus* usually opposite to that of the victim. However, reports of a female Mahrt and a male victim dominate. Often the Mahrt is described as a beautiful, partially naked and slippery woman (like a Succubus). In Low German folklore they are the cause of bad sleep, which they cause by sitting on the sleeper's chest or back and squeezing its victims throat or causing an unpleasant pressure on the chest. This is the *moortreiten, moorrieden,* mentioned earlier, or *Albdrücken* (the pressure of the Alb). The Moor or Mahrt can also cause the same experience as the Succubus or Incubus; causing an erotic tension so strong that the victim has an orgasm.

In the legends, the Moor first enters bedrooms in a different guise through a tiny hole, never through windows or doors – despite a painting of a fleeing *Nightmare/Incubus* by Fuseli – but through cracks, keyholes or even smaller holes where for example a nail is missing. Sometimes the Moor appears in the form of an animal, such as a caterpillar, weasel, cat or white mouse, but the creature can also appear as a swimming swan, a plume of smoke or, more rarely, as objects such as an apple, a pear, a straw or a needle. In contrast to other European conceptions of the Alp-type nocturnal visitors, the Moor is not documented in Low German as a black, hind-legged, marten-like beast or as a devil. There is a widespread assumption throughout Germany that godparents can turn children into *Moortrieder*. Pastors can also be responsible for this, as can other relatives. The Moor usually chooses people as its victim, but horses can also be tormented by them. When such a nightly encounter happens, the horses are restless and sweaty. The next morning their manes show the so-called *Moorklatten* – matted hair. In addition, the Moor is said to be able to push trees and leave a *Moorquast* there. These are found in the tops of birch trees and resemble a broom. In Low German, "Moorquast" refers to a witch's broom.

To repel a Moor
A Moor often chooses a particular victim whom she rides more often than others. By plugging the hole through which the Moor enters the house, she is caught, because a Moor can only get out the same way she came in. Some legend has it that this capturing of the beautiful Moor can be followed by the "marriage" of the Moor and the ridden man. This marriage often turns out to be problematic, because the man is not allowed to open the closed hole again or show it to her, and if he complies with her requests she slips out, only to come back regularly to look after her children. The husband usually does not see her again. By calling out the name of the Moor herself, she can be forced to end her ride. Sometimes a victim wakes up while she is riding him and grabs her; however, due to her slippery skin, in most cases she escapes. Occasionally the etheric double of a lover or fiancé rides her or his future partner, but is mistreated as a Moor and sometimes dies as a human being from the injuries of the etheric double.

Moosgeiß

The *Moosgeiß* is mentioned by P. Hillebald Ludwig Seeb in *Sagen Niederösterreichs* (1892). He describes the creature as a kind of ghost bird that does not sing but bleats like a goat. The Moosgeiß is an evil spirit that lures wanderers into the Moos (here meaning "bog", "swamp", instead of "moss", like in *Moosweiblein*).

Moosweiblein

In Germany various names are used for *Moosweiblein* (little moss-woman/women). They are a special class of small sized forest-spirits. Other names containing the component Moos are for example: *Moosweibchen, Moosfräulein* and *Moosfräule*. The name component *Holz* (wood) occurs in the names *Holzfräulein, Holzfrau, Holzfräule, Holzfralerl, Holzfrala, Hulzfral, Holzweiblein, Holzweibchen* and *Holzweibel*. Name variations with the first syllable *Busch-* (bush-) are, for example, *Buschweibchen,*

Buschweiblein, *Buschfräulein* and *Buschjungfer*. The name component *Wald* (forest) occurs in the names *Waldweiblein*, *Waldweibchen*, *Waldweibel*, *Waldweib*, *Waldweibigen*, *Waldfrau* and *Waldfräulein*. Other names include *Rüttelweib*, *Rüttelweiblein* and *Lohjungfer*.

Appearance

The appearance of Moosweiblein is variously described. Generally, they are small in stature. Exact sizes vary but is usually reported as the size of three-, four-, or five-year-old children. They are ugly, providing an unattractive sight. In some cases they are quite mossy, with no definite shape, or at least shaggy, with hair all over their bodies. Some Moosweiblein are also hunchbacked. Generally they are described as very old and gray. Their faces are old and wrinkled, sometimes gray, with black eyes, that may sometimes be half-blind. The head, when touched, feels ice-cold. Moosweiblein have long snow-white hair in wild disarray, more rarely black hair or yellow hair. Moss sometimes grows on their faces or feet. Moosweiblein have fine, mewling voices. The clothing of the Moosweiblein can be as varied as their appearance. Sometimes they are ragged or even naked, dressed in black, or wearing old gray clothes. Most often, however, they are clothed in moss or wear clothes made of moss, especially tree moss. Sometimes they use other forest plants as well, or they are dressed in moss in such a way that it surrounds them like a blanket, or fur. They also dress in flax stalks, and are sometimes entirely wrapped up in them. The accouterments of the moss-wife often include a tied-up apron, which may sometimes be of a tawny color. The Moosweiblein always walks barefoot. They sometimes carry wood in a basket on their backs, or brushwood in their apron. These baskets are made of unpeeled willow. In addition, Buschweibchen and Holzfräulein lean on a knotty stick to support their swaying gait.

Social life and activities

The habitat of the Moosweiblein is the forest and they prefer the dark places in the woods, or the deepest parts of it. Sometimes they are seen on the heath as well. Their dwelling is a hole in the ground, a hollow tree, a little house made of tree roots and moss etc.. They sleep on moss and also bed their children on moss or bark. Moosweiblein allow humans to gather wood in the forest if they receive a piece of bread or a dumpling as a gift beforehand. Moosweiblein often live in extended families. They are usually married to *Holzmännlein*, but also engage in love affairs with humans. They spin tree moss with spindles, sit spinning at crossroads, or knitting in the bush. They wash their clothes at small ponds, but prefer to be unobserved while doing so. Moosweiblein know how to bake cakes. When they bake, the mountain tops steam. Rising mountain mist in spring and autumn is considered the Moosweibleins hearth smoke. When asked, the Moosweiblein also give their cakes to people. When bread or flour is scarce, however, they tend to feed on tree roots. The Moosweiblein sing sweetly, yet unintelligibly, usually at noon or midnight. When it hails in April, the Moosweiblein soar over the mountains. They love to jump on haystacks and play like children and they can fly in a whirlwind. They leave the forest only once every hundred years. If they do so while at the same time a large piece of bark is peeled from a tree, it always means that a Moosweiblein will die.

Interaction with humans

Moosweiblein are herbalists and know how to give as well as cure diseases. If they are mocked by people, they send them afflictions. This can happen in different ways. They can press on people, so they become sick and miserable and squat on them so that people become paralyzed. They can also breathe on them, from which people get bumps or boils on their faces. In addition, moss-wives possess knowledge of the future. Moosweiblein reward people by giving them wood chips or leaves, which turn into gold. They also give *Garnknäuel* (balls of yarn) that do not end, unless the end is deliberately sought for, or they give spun yarns and knitted goods that bring good luck and blessings to the house. Moosweiblein also show their gratitude with well-intended advice and warnings. In addition, they guard children in the forest, lead people out of the forest at night preventing them from going astray, or let them find deer and roe deer antlers. On the other hand, Moosweiblein steal bread and dumplings from people, the bread fresh from the oven, the dumplings from the pots. Caraway bread, however, they do not tolerate, which is why they exclaim: *"Caraway bread, our death"*. The same applies to "pipped" bread, i.e. bread into which the fingertip has been pressed. They also cannot touch counted baked goods. On the other hand, part of the hay cuttings and the water which forms drops on the rim of the vessel when scooped, as well as part of the linseed, flax stalks, ears of grain, tree fruit, the flour that gets stuck to the bucket frame, and leftover bread crumbs, all rightfully belong to the Moosweiblein. Sometimes Moosweiblein come to people's aid with good deeds and advice. They stop by at people's homes and do various jobs, such as spinning flax and wool at night, scouring, feeding, milking, mowing, helping to make hay and cut grain. If the Moosweiblein receive food from shepherds, they bless their herd, which then give more milk. They also protect their tools from thieves. As house spirits, moss women bring good luck and blessings, but they also like to receive food offerings in return. Cursing and the vices of people are abhorrent to them. They love silence, hate quarrels and curses, and are driven away by them, just as they disappear never to be seen again when they are given new clothes.

Mountain-spirits or Berggeister

Mountain-spirit (lat.: *Daemon subterraneus*, "underground demon"; also *Daemon metallicus* "mountain deamon/Berggeist" or *Kobold* according to Jacob Grimm) is the generic term for different nature-spirits, which are to be found in mines or mountains. Especially in German speaking countries and regions they play an important role in folklore and especially in the beliefs of the miners. The mountain-spirit is however a worldwide phenomenon. Well-known examples are the *Bergmönch* (mountain monk), the *Bergteufel* (mountain devil) and the *Goblin*-like *Bergmännchen* (little mountain men). In Norway the term *Bergande* exists, apart from *Trolle* (Trolls) and the well-known Welsh *Knockers*. Later, the term was extended in a broader sense to also include spirits who just happened to live in mountainous areas such as *Rübezahl*. Other common names for mountain-spirits are *Knappenmandl*, *Grubenmännlein*, *Lötterl* (Slovenia). Names for individual mountain-spirits are *Nickel*, *Skarbnik* (Treasure Keeper, Upper Silesia), *Gübich* (Harz), *Gangerl* (area around Budweis). A malevolent mountain-spirit of Swabian salt pits is the long-nosed *Halgeist* or *Haalgeist* (both meaning "salt ghost") which throws everyone over the mountain who dares to make fun of its large nose. Ludwig Bechstein in his *Deutsches Sagenbuch* mentions the *Herdmanndli* as the mountain-spirits of the Swiss mountain Pilatus. The term *Bergmännlein* was first mentioned in 1487 as the name of a mine in Schneeberg. At about the same time, a woodcut illustrating the oldest poem on mining in the Erzgebirge region, *Judicium Jovis*, by the humanist Paulus Niavis, depicts three naked, childlike creatures, without clear sexual characteristics, who are interpreted as protective spirits of mining. Possibly this kind of representation is based on the ancient *Penates* who watched over the pantry and the supplies of a household. Elsewhere, Niavis also reports that the miners in Schneeberg knew of dangerous *Unter-Tage-Dämonen* (underground demons) *"that do violence to people"*. In a Prague miniature from 1525, about the granting of the right to mint coins to the miners of Kuttenberg by Wenceslas II, a small, naked figure also crouches at the feet of the king, which stretches out a pit light to greet the miners.

Good and devilish mountain-spirits

The founder of mineralogy, Georgius Agricola (1494-1555), in his scientific writings about mining: *Bermannus* (1530), *De animantibus subterraneis* (1549) and *De re metallica libri XII* (posthumously published 1556), stressed that the presence of mountain-spirits is confirmed by experience. He tried, among other things, to bring the traditions of the miners known to him into line with the views of medieval demonologists such as Michael Psellos (1017 or 1018-1078) and Johannes Trithemius (1462-1516). Psellos, for example, divided demons into six classes, of which he considered the fifth, the "underground class", to be among the most vicious and dangerous, along with the "light-haters", because they were equipped with a solid body. Agricola countered that there were also harmless and good natured mountain-spirits besides such evil spirits. In his opinion there were two kinds of mountain spirits:
* *daemon subterraneus truculentus* (dark, coarse, or wild underground daemon): *Bergteufel* (mountain devil).
* *daemon subterraneus mitis* (mild, peaceful underground daemon): *Bergmennel, Kobel,* and *Guttel.*

Contrary to the theologians of his time, Agricola counted these spirits also among living beings and not among purely spiritual beings. As an example of a "mountain-devil", Agricola mentions here for the first time a ghost with wild eyes and a long neck (like a horse), that is said to have killed twelve workers in Annaberg with his poisonous breath, whereupon the mine, despite its high silver content, was abandoned. In the early German translations, however, there is direct reference to a spirit in the appearance of a *"horse with a long neck and wild eyes"*. Another example is a ghost in a black frock who is said to have lifted up a worker in the St. Georg mine on the Schneeberg and transferred him to a silver-rich cave, *"not without doing him evil"*. In more recent transmissions, however, there is only talk of a suspended tool which the spirit brought *"not without physical exertion"* up into a higher distance. Even if Agricola does not call him that, this spirit is obviously the *boshaften Bergmönch* (malicious Mountain-monk) who later found his way into the miner's legends, especially in the Harz Mountains, the Erzgebirge in Saxony and Transylvania.

Agricola opposes these dangerous, vicious loners with the sociable Bergmännchen. They show the characteristic behavior of *Goblins*: they giggle cheerfully and make themselves noticed by noises (knocking etc.), or stone throws, run here and there and imitate working people. Mostly they are invisible. Otherwise, they appear in the form of old men, measuring only three feet and wearing the typical miners' work clothes with hooded coats and ass leather. This appearance became canonical for *dwarfs* from now on. Even if they tease the miners sometimes, they harm them rarely – only after they were insulted by laughter or insults. The miners have nothing against the presence of the Bergmännchen. On the contrary, they are considered a good omen for rich finds (hence their nickname *Guttel* from *gut*, "good"). Agricola itself compares them with the above-ground *household-spirits*, that help people with all kinds of domestic jobs, work in the stable etc. (similarly like *Wichtel* or *Heinzelmännchen*), as well as with the Scandinavian *Trolls*, however the latter also in a harmless, "domesticated" version (now better known as *Tomte*).

Christian demonization of mountain-spirits

This clear division into friendly and hostile mountain-spirits, has already been partly blurred again by Agricola's contemporaries. Even the translators of his *Bermannus* called the misanthropic mountain-spirits *Bergmännel* again. In his *Cosmographia*, only Sebastian Münster maintained the strict separation between *Klein Teüfelin* (little mountain devil) and *Bergmenlin* (litte mountain man). In the religiously heated climate of the Reformation and Counter-Reformation, the diabatization of the miner's spirit was constantly advancing: Martin Luther attributed the dread of the *Bergmönch* in particular to Satan's direct influence, who also tried to bring the miners to their doom through lies and deception. The reformer and preacher Johannes Mathesius still knows the terms *Cobelt* and *Gütlein*, but their philanthropic nature seems forgotten. All of them are mere ghosts. Also in the work of the Catholic Olaus Magnus, the mountain-spirit is demonized as some kind of devil, with big ears, or horns, beak-like muzzles, claw-like hands and birds of prey feet – its positive actions becoming irrelevant.

Paracelsus' equation of mountain-spirits with Gnomes

Paracelsus created new impulses, but also confusion, by placing mountain-spirits in the framework of the *Tetrasomia* (four-element doctrine) and declaring them Elemental-spirits. He described the mountain-spirits as *Pygmäen* (Pygmies), who, apart from their small stature, have almost nothing to do with the Pygmies of ancient tradition, or, for that matter, with a Greek foreign word of unclear meaning, such as *Gnomes*. Unlike Agricola, Paracelsus by no means attributes a solid body to the earth-spirits, but considers them, on the contrary, to be extremely subtle and almost bodiless, since they can move through the densest of all elements, earth. Similar to *Salamanders* (Fire-Elementals), that consist of a fiery substance of light. But since they can also move effortlessly through less dense elements, like the *Undines* (Water-Elementals), they sometimes come into contact with people. In such cases they may appear in the form of *Irrlichtern* (Will-o'-the-wisps), ghosts or traditionally as helpful little males. Like the other elemental spirits, the Gnomes have no soul. They can only achieve this (having a soul) by marrying a human being. The possible descendants of Gnomes and humans are called dwarfs.

Post-Renaissance evolution

After the Renaissance period, the solitary mountain-spirit in the German speaking countries over time assumed more and more traits of the sociable Bergmännchen, so it now frequently appears in the shape of a little old man in miner's clothes. Likewise, it can lead the miners to the discovery of new mining-places and helps them occasionally in person with the mining of the ore. Sometimes, the miners bring it sacrifices (daily food and a chandelier, a red skirt once a year). If this offering is omitted, the ore runs dry, or worse, the miner is killed by the mountain-spirit. In general, the mountain-spirit rewards diligence and honesty, but punishes greed and breaking one's word. Like the Gnomes of Paracelsus, he can walk through rock, often appearing also above ground, at the shafts, in the mountains and in the forest (where still unknown rich ore veins can be found). Mostly the mountain-spirit is regarded as male, but sometimes also as female, as a beautiful *Fairy* or *Weiße Frau* (White Woman), who may fall in love with a miner. Rarely the mountain spirit is a *Woodwose* (founding legend of *Wildermann* in the Harz Mountains), or a *water-sprite* (in a lake near Erzberg, Hochsteiermark Austria). Also the Goblin-like Bergmännchen appear more and more as Fairy-like beings: their clothes are (for miners) either white, gray, or silver, or strikingly colorful (red, green). Their festivities and dances do not only take place in underground caves and palaces, but also on meadows in the moonlight. Occasionally (for example, in Banská Štiavnica/Chemnitz, central Slovakia) the mountain-spirits even appear in the shape of barefoot dancing girls. In addition, the mountain-spirits are said to also appear as small animals, e.g. rats (which run out of mountain crevices), or as black birds, flies and hornets, etc.

The mountain-spirit as treasure keeper
An important function of the mountain-spirit is that of treasure keeper. In underground caves and palaces he guards immeasurable treasures of precious metals and gems, often in the appearance of a demonic being, such as a black dog, snake, dragon, or the ghost of a wicked and damned miner. Sometimes the treasurer is an executioner as well, with a red cloak and a bared sword, who only kills the cowards that retreat from him, but lets the brave pass. The Upper Silesian *Skarbnik* has many similarities, both with the Bergmönch and with Rübezahl, but tends to behave even more viciously. It usually appears in the form of a miner, but has pitch-black or red-hot eyes. Just by looking at them, he can make intruders incurably ill. While the miners generally depend on the goodwill of the treasurers to make rich finds, the *Walen* (mysterious ore seekers) in the legends often have power over the treasurers. Occasionally, however, it is also the *Mistress of the Mountain* who rules over the other mountain-spirits, and who guards the treasures. She can allocate them as she pleases (e.g. to her lover), or make them disappear.

Murbl

In Tyrol, Austria, the *Murbl* is a strange and demon-like worm or snake, sometimes compared to the *Haselwurm*, a creature which many people claim to have seen in the Wurmbach valley. According to local dramatized lore even the bravest person would run away if he or she saw the worm. The existence of the Murbl was regularly confirmed by shepherds who claimed to have seen it. Old tales claim that the place was once populated by many of such monsters, which is why the brook that runs through Wurmthal is called Wurmbach (Worm-creek). At the beginning of the Wurmbach, not far from the Arzleralpe, at the so-called Arzlerberg, such a worm is said to inhabit a large hole which opens under a forest tree. This hole is described as not being longer than a good

1½ shoes, which is very small for a creature that apparently is so much feared and respected. Where the Haselwurm is always described as a special snake or snake-like creature, some people who encountered the Murbl thought it was a child, clad in colorful diapers with red ribbons, because its head had due to its roundness much in common with a child's head. The Murbl was described in *Mythen und Sagen Tirols,* collected and published by Johann Nepomuk Ritter von Alpenburg, Zürich, in 1857.

N

Nachtahnl

In Austria, the Leibnitzer Feld, the valleys of the Sulm, Laßnitz and Kainach, are haunted by a night spirit known as the *Nachtahnl* (also: *Waschfrau*: Washerwoman or *Nachtfrau*: Night woman). The Nachtahnl has a smooth, shiny complexion and beautiful hair that reaches almost to the knees. But she does not appear to everyone in her beautiful guise; on the contrary, it is said that to the mocker she becomes larger and more frightening the closer this person approaches.

The Nachtahnl likes to lurk near springs, ponds, especially in swampy lands and lakes. Here this figure often appears at night when she cleans the laundry of the deceased, who were buried disrespectfully in dirty clothes, and dries the clean laundry in the moonlight. Many have seen her, how she, dressed in a white dress, performed the services of a washerwoman. Whoever disturbs her, or whom she meets on the way, she chases away, or she does not let the person leave the place and forces him or her to her service. Also, one should never mock or imitate the Night Mistress, for she always punishes such audacity severely. Many a person who dared to do such a thing received a hard slap in the face from the Nachtahnl, and all who felt the force claim that the Nachtahnl has an iron hand. Sometimes the Nachtahnl is seen with a child. Once a servant met the ghostly figure sitting by a fence; it had a child on its lap and was feeding it from a bowl. When the Nachtahnl saw the servant, she got in his way and chased him away.

Nachtgiger

The *Nachtgiger* is the name of a monster-like child-fright figure in Franken (Franconia), Germany, comparable to the *Butzemann* or the *Nachtkrabb* in the Austrian-South German area, meaning. In some Franconian areas – dialect-dependent – they are also called: *Nachtgeger*, *Nachdgiecher* or *Noochdgieger*. Nachtgiger means "Night-rooster": (Franc.: *Gieger* + *Nacht* = *Nachthahn* or *Nachtgockel*, both also meaning (Night-rooster). A variant in the West-Central Franconian area, for example in the places Dürrwangen, Großlellenfeld and Pleinfeld, is the *Holzgeger* or *Holzgieger*. This creature is to go around particularly at night and fetch children, who are impudent or still alone on the way. The Nachtgiger does not seem to be able or to want to penetrate into the houses thereby, it is content with what it can find outside, starting from 10 o'clock pm. Allegedly, the Nachtgiger eats children. Thus the figure of the Nachtgiger is especially used to scare children and make sure that they do not roam around alone at night or that they go to bed "well-behaved". Adults who *"turn night into day"*, i.e. are out and about until the early hours of the morning, are also called Nachtgiger.

Nachtkrabb

Nachtkrabb or *Nacht(t)rapp* is the name for a Bogey-figure in southern Germany and Austria, that serves a similar function to the Sandman. Similar legends exist in Hungary, the Czech Republic, Poland, Sweden, Norway and Russia. The Nachtkrabb supposedly grabs children who are still outdoors after dark and flies away with them, so far that they never find their homes again. The Franconian equivalent is called *Nachtgiger*. Only in the more northern areas of southern Germany is this figure called *Sandmann*. The origin of the legendary figure has not been conclusively clarified. Several versions of the Nachtkrapp exist. In most legends, the Nachtkrapp is described as a giant, nocturnal raven-like bird. In Norse mythology, the Nachtkrapp (Swedish *Nattramnen*, Norwegian *Nattravnen*) is depicted without eyes, which if looked into can cause death. It is also depicted with holes in its wings which cause illness and disease if gazed at. Some of the most common legends claim that the Nachtkrapp leaves its hiding place at night to hunt. If it is seen by little children, it will abduct them into its nest and messily devour them, first ripping off their limbs and then picking out their heart. According to other legends, the Nachtkrapp will merely put children in his bag

Habergeiss (1939) Rolf von Hoerschelmann (1885-1947)

Wolpertinger (1836) from Spiegel der Geschichte oder Magazin aller Merkwürdigkeiten

and take them away. Tales about the *Wütender Nachtkrapp* (German, lit. angry night raven) are less common. Instead of abducting children, it simply crows loudly and flutters its wings, until the children have been terrorized into silence. The word *Krabb* (also *Krapp, Krabbe, Grabbe, Rappe,* from Old High German *hraban*) is in Upper German dialects a name for the raven, or other corvids. It was obvious that these carrion-eating swarming birds were also said to have all kinds of sinister effects, for example that the raven would kidnap children at night. According to Grimm's *Deutsches Wörterbuch* (German Dictionary), the term *Nachtrabe* (night raven) was not exclusive for the raven but covered various birds, including owls and the night heron. The night heron's genus name *Nycticorax* derives from the Greek for "night raven" and refers to the largely nocturnal feeding habits of this group of birds, and the croaking crow-like call of the best known species, the black-crowned night heron. It is possible, however, that the term, similar to the raven, refers only to the "raven-black" color.

Local variations

In southern Swabia, the *Nachtkrabb* is a black legendary figure that puts children in a sack – like Krampus – and takes them away when they are still outside after dusk. In Austria, the *Bogey*-figure is known as the *Nachtkrapp*. It is described there as a huge, raven-like bird that kidnaps and eats children. In central Thuringia, children are warned about the Nachtraben, which always appear in a flock and catch and take away children who are not at home after dark. The *Guter Nachtkrapp* (German, lit. good night raven) is a curious exception within the stories about the Nachtkrabb. In Burgenland myths, this bird enters the children's rooms and gently sings them to sleep.

Fastnachtsgestalt ("Shrovetide figure")

As a bird-like figure, the Nachtkrabb is also one of the carnival figures of the Murrhardt Fools' Guild; it can already be found on a mural in the Murrhardt monastery. The real model of the Murrhardt carnival figure is probably the *Waldrapp* (crested ibis or bald ibis), a dark-feathered bird with a naked red face and a long, red, curved beak that lives in colonies and is capable of making somewhat eerie noises. It was also native to Central Europe until about 350 to 400 years ago, and may have inspired the imagination of carnivalists. Not only in southern Germany, as the Venetian masks with long red beaks are also said to go back to the Waldrapp.

Nachtpferd Zawudschawu

Like many countries, Switzerland too has its ghost horses. In the city of
Sion in Valais, a nocturnal three-legged horse was often seen thundering
through the alleys in the moonlight. On the swampy moors in the
Gruyère, in Freiburg (Fribourg), a wild horse called *Zawudschawu* grazed
at night. It was black as ebony, only its wild mane and long tail were snow
white. Often, when frail old men, no longer able to walk properly, took
the path across the moors of Buriander, it would come to them in a proud
running pace and settle down on its front legs, inviting them to mount. If
Zawudschawu did not like the person on its back, the animal would run
at a furious gallop to a swamp and throw the rider into the water.

Nachzehrer

The *Nachzehrer* (lit. one who consumes afterwards) is a corpse chewing
on its own shroud or body parts after death. It is also known as the
Dodelecker or *Dodeleker* (dead-licker), or *Gierrach,* and it is the common
name, in German folklore, for a *Revenant* who shares a number of
essential characteristics with *Vampires.* Contrary to a long-held belief in
folklore, the area of distribution of the Nachzehrer is by no means limited
to the partly Slavic areas of eastern and northeastern Germany. He was
also widespread in the west as far as the Rhineland. There, when old
cemeteries in the Eifel were abandoned, skeletons were discovered lying
face down – a clear sign of the burial of a corpse that was thought to be
dangerous. Similar to the Polish *Wieszczy,* a child born with a caul might
become a Nachzehrer, especially if the caul was red. The legends and
oral traditions describe the Nachzehrer as follows: Unlike the Vampire,
who must leave its grave, the Nachzehrer lies or sits underground
and sucks the life force from the living – usually his survivors, or the
inhabitants of his village. With this conception, it is to be considered
that also most traditional reports on Vampire attacks do not speak at all
of bloodsucking, but rather diffusely of the "strangling" or "weakening"
of the victim. The Nachzehrer performs his sinister work by calling out
to his victim, or by establishing a telepathic connection with it through
the "open evil eye". Often he chews on his shroud or even on his arms
until everything is gnawed away. As long as he is still chewing, people die
either from emaciation or from a plague. However, those who died as a
result of the work of a gnawing man did not become undead themselves.

Protection from the Nachzehrer

In order to effectively banish a potential Nachzehrer, appropriate measures had to be taken before burial. Under no circumstances were the eyes or mouth allowed to remain open, which is why the eyes of the deceased had to be closed without looking into them, because then telepathic contact would already have been established between the Nachzehrer and its future victim. Under no circumstances was the mouth of the dead person allowed to come into contact with the shroud or any other piece of cloth. Often the corpses were bound, sometimes only symbolically, such as with a rosary around the wrists. Banishing metal objects (scissors, nail files, knives) were often placed on the chest of the dead person and dried legumes or pebbles were thrown into the coffin. According to folk-belief, the undead had to count these before he could begin his sinister activities. But, since he was possessed by the Devil, he could never get beyond two peas or stones, because he was not allowed to pronounce the sacred number "three" (symbol of the Trinity). If one nevertheless meant to state an injury coming from the Nachzehrer, the grave could be opened. Then the measures known from the southeast European Vampire belief took place, such as beheading, cutting the heart out and impalement. Possibly the idea of the Nachzehrer originated from a more primitive Vampire belief. Even in Romania and Serbia, the homeland of the classical Vampire, one encounters the idea of the Nachzehrer, who sits or lies in the grave and sucks the life force out of the living, and while doing so spreads epidemics. For this reason, folklorists assume that the belief in the Nachzehrer arose no sooner than at the end of the Middle Ages, in direct connection with the plague epidemics. In the 14th and 15th centuries – the era of the Black Death – there were also far more reports of grave openings and "executions" of suspicious corpses, because these were now no longer attributed only a vampiric ability to harm the living, but were seen specifically as the causers of the plague.

Napf-Hans

Napf-Hans or *Jean de la Boliéta* (in English: *Jack o' the bowl*) is a figure of Swiss folklore. He is a helpful *household-spirit* resembling a *Kobold*. In return for a bowl (*Napf* in German) of sweet cream left out for him each night, he would lead the cows to graze in places considered dangerous to humans, while none of the cows ever suffered any injury. The path used by him was always clear of stones no matter how rocky the mountainside, and this came to be known as Boliéta's Path.

Neuntöter

Neuntöter (pl. & sing.) is the name of a ghoulish type of *Revenant* or *Vampire* from northern Germany. Someone destined to become a Neuntöter is already born with teeth or even a double row of teeth. According to Claude Lecouteux in *The Secret History of Vampires* (2010), these people die young and will cause the death of nine of their closest relatives – Neuntöter literally means "Nine-Killer." The Neuntöter drew to himself those whom he liked best, or who had experienced some unfortunate circumstance at his or her death: a cat had been allowed to walk over the corpse; the eyes of the deceased had refused to close; the shawl of a woman who had laid out the corpse had brushed the corpse's lips; and so on. Neuntöter feed on dead bodies that they create by spreading diseases like the plague. They were known to destroy entire villages by spreading diseases and pestilence. According to legend, it took nine days for a person to turn into a Neuntöter after the body was buried. They were covered with open sores and smelled strongly of excrement, but they could be warded off with lemons, which they detested. The creature could be destroyed by chopping off its head.

Nixe, Wasserfrau, Wassermann

The *Nixe* (pl.: *Nixen*) or the *Nix* (pl.: *Nixe), also Wasserfrau (Water-woman), Wassermann (Water-man)* is a widespread term in the German-speaking world for a female or male humanoid and often shape-shifting water-spirit, also known as *Nixie, Nyx, Näcken, Nicor, Nokk,* or *Nokken.* The word has been documented in the Old High German form *nihhus/ nicchus* since the end of the 10th century and has parallels in many other Germanic languages. They are related to Sanskrit *nénēkti*, Greek *νίζω nízō* and *νίπτω níptō*, and Irish *nigh* (all meaning to wash or be washed). The form *Neck* appears in English and Swedish (*Näck* or *Nek*, meaning nude). The Swedish form is derived from Old Swedish *Neker*, which corresponds to Old Icelandic *Nykr*, and the Norwegian *Nynorsk*. In Finnish, the word is *Näkki*. In Old Danish, the form was *Nikke* and in modern Danish and Norwegian Bokmål it is *Nøkke/Nøkk*. The Icelandic and Faroese *Nykur* are horse-like creatures. In Middle Low German, it was called *Necker* and in Middle Dutch *Nicker*. The Old High German form *Nihhus* also meant "crocodile", while the words *nikwus* or *nikwis(i)* mean "to wash or being washed". The Old English *Nicor* could mean both a *water monster* like those encountered by Beowulf, and a *hippopotamus.* The Norwegian

Fossegrim and Swedish *Strömkarlen* are related figures, sometimes seen as by-names for the same creature. The southern Scandinavian version can transform himself into a horse-like *kelpie*, and is called a *Bäckahästen* (Brook-Horse), whilst the Welsh version is called the *Ceffyl Dŵr* (Water-Horse). Under this vast variety of names, they were a common appearance in Germanic and Scandinavian folklore. The related English *Knucker* was generally depicted as a *Wyrm* or *dragon*, although more recent versions depict these spirits in other forms. Their gender, bynames, and various transformations vary geographically. The German Nix and his Scandinavian counterparts were male. The German *Nixe* was a female *River-Mermaid*. Similar creatures are known from other parts of Europe, such as the *Melusine* in France, and the water-spirits in Slavic countries (e.g. the *Rusalka*).

What exactly was and is meant by *Nix(e)* strongly depends on the respective temporal, cultural and regional context. In the occult lore Nixen for example are often used as a synonym for *Undines* or *water-elementals*. In order to understand the historical use of the term, the relevant source texts must be evaluated, and information from more recent stories must not simply be projected into the past. In later folk tales, Nix and Nixe can appear in human or animal form and usually have ambivalent or even negative connotations. It was only through their reception in the Romantic period that the Nixe could at least also be portrayed positively.

Nix & Nixe
Along with *Wasserfrau*, Nixe is a widespread term in the German-speaking world for female water-spirits. The masculine form Nix is, however, rarer than the designation *Wassermann*. In folk tales, Nix and Nixe often live as a family in an underwater home. From there, the Nixen-daughters come ashore and mingle with people, for example to go shopping or to amusement events. They can only be recognized by the wet hem of their clothes. There is a widespread legend, according to which a group of Nixen regularly mingled at an evening dance party, but eventually returned home to the water too late and are killed for it by their Nixe father. The Nixe is usually described as a beautiful woman of ambivalent character: On the one hand she can warn of storms or give gifts to children, on the other hand she can drown fishermen or kidnap children. Common is the story according to which a Mermaid needs a

human woman as a midwife and rewards her richly for this. Nixen can also appear as household-spirits. The Nix, on the other hand, is a figure with a largely negative connotation; he is said to enjoy drowning children. This use as a figure to frighten children is intended to keep children away from the water. The Nix, or Wassermann, is also said to try to abduct girls and women out of sexual interest. The Nix is usually described as an ugly man or as animal-shaped, rarely as an attractive youth. The Czech magician Franz Bardon described him however as rather small in stature (*Wassermänchen* = little Waterman).

Nixe of the Lahn
The alleged sighting of a Nixe in the German river Lahn in 1615 generated an extensive scholarly and artistic reception, which in turn became the subject of scholarly research. On 13 October 1615, a Nixe was seen in the Lahn at the Elisabeth-Mühle (Elisabeth Mill) in Marburg. The creature did not look like a woman, but formed itself continuously out of the water, resembling a rope or a snake. People who tried to grab her would find their hands frozen. In the same year, the Marburg printer Rudolf Hutwelckers published an anonymous broadsheet with the title *Nympha Marpurgensis Lanicola* (the Marpurger Waternix). This is a Latin didactic poem in epic verse, in which the Nixe introduces herself to the listener. She professes to be harmless and not to herald any bad omens. With the publication of such a Nymph text, Hutwelcker presumably wanted to profit from the discussions going on at the time about the elemental spirit doctrine of Paracelsus *(Liber de Nymphis)*. An explicit criticism of Paracelsus and his followers is subsequently found in Johann Hornung's *Cista medica*, published in 1626. Hornung had included in this collection of medical treatises both the Nixen-poem and three critical responses to it by Andreas Libavius. Libavius explained the sighting naturalistically as a misinterpretation of gases and vapors, thus opposing both the demonological interpretation of the theologians and the natural philosophical interpretation of the Paracelsists. With his anti-Paracelsian polemic, Libavius attacked above all the Rosicrucian tradition that was forming at this time. The Nixen-poem was still being used in the medical literature of the time. The *Lahn Nixe* was still debated in specialist Latin texts until the middle of the 18th century. It became known to a wider public through the Danish scholar Ole Worm, who adopted the details of the *Cista medica* in his *Danicorum Monumentorum libri sex*, published in 1643. Worm had drafted a scientific taxonomy of the *"Nöcken"* or *"Nods"*,

and used the Marburg *"Wasser Nichts"* as evidence that these creatures
were not only found in the sea, but also in rivers. In 1837 Hans Christian
Andersen probably drew on the *Monumenta Danica* as a source for his
world famous fairy tale *The Little Mermaid*. Also in the 19th century, the
sighting-report was included in German saga collections. Hermann von
Pfister-Schwaighusen, for example, reports of the *"Nickse"* in the Lahn in
his collection *Sagen und Aberglaube aus Hessen und Nassau* (1885). The
Brothers Grimm drew on the works of Hornung and Worm as sources
for their saga *Nixenbrunnen* and their fairy tale *Die Nixe im Teich*. The
Grimms were the first to use the tale as a source.

Nörgelen

In the folklore of Tyrol a comical contrast to the graceful figures of
the *Saligen Fräulein* is formed by the teasing little folk of the *Nörgelen*,
Nörggeln, Norgen or *Wichtelen* – as they are commonly called. They were
Erdzwerge (Earth dwarfs), small, old men with big bellies, big heads
and greasy noses. The *Putz, Kasermannl, Pechmannl* or *Wild Mannl* are
different specifications of the same legendary creature. The Nörgelen had
a long, ice-gray beard and a disproportionately large hat pressed deep
over their faces. Their feet resembled those of geese and ducks, which is
why they could not take proper steps while walking, but merely sort of
rolled along. They must have been well aware of the great defects of their
shape, because they tried to hide them carefully. This was often difficult,
because their gray or grass-green dress was usually more threadbare
and ragged than the skirt of many a poor student. Only on particularly
festive occasions did they wear a bright red gala jacket with large golden
buttons. Apart from that, cleanliness was not their virtue and one should
not be surprised that their usual lodging were in caves and holes in the
ground, from where they made their etiquette visits to the farms and
mountain huts. Such so-called *Norgenlöcher* (Holes of the Norgen) can
be found scattered all over Tyrol. They are found above the Sachsenhofe
on the Vellauerberge near Meran, to Woalda in Passeier. The *Alpe Norgles*
and the *Norgehöhle* at the Swiss border have their names from them and
in the so-called Hagen near Meran still today a lane is called after them:
the *Norgengasse* (Norgen alley). Especially in Upper Vintschgau, in the
Planail valley, on the mountain stretch between Matsch, Schnals, Passeier
and Ötztal, there were many Norgen places, which all points to a wide
spreading of the legend.

O

Oligsmännchen

The *Oligsmännchen* is a water devil in Luxembourg folklore. At the
source of the Oligsbaach, which after a very short course plunges into
the Alt- or Gaanerbaach in Emeringen and often turns into a raging
torrent, the Oligsmännchen sneaks around. Anyone who shows up at the
meadow after sunset is irretrievably lost, because in no time a sinister
old man grabs this person by the hair and pulls him or her underwater.
This spirit creature was described by Nikolaus Gredt in *Sagenschatz des
Luxemburger Landes,* Luxembourg 1883.

Ossaert

An *Ossaert* (also: *Oschaert, Osgaard*) is a mocking *water-sprite* and appears
in folktales from the southwestern Low Countries like the Dutch province
of Zeeland and the bordering region of Belgium. The Ossaert is usually
invisible when it jumps on its victim's back, preventing the victim from
moving or making the person collapse from exhaustion – just like the
German *Aufhocker*. Sometimes only the voice of the creature is heard, in
other cases the Ossaert is described as a black monster with huge claws and
red eyes, like a hellhound. The phantom also appears as a blue light and is
sometimes associated with a *Werewolf* or *Nightmare*, but he can virtually
take any shape and any size. People have encountered him in the shape of
a dog, rabbit, horse, a donkey with enormous fiery eyes the size of plates,
or a bull with the head of a man. It is possible that the name Ossaert has a
link to the latter, as *Os* in Dutch and Flemish means "Ox". To prevent the
Ossaert from spoiling the caught fish, the first fish was sacrificed to him.

Otso or Metsän kuningas

Like the name of God is never pronounced directly in Hebrew, in Finnish
mythology the spirit of the bear was feared so much that there are only
names that indirectly refer to it. *Otso, Ohto, Kontio, Metsän kuningas*
(King of the Forest), and *Mesikämmen* (Honey palm) are some of the
many rarely uttered circumlocutory epithets for the spirit that was never
directly named. Generally, the spirit of the bear was referred to as *friend,*

brother, *uncle*, or *forest-cousin*, or ways were thought up that would bypass the need to refer to the spirit at all, even indirectly. Some sub-traditions considered the bear as a relative who had fled the community and been transfigured by the power of the forest. If a bear had to be killed, a sacred ritual of Peijainen was held, and the bear's spirit in the form of its skull remained in a sacred place, where people would make offerings to it.

Oude Rode Ogen

Oude Rode Ogen (Old Red Eyes) or the *Beast of Flanders* was a spirit reported in Flanders, Belgium, in the 18th century, who would take the form of a large black dog with fiery red eyes.

P

Painajainen

In Finnish folklore the *Painajainen* (Presser) was an *Alp*. According to Thomas Keightley the Painajainen *"resembles a white maid, and its brightness illumines the whole room. It causes people to scream out woefully; it also hurts young children, and makes them squint. The remedy against it is a steel object or a broom placed under the pillow."* In Finnish lore however, the Painajainen is also depicted as a dark or black *Bogeyman*, such as a phantom, a Troll, an animal, or a bird, which rose up on the sleeping person's chest, paralyzing them and even trying to suffocate them. The Painajainen is equivalent to a Deattán-holder in Sámi.

Para

The *Kobold* of Finland is called a *Para* (from the Swedish Bjära). According to Thomas Keightley the Para steals the milk from other people's cows, carries and coagulates it in his stomach, and then disgorges it into the churn of his mistress. A strange ritual was performed to reveal the woman in whose service the Para was stealing things. The victim of a Para would take a certain kind of mushroom, that, fried with tar, salt and sulphur, and then beaten with a rod, would make the woman who owns the Kobold quickly appear and entreat to spare him. Relying on Keightley they were apparently women who were the mistresses of the Paras.

Peko

Peko – Finnish spelling *Pekko*, *Pekka*, *Pellon* or *Pellonpekko* (Field-Pekko) is an ancient Estonian and Finnish god/daemon of fields, crops – especially barley – and of brewing. He is mentioned by bishop Agricola in 1551 as the god of Karelians. In the area of Setumaa, between Estonia and Russia, inhabited by the Seto language-speaking Setos, the cult of Peko was alive until the 20th century. Today, the Seto people (an ethnic group of Estonians in the south-east of the country) also revere Peko as their national hero and king, and the name and figure are widely used as a national symbol. Peko is sometimes associated with Estonian Pikne (Pitkne), Baltic Perkūnas or even the Christian Saint Peter. The main communal cult is divided into a spring and an autumn festival. Before the Pentecost celebrations, the young adult Setukese held a ritual fight before sunrise until the first drop of blood flowed. The first one to be injured became the guest of honor at the next year's festival. The second festivity in honor of Peko was held after the harvest. Older men made offerings, and the formula *"Peko, Peko, come to drink the beer"* was common. However, ritual gatherings were also held to worship Peko throughout the year, including at Candle Mass and the Midsummer Festival. Wooden figures of Peko in particular were an important part of the Peko cult. (Black) candles were lit in his honor. Usually, the wooden effigies of Peko had holes on the top for candles. Carved idols of Peko were kept by the Setukese in the granaries – usually protected from foreign eyes. A third holiday was held around August 4, in which the people of Setomaa sing the local anthem, host a musical competition, and elect the next representative of Peko for the year (known as ülebtsootska, the "vice-king"), before they end the celebrations with a military parade.

Perchta

Frau Perchta, or *Frau Percht*, is a legendary figure found in various ways in continental Germanic and Slavic mythology. She probably emerged from the Nordic goddess Frigg by assimilating Celtic substratum. The earliest certain written records of Perchta date from the 13th century, one probable record from the 12th century, and one worthy of consideration from the 11th century. In Central Germany, the mythical figure Frau Holle corresponds to her. The Grimms say *Perchta* or *Berchta* was known *"precisely in those Upper German regions where Holda leaves off, in Swabia, in Alsace, in Switzerland, in Bavaria and Austria"*. The figure of Frau Percht occurs mainly in the East Upper German language area and to a lesser extent in Slovenia and the Czech Republic. In the area of the Low and Middle German dialects she is unknown. There Frau Holle dominates, as well as – further North – other figures, such as Frau Fricke or Frau Gode or Wode. There are only a few overlaps between the Percht and Holle areas. The name *Percht* is possibly derived from Old High German *peraht* (bright, shining) and means "the Shining One". Other conjectures suggest that the name Perchta or Percht is of Celtic origin. According to Jacob Grimm (1882), Perchta was spoken of in Old High German in the 10th century as *Frau Berchta* and thought to be a white-robed female spirit. She was known as a goddess who oversaw spinning and weaving, like in the myths of *Holda* and *Spillaholle* in Continental German regions where she was believed to be the feminine equivalent of *Berchtold*, and she was sometimes the leader of the *Wild Hunt*. Name variants of Perchta and alternative forms are for example: *Bercht, Berchta, Pertica, Per(ch)tiga, Stampfe, Paxto-Stampfo* or *Sperchta*. These names, however, are only found in small areas and in mixtures with the actual name Perchta. Occasionally, mythical motifs from the Midwinter customs connected with the Perchta have been transferred to Christian saints. For example, Perchta is not found in the Passau area, but in the traditional legends *Saint Lucia* has adopted many of her attributes. This can be explained by the fact that in the 14th and 15th centuries December 13 – Saint Lucia's day of celebration – was the shortest day of the year, according to the Julian calendar. Saint Lucia is thus a "pre-existent substitution figure" in relation to Perchta.

Perchta punishes laziness and violations of the *Festspeisegebot* (banquet rules). The punishment can range from simple nightmares to slitting the belly. The belly of the victim is then gladly filled with stones to sink it into a well. In addition, Perchta's breath can kill or blind. Conversely, it rewards diligence and helpfulness. In addition to full spools, golden threads, and bundles of flax for spinners, she also gives away coins that maids find in buckets (mainly at the well). But she is also said to be responsible for the growth of grain. Wells or ponds are also the places where Perchta tends the souls of the not yet born. In this sense, she is also considered to be the leader of the flock of unborn and unbaptized deceased children. Under the name *Butzebercht*, Perchta is also depicted as an old woman who has a crippled foot (grown too large from spinning or also said to be duck- or goose-shaped).

Perchta appears mainly in the Rauhnächten, that is, the time between the Winter Solstice and January 6. Her day is mainly January 6th (Epiphany or Alemannic High New Year). Perchta is said to travel through the air during this time. The similarity of names between Frau Perchta and *Knecht Ruprecht* suggests a connection between the two figures. This is also supported by their rewarding and punishing behavior, as well as the fact that both prefer to appear during the winter months. In descriptions or depictions of Perchta, the attributes of iron and nose are strongly emphasized. The ax with which she hacks into the body of her victims is made of iron, for example. She also rattles an iron chain in many narratives. This conspicuous emphasis on iron may indicate a pre-Germanic substrate. For example, Celtic Noricum was the largest supplier of iron to the Roman Empire. There, the goddess *Noreia* was highly revered. Among other things, she was also considered the goddess of mining. It is also almost universally emphasized that Perchta has a large nose. The motif nose can be interpreted as a bird's beak and probably refers to an old bird goddess, who was worshiped in numerous variants in Southeastern Europe.

Perchtenläufe
The so called *Perchtenläufe* (Perchten runs) are first attested in writing in 1582. They are not mentioned in the *Anti-Aberglaubens literatur* (anti-superstition literature) from the period between the 13th and 15th centuries, which condemned even minor food offerings to the Percht as a mortal sin. However, similar processions are known in numerous areas of Europe, such as the *Graubündner Stopfer* and the *Klöpfler*, which originated in the Bavarian-Austrian area. This could indicate that previously existing customs in the 16th century were now justified by the fact that one wanted to hunt the Percht, which was still tolerated to some extent, since the custom was directed *against* the "demon". However, it was probably not an actual Perchta custom. It was not until the age of the Counter-Reformation that this tolerance was over, and the Percht runs were rigorously suppressed by the Catholic Church and the secular authorities.

Petermännchen

Petermännchen is a *Kobold* inhabiting Schwerin Castle, in Mecklenburg-Vorpommern, Germany. He had one of his places of activity in the cellar vaults of Schwerin's landmark. According to one tradition, the vaults of the castle were connected by passages with Petersberg in Pinnow, where the good-natured Kobold with a sinister expression worked as a blacksmith. Petermännchen is described as dwarf-shaped figure, equipped with a lantern, sword and bunch of keys. He is said to have punished thieves and intruders with plagues, jokes and nocturnal rumbling, and to have driven them into flight, while rewarding honest people. In addition, the Kobold woke up soldiers who had fallen asleep and were assigned to night watch.

Picullus

Picullus is an entity in Prussian mythology and later folklore, which – as is often the case with pagan deities – started as a god or god-pair and under pressure of Christianity eroded into an air-demon or minor deity/devil who could teach magic. The name is identical with Old Prussian: *pickūls* and Latvian: *pikuls* "devil", which was borrowed from a Slavic language (e.g., Polish *pkiel* "devil, hell"). It is usually described as an angry, evil spirit, similar to the Lithuanian *Velnias*. The oldest mention of Picullus' god-form *Patollos* is mentioned in 1418 by Bishop of Warmia in a letter to the Pope *(Collatio episcopi Warmensis)*, according to which the pagan inhabitants of Prussia worshipped the *Patollum* and *Natrimpe* and other monstrous spirits. Nothing is said here about the function of Patollus or Natrimpe. A more detailed description of Patollos can be found in the *Prussian Chronicle* by Simon Grunau, although he is considered unreliable. Grunau writes how the brothers Widowuto and Bruteno came from Sweden to Prussia and that Widowuto became king, while Bruteno became the *Crywo cyrwaito* or high priest of the three gods *Patollos*, *Potrimpos* and *Perkunos* in the sanctuary of Rickoyto. In it stood a great oak tree, green in winter and summer, around which these three idols were worshiped in the form of three "jewels" which were the skull of a man, a horse and a cow. According to Grunau, the three gods were also depicted in the flag of Witowud: *"... the third image was an old mahn with a long groen bard and its color all deadly, was crowned with a white cloth like a morbant (turban) ..."* In addition, Grunau also notes that *Patollo* was the supreme god of the Prussians. He was a frightening and ruthless god

of the dead, who would haunt and taunt the living if they disobeyed their
pagan priests or buried the dead without proper sacrifices to the gods.
Most researchers believe that, despite varying names, Patollo(s) and
Peckols were probably the same entity, in charge of the underworld and
the dead. Later sources do not mention Patollos, but a *Peckols* or *Picullus*,
who is described in the *Sudovian Book* (ca 1520). The booklet describes
Peckols as the god of hell and darkness, and Pockols as an airborne
spirit or devil. The same pair is also found in the church decrees of 1530
(*Constitutiones Synodales*). There, *Pecols* was identified with the Roman
god of the underworld, Pluto, and *Pocols* with the Greek deities of anger,
the *Furies*. In the 17th century Christoph Hartknoch and Matthäus
Prätorius testified that people still believed in *Picolli* and *Pykullis*.

Pinčiukas

Pinčiukas is a kind of devil in Lithuanian folklore, rather small in size
and more of a prankster than really evil. Sometimes he is imagined as a
sneaky creature with goat-like features, who can trick you in order to get
what he wants. If you're not a good child, he might come to poke you with
a pitchfork. Pinčiukas may also act like an *Alp*, causing sleep paralysis
or nightmares. He is believed to have invented how to make vodka from
a she-goat's urine – so called "devil drops", that make it easier for this
devilish creature to control human beings! Pinčiukas could very well be
some culturally morphed version of *Picullus*.

Piru

In Finnish folklore, a *Piru* (also *Pirun*; pl.: *Pirut*) is often featured as a
nasty spirit of the forest, with which a smart aleck either wins or loses
a battle of wits, giving or receiving a forfeit in return. In many cases,
poltergeist and haunting phenomena are described as *pirus*. The Devil
may be referred to as (proper noun) *Piru* or *Pääpiru*, and today *piru*
is also a mild swearword in Finnish. Piru can also mean an evil being
serving the Devil, or an otherwise lesser evil being or demon. The word
"piru" is possibly a diminutive, a pejorative derivation of the word *perkele*,
meaning devil. The word *perkele* is related to the Slavic *Perun*, meaning
thunder god. A separate borrowing of the word Piru from Perun has also
been suggested in the past, but is no longer considered likely. In Finnish
literature, Perun is first mentioned by Mikael Agricola in his translation

of the Bible. He used it to refer to the Devil. However, in Finnish folklore, Pirut often appear as a group of small evil creatures resembling *Gnomes, Trolls* and *Goblins*, and sometimes as individual beings.

Unlike place-bound ghosts, Pirut and demons may wander around looking for suitable victims. They can strike suddenly and possess people, i.e. take up residence in humans. The possessed person may behave in a crazy way or become ill, or their personality may change completely. The possession can be removed by a skilled exorcist. Pirut also may possess a house, i.e. come to live in it and disturb the people in the house. Even in this case, an exorcist or spells have been needed to expel the Pirut. There are stories from Finland that Piru has come to wedding dances in the guise of an unknown man. He may have danced with the bride, who afterwards fell ill or was disgraced by this act. Piru may also impersonate a woman and corrupt a man. When Piru abducted a child, the child and Piru ended up as invisible vagabonds. The only food the child would eat from then on, was food linked somehow to a curse or something negative. For example, if the child or Piru made a cow tip over a milk jug and the milkmaid cursed. The Devil then allowed the child to lick the spilled milk from the ground. If the maid blessed food or milk, the child was punished by Piru or left without food. It was also believed that if you stayed in the sauna overnight, Piru would get angry and could even kill you. In Finnish folktales of the Christian era, Piru is seen as the punisher of wrongs.

Platschmrechen

In the Mühlbach valley, situated between Mutfort and Kontern (Luxembourg), a splashing sound can sometimes be heard at night along the Syr, or along the Mühlbach. It is the *Platschmrechen* (*Platschmariechen*: Splashing Marie), a ghostly washerwoman, from whom one should carefully keep away. If one wants to approach her to observe her, she suddenly disappears. Also, sometimes it seems to be her pleasure to tease the curious. If she is sitting by the Syr and one wants to sneak near her, suddenly the splashing can be heard at the mill stream; but if one then hurries to the mill stream, she will quickly move to some other location at the Syr, where the splashing can be heard again.

Picolus or *Peckols* (1863) illustration by Louis Le Breton in *Dictionnaire Infernal*

Poltergeist

Poltergeist, derived from the German *poltern* (making noise) and *Geist* (ghost), is a paranormal phenomenon consisting of various noises, displacements, apparitions or disappearances of objects and other phenomena a priori inexplicable. In general, they are considered as "small haunting" phenomena that would be related to the presence of a disturbed adolescent, as opposed to "large haunting" phenomena that involve the intervention of the spirit(s) of one or more dead people, although the distinction is not always obvious. In the French *Vallée Classification System*, poltergeists fall into the category of "physical effect anomalies" or AN type II. The term poltergeist appeared in 1540 in the *Novum Dictionarii genus* (New Dictionary) of Erasmus Alberus. It is used, for the first time in German, by Martin Luther during the Protestant Reformation, to designate events that would be caused by disembodied spirits or by the Devil. Catherine Crowe first used it in English in 1848 and it was the Romanian medium Eleonore Zugun who, in the middle of the 20th century, popularized it by calling herself "Poltergeist's daughter". Paradoxically, the Germans are now more willing to use the term *Spuk*.

Nature of the phenomenon

The manifestations of a poltergeist present all – or part – of a considerable range of effects defying reason: violent blows, or knocking, tapping or banging noises, various other noises, all without any identifiable cause; unexplained throwing of stones or debris, targeting the inside or outside of a house (Lithobolia, the Stone-Throwing Devil); displacement or projection of objects (that sometimes get broken), up to their levitation or apparent teleportation through solid walls. More rarely: spontaneous combustion; actions on people: contacts, scratches, bites and levitations, use of a spectral voice (use of victims' "false vocal cords") and appearances. Here is Ernest Bozzano's description of it in Les Phénomènes de hantise:

> *"In addition to the phenomena to which we have referred, moving furniture, slamming windows and doors, breaking dishes, these are very often doorbells that keep shaking loudly for no apparent reason, even after they have been isolated by the removal of cords and wires. Equally frequent are cases of "stone rains", with very remarkable characteristic features, such as when the stones travel trajectories contrary to physical laws, or stop in the air, or fall slowly, or reach a determined goal with very*

unusual dexterity, or strike without harming, or then bounce back, as if they were grabbed by an invisible hand; also the stones can be hot, or even burning. In other circumstances, the sheets are violently ripped off the beds of the people lying down, the latter being lifted and gently placed on the floor, if however the beds themselves are not knocked over."

The demonstrations generally seem to be totally devoid of cause and logic. Despite material damage, sometimes significant, the people present are rarely injured. The phenomenon is reported in all regions of the world, in Europe and the United States, but also in China, Africa, South America, Japan, India, New Zealand, Patagonia, the West Indies, Java, etc. It is also present at all times: the researcher Hereward Carrington identified 5 poltergeist cases before the year 1000, and 130 between the 16th century and the end of the 19th century.

Folklore and popular belief
In Western popular belief, especially in the USA and Europe, poltergeists are often seen as the souls of deceased people who died or were killed in a sudden, mostly violent death. Today Hollywood is mainly responsible for that association. In European folklore, poltergeist phenomena were often attributed to the activities of *Elves*, *Goblins* and related *Fairies* or *household-spirits*. In Japan and China, poltergeist activities are attributed to certain demons such as the Bakeneko, Nekomata, and Rokurokubi. Due to the violence and destructiveness associated with poltergeist activities, poltergeists are always perceived and classified as malignant. Poltergeists are also known in some regions as *Neckgeist* or *Klopfgeist* (*Klopgeest* in Dutch).

Pompwief

At Sellingen in the province of Groningen in the northern Netherlands, the *Pompwief* haunts a local pond. The Pompwief may have been haunting the pool for centuries or even a thousand years, as she is not actually a ghost of a deceased woman but a swamp-spirit. The Low Saxon word "pomp" does not mean pump, but a small pond. So Pompwief literally means "Pond-woman" – a creature belonging to a class of nature-spirits that dwell near water or swamps of which we find many local varieties all over Europe.

Puck or Puk

In European folklore *Puck* or *Puk* is a domestic and nature sprite, demon and Fairy. In Schleswig on both sides of the German-Danish border, the figure is also known as *Nis Puk* or *Nomis Puk*. The Puk or Puck (Lower Saxon: *Puk*, Norwegian: *Nisse*) is a dwarf-like figure of indeterminate gender of the Nordic folk tales. Puks live together with humans and belong to the group of *Elves* from Germanic mythology. Puk itself was possibly borrowed from Baltic folklore (*Pukis*), but is also associated with the Celtic *Púca*. In fact the etymology of Puck remains uncertain, though in general names of spirits that start with *pu* or *bu* usually are Bogeys or have a Bogey-ingredient. The modern English word is attested already in Old English as *Puca* (with a diminutive form *Pucel*). Similar words are attested later in Old Norse *Púki*, with related forms including Old Swedish *Puke* or *Pocker* (devil), Icelandic *Púki* or *Púkinn* (little devil), and Frisian *Puk* – but also in the Celtic languages (Welsh *Pwca*, Cornish *Bucca* and Irish *Púca*). There is also a theory that states the name is derived from *Pogge* (a toad), which in popular opinion was the impersonation of the Devil. Most commentators think that the word was borrowed from one of these neighboring Northwest European languages into the others, but it is not certain in what direction the borrowing went. The Puck or Puk shows the following characteristics:

- To humans, it normally appears invisible due to its cap, which is a camouflage cap. At times it assumes a kind of spirit form that allows it to communicate with the dead.
- If the Puck is treated well with regular food and drink, it is able, in conjunction with other legendary figures such as dwarfs and giants, to positively influence the well-being of the inhabitants and their animals, even to the point of wealth. However, if it is treated badly, it causes serious damage to the inhabitants, which not infrequently ends in madness or death.
- Puke usually dwell in the attic. Sometimes a Puk remains in an abandoned house, but it happens that it makes the move together with the people.
- A Puck lives in houses as well as on ships, where it is called: *Klabautermann*. Everything that applies to the *land Puke* also applies to the Klabautermann.

The British Puck

In Britain and Ireland, Puck fuses with the *Pooka* or Púca and, in the 17th and later centuries, Puck is also known as the male spirit *Robin Goodfellow*.

Puck could be a mischievous, slightly rebellious *Fairy*, playing tricks on travelers, and could transform itself and liked to frighten young girls and push old ladies. A Puck had the capacity to take many forms but it generally took that of a man. It could take on both terrifying and pleasing forms, for example: a horse, a rabbit, a goat, a *Goblin* or a dog. No matter which one, its fur was almost always dark. It often took on the appearance of a large black horse with fiery yellow eyes and a long wild mane. In this form, it roamed a large territory at night, breaking through gates and terrorizing the inhabitants of remote farms. If someone was lured onto the back of a Puck, he or she had to be prepared for a wild ride, although unlike the *Kelpie*, that would take its riders directly to the nearest stream or lake to drown them in order to devour them, the Puck would not really hurt anyone. Shakespeare made the ability of Puck to be a shapeshifter famous in *Midsummer Night's Dream.' Act III., Sc. 3*:

"I'll follow you, I'll lead you about a round,
Through bog, through bush, through brake through brier,
Sometime a horse I'll be, sometime a hound,
A hog, a headless bear, sometime a fire;
And neigh, and bark, and grunt, and roar, and burn,
Like horse, hound, hog, bear, fire, at every turn"

As a prophet and household-spirit

In some regions, Puck was cited with considerably more respect than fear; if treated with due respect, it may prove beneficial to those who encounter it. Puck as a nature-spirit is a being of the mountains and hills, in these regions there are stories that he would appear in the early November to give prophecies and warnings to those who consult him. It was believed that Fairies could help tidy the home; hence Puck (as Robin Goodfellow) was often depicted as a household-spirit, carrying a broom and supporting domestic workers with their chores. It was also understood that he could enforce order on the household by punishing idle maids who did not meet his high expectations by pinching and nipping them. Consequently, Puck/Goodfellow was often praised, or indeed feared, as the strict disciplinarian of the home and its workers. According to Reginald Scot he had a 'standing fee' of a 'mess of white bread and milk', which he expected after supporting housewives with their chores. If his payment was forgotten, Goodfellow was believed to steal from the home that owed him, often stealing grain and milk from the dairy.

Pūķis

In Latvian folklore *Pūķis* (dragon) was believed to be a familiar of a sorcerer. A Pūķis would steal grain and other riches and bring them to its owner. He would be kept in a separate room where nobody could enter without the owner's permission. Dragons would be fed the first bit of every meal. If a dragon felt that he was not revered enough he would turn on the owner and burn the house down. Sometimes dragons could speak. In Latvia and Lithuania belief in the dragons was inspired by fiery meteorites. The term Pūķis is borrowed from Old Norse *púki* (demon, evil spirit), from Proto-Germanic *Pūkô*; compare Swedish *Puke* (house-spirit).

Q

Querxe

Querxe is an East-Central German term for *dwarfs*. The term refers in particular to the members of a people of small stature from the Lusatian saga world. The setting of the Querx sagas is the mountainous Upper Lusatia. The center is the area around Zittau, but they are also known in Vogtland and Bohemia. The Querxe are, just like the *Heinchen*, *Veensmännlein* and *Lutken, mountain spirits* that almost always appear en masse as a people. Querx is a name form of the dwarves, for which the spelling *Querks* is also found. Other Middle German name forms are *Querz, Querg, Quarg*, as well as the plural *Quarkse*. In Franconia they are called *Querkel* and in the Thuringian Forest *Querlich*. Jacob Grimm also mentions the name *Querch* for dwarf in his *Deutschen Mythologie*. The name is etymologically identical to High German *Zwerg* and does not differ from them in content. Both Zwerg and *Querg* (and variants) derive from Middle High German *Twerc*. The development of the first part of the name corresponds to that of East Middle German from Middle High German *Twarc*, and the New High German *Quark*, a loanword from Slavic; the Lower Sorbian *Twarog*.

According to legend, the Querxe owe their origin to the Querxborn-spring, located on the broad mountain near Zittau. From this *"clear, fresh spring"*, some of them are said to have gushed forth. It was believed the Querxe were particularly at home at Querxborn and one could see them *"one after the other going in and out the entrances to the dwellings of the dwarves: their 'Querxlöcher'"* (*Loche* means "hole"). The mountain itself was called a *Zwergberg* (Dwarf mountain) in the *Kirchenbuch von Bertsdorf* (Church Book of Bertsdorf) in 1619. There were also Querxlöcher in Silesia, on the Prudelberg near Stonsdorf; in Upper Lusatia on the Dittersberg near Schönau auf dem Eigen and in Warnsdorf in Bohemia.

If the Querxe went to the surrounding villages to secretly steal food from the farmers, they used to put on a *Nebelkappe* (fog cap) to make themselves invisible. They loved baked goods, but could not stand caraway seeds. Therefore, to protect their bread from getting stolen, the locals always baked bread with a few caraway seeds in it, which the Querxe therefore did not touch. The Querxe sometimes brought gifts to the people, mostly cakes or rusks. Sometimes they were also valuable gifts, that as talismans brought luck and blessings into the house. The family of *Ponickau* is said to have possessed such a talisman, which the woman of the house once received as a gift from the dwarves. A Querxe-talisman is also attributed to the family of *Bünau*. Unlike the von Ponickau family, however, they are said to have received it at a Querxen-wedding.

Like the *Lutken*, the Querxe often came to the villages and the people became accustomed to them. They left Lusatia when Christianity arrived there, because they could not stand the sound of church bells and went to Bohemia, which is why the Bohemians still bake caraway bread today. When they left Hainewalde, they said they would only return *"wann die Glocken wieder würden abgeschafft sein und wann Sachsenland wieder käm' an Böhmerland; dann, meinten sie, würden auch bessere Zeiten sein."* (When the bells would be abolished, and when Saxony would rejoin Bohemia; then, they thought, there would also be better times.)

R

Roesschaert

In West-Flemish folklore *Roesschaert* is a shapeshifting demon whose
most dominant shape is that of a huge, demonic, black phantom-dog with
bells around its neck. It especially haunted the people of Blankenberge
and used its shapeshifting abilities in performing cruel pranks upon them.
The 1874 *Almanac van Blankenberge* tells of the dreadful storm of 1791. It
destroyed the hut of a suspected witch on the beach, and the inhabitants
were overjoyed, smashing what little was left of the ruins. Then a spine-
chilling sound was heard, coming out of the dunes and a huge black dog
with bells around its neck came running down the dunes and grew larger
and larger. People were convinced the witch had changed herself into this
devilish dog: *"'t Wierd alsan moa grotter en grotter en 't riep: roes, roes,
roes. En azo krêeg 't de noame "Roesschaert". En iederêen was overtuugd dat
d'ekse eur veranderd ad in een bêeste".* (The witch grew bigger and bigger
and at the same time she shouted: roes, roes, roes. And everyone became
convinced that the witch had turned herself into a beast.) This Flemish
sentence, taken from a folk-tale, takes the witch/dog shouting *roes, roes,
roes* as the etymological source of the name Roesschaert. Several other
completely different opinions about the origin of the name Roesschaert
have been proposed, but no convicting consensus has been settled.

Ròggemouer

In the northeastern part of the Dutch province Groningen, bordering
German East-Frysia, the *Ròggemouer* (Rye-mother) is a Lower-Saxonian
field-spirit. She appears in the rye-fields when in the summer the rye has
reached its maximum height and guards the fields: *"As the rògge groot
wòrdt, so dat ie der hoast nait meer over kieken, din zit ter altied 'n gaist
in, dij der op past".* (When the rye grows so high that you can hardly see
over it there is always a spirit in it watching over it). The Ròggemouer
thus functions as a classic German *field-spirit*, yet she is also handy as
a child *Bogey* to prevent children from entering the field. She is located
by watching over the field. There is always a spot where the rye seems to
move more than in the rest of the field. Folk-belief locates the spirit on
that particular spot.

Roggenhund or Kornhund

The *Roggenhund* (rye dog) or *Kornhund* (corn dog) is a German field demon and dog-shaped wind-spirit feeding on flour. The name is one of the many names attributed to the more commonly used Roggenwolf (rye wolf). Its attributes are also the same, though there might be a certain accentuated quality. Other names are, *Heupudel* (hay poodle), *Schotenhund* (husk dog), *Scheunbetze* (barn dog), *Dreschhund* (threshing dog), *Weizenbeller* (wheat barker) or *Kornmops* (corn pug).

Roggenmuhme

The *Roggenmuhme* is a female corn demon and child terror of German folklore that resides in the fields and acres. The daemon walks up and down the field, feeding on the grain and plucking out the unripe ears. If she is angry with a farmer, she ploughs up his field and punishes him in this way. In general, however, the Roggenmuhme's passage through the field ensures fertility. At harvest time – following a classic field daemon pattern – she flees into the last sheaf. The Roggenmuhme also receives a share of the harvest, which is either left standing or thrown into the field. This custom is said to make the Roggenmuhme act benevolent and bring about a bountiful yield the next year. The dwelling of the Roggenmuhme is thought to be under the earth, in the "root realm" or in a cave. The Roggenmuhme resembles figures like *Frau Holle* and *Perchta* in that she punishes lazy maidens who have not spun off their distaffs during the *Zwölfnächten* (Twelve Nights; a period between December 20/21 and Januari 5/6). This is why she is also called *Rockenmör*. The breath of the Roggenmuhme brings sickness and death.

Roggenmuhme means *rye-aunt*

Muhme is an older German kinship term and mostly means *aunt* or *niece* (as the aunt's daughter), but can also denote social proximity in general, such as how children today are instructed to use the word "aunt". The male equivalent of Muhme is *Oheim*. The Roggenmuhme is addressed by a huge number of different names, related to different regions, or one of her attributes. These can often have certain recurring name components.

• Names with the name component *Roggen-*:
  Roggenmutter (rye mother), *Roggenfrau* (rye woman), *Roggenweib* (rye wife), *Roggenweibchen* (little rye woman), *Roggenwief* (rye wife),

Roggenalte (rye elder), *Roggenhexe* (rye witch), *Roggenmöhme,
Roggenmöhn, Roogenmäuk, Roggemöh, Roggomön, Roggenmüne* and
Roggenmiene (all meaning *rye-aunt*).

- Names with the name element *Korn-*:
  Kornmutter (corn mother), *Kornmoder* (corn mother), *Kornmuhme*
  (corn aunt), *Kornmöhm* (corn aunt), *Kornmähne, Kornfrau* (corn
  woman), *Kornweib* (corn wife), *Kornwyf* (corn wife), *Kornwif*,
  Kornweiblein (little corn wife), *Koarkewiffke* (little corn wife),
  Kornweibel (corn wife), *Kornalte* (corn elder), *Kornengel, Koansbab* and
  Kornbaba. It should be noted here that, depending on the region, the
  word *Korn* either referred to the totality of grain, or was used for the
  local main cereal. Especially in central and southern Germany, the use
  of *Korn* for *Roggen* (rye) is traceable for 1865.

- Names with other cereals as part of the name:
  Other cereals are also reflected in the name of the Roggenmuhme. These
  are *Weizen* (wheat) in *Weizenmutter* (wheat mother) and *Weizenmuhme*
  (wheat aunt), *Gerste* (barley) in *Gerstenmutter* (barley mother) and
  Gerstenmuhme (barley aunt), *Hafer* (oats) in *Hafermutter* (oat mother)
  and *Habernitza*, but also cereals in general in *Getreidemuhme* (grain
  aunt), *Getreidehexe* (grain witch), *Saatmuhme* (seed aunt), *Preinscheuhe*
  and *Breinscheuhe*.

- Names with other crops, arable plants and agricultural terms as name
  components:
  Various other field crops are used as name components of the
  Roggenmutter, such as *Erbse* (pea) in *Erbsenmuhme* (pea aunt), the
  Erbsenmöh and *Erbsenweib* (pea wife). Flax is a name component of
  the *Flachsmutter* (flax mother). Named after *Radel* (a field weed) are
  Radelweib, Rahlweib, Raalweib and *Ralenweib* (all meaning *Radel-
  woman*). Other names are associated with fields and harvesting, such as
  Erntemutter (harvest mother) and Feldweib (field mother).

- Other names:
  Additionally the Roggenmuhme is also addressed to as *Alte* (Old),
  altes Weib (old wife), *Großmutter* (grandmother), *große Mutter*
  (great mother), *alte Hure* (old whore), *große Hure* (big whore),
  Heimmutter, Pannwief, Dratweiberl, böses Weib (angry wife), *böse Frau*

(angry woman), *Beumöhn*, *Muhme* (aunt*)*, *weiße Frau* (white woman)
und *wilde Frau* (wild woman).

Appearance

The Roggenmuhme is often described as being all black or snow-white,
in addition to being of superhuman size. The arms of the Roggenmuhme
are long or of iron. Her fingers are fiery or iron. The Roggenmuhme
is also said to have claws, which may also be of iron. She has (many)
unusually large breasts. They are thus long she can swing them over her
shoulders and they may be black, of wood, iron or silver. The breasts can
also be pointed and hard, have glowing iron tips or burn, and can be
filled with tar, poisonous milk or blood. Because of the prominent feature
of her breasts, the Roggenmuhme is therefore also called by names as
Zitenweib, *Tittenwief*, *Tittewiv*, *Tittenwiv* or *Tittewîf* (all meaning *tit-
wife*). In addition, she can change her shape, for example into a turtle, a
snake, a frog, a wolf, a black cat, a horned beast or a dog with a blanket.
Sometimes she is described more recognizable as simply an old and
wrinkled woman. She can have needles or pointed growths coming out
of her face, has a crooked nose and wears glasses. In some cases, she
is even described as headless, or believed to have a heart of iron. The
Roggenmuhme is often dressed in black, but may also be dressed entirely
in gray. Her appearance is ragged. Sometimes the Roggenmuhme wears a
red skirt or a red dress and a red cap with it. She also has a blue cloak and
may wear wide flowing skirts. Often the Roggenmuhme wears a white
headscarf like a reaper. Sometimes she walks on crutches.

Roggenmuhme as a weather phenomenon

The Roggenmuhme is associated with several weather phenomena. When
the wind passes through the cornfield, the *Kornmutter* moves over the
grain or the *Kornweiber* walk through the grain. She is also *die fahrende
Frau* (the travelling woman) or *fahrende Mutter* (travelling mother),
when in the whirlwind, the Roggenmuhme is travelling with her *Doggen*
(very large dogs of a German or Danish breed). Thunderclouds are
named after her as *alte Weiber* (old wives) or *Regenmütter* (rain mothers).
The Roggenmuhme is also known as the *Regenmuhme* (rain aunt).

Roggenmuhme as noonday spirit

The Roggenmuhme appears as the German version of *Lady Midday*,
between 12:00 and 13:00; an hour, in German dialect also called *im*

Untern or *Onnern*. Hence she is called *Mittagsfrau* (midday woman), *Mittagsmutter* (midday mother), *Untermutter* (mother of the midday), *Untermuhme* (aunt of the midday), *Enongermur, Enungeschmor, Enongeschmor, Enongermoer* or *Einuhrsmutter* (mother of one o'clock). Whomever she meets in the fields at noon, she kills, or frightens with strange sayings. If she finds women in bed between 12:00 and 13:00 (siesta time) and between 18:00 and 20:00, she does their field work. If she does not find the women in bed at the specified time, there will be a misfortune.

The Roggenmuhme as a child scare and torturer

The Roggenmuhme is particularly frequently mentioned as a demon that scares children. Her activities in this role are extremely varied. In their Legend No. 90 *Die Roggenmuhme*, the Brothers Grimm relate that the Roggenmuhme exchanges human children for *Wechselbalgen* (changelings), but brings back the right child if the *Wechselbalg* is not suckled. Elsewhere it is said that she steals illegitimate children at midnight. The Roggenmuhme lies hidden, as a predator, in the field for all those children. She also abducts children who want to pick *Kornblumen* (cornflowers) in the field. After the *Kornblumen* she is also called *Kornblumenfrau* (cornflower-woman), *Krullmoer, Krüllkemoer, Krullkesmouder, Krüllkesmutter, Tremsenmutter, Tremsemutter, Trensemutter, Trimpsenmutter,* or *Trämssemutter*. If children do not get into the field on their own initiative, the Roggenmuhme lures them into the field as the *Ziehmuhme* (pull aunt) or *Kindermuhme* (child aunt). She especially lures by her beckoning. Children are also carried off by her by putting them into her sack or carrying basket. Kidnapped children she hides under her wide flowing skirts or brings them to the *Wurzelreich* (root kingdom). The Roggenmuhme also drags children to her with an iron stove-crutch and has them guarded by a toad. She leads children astray in the field, lets them starve to death or comes with her *Elfen* (Fairies) and lays the children on flower-pillows, whereupon they fall asleep and do not awake. The latter is more reminiscent of *Feen*. As a *Hexe* (witch), the Roggenmuhme appears when she bewitches children or has the evil eye, as a *Nachtmare* (Nightmare) when she sends evil spirits to disobedient children's bedsides at night. The Roggenmuhme is a witch of the night. Often children have to suck on the aforementioned deadly breasts of the Roggenmuhme or get them beaten around their ears. Otherwise they are also pressed against the breasts of the Roggenmuhme

and thus come to death. Generally she crushes children in her embrace.
The Roggenmuhme also crouches in the corn in wolf form and is
accompanied by little dogs that lure children into her iron embrace. She
is also considered to be the mother of a class of field daemons called
the *Roggenwölfe* (rye wolves), which eat the children. Both of these are
recalled by the name *Wolffrau* (wolf woman). In addition, she feeds
children to her burning horned cattle. The Roggenmuhme also pursues
the children on horseback or runs as fast as a horse herself. In the latter
case, she rushes children to death in races. She can also fly and in this way
takes the children to the sea to drown them there. If she accosts children,
they must die.

Sichelweib

The ways the Roggenmuhme is said to torture children is absolutely
horrible. The Roggenmuhme requires children to eat a slice of bread
spread with tar. If they do not comply, she cuts off their heads. She
also smears children with tar from a bottle or smears their eyes with
tar. She also scratches out children's eyes or blows out their eyesight,
just as the *wilde Jägerin* (wild huntress) *Frau Holle/Perchta* is used to
do. The Roggenmuhme strangles children, twists their necks or cuts
off their heads, and also cuts off their necks or noses and ears. She also
beheads children with the sickle. That is why the Roggenmuhme is also
called *Sichelweib* (sickle-wife), *Sichelfrau* (sickle-woman), *Sichelmuhme*,
Sichelhals, *Zekelwief* and *Secherwief*. For the same purpose she also
uses a knife or a saw. With the scythe she mows off the children's legs.
Fingers are also cut off. Generally, the Roggenmuhme tears off children's
legs. Sometime she ties children into a bundle with a thread or she
ties children to a twine thread and then beats them up. She pinches
children with iron pincers or makes use of a pinch. She stabs children
with pikes, of which she has three, one by the head and one in each
hand. The Roggenmuhme also stabs with stalks or drives nails into
children's heels. In her hand the Roggenmuhme carries a rod or whip,
which is to be valued as a lightning rod. She also has a scepter or an iron
Kantshu (normally a short leather whip) to whip children. Or she puts
them into the nail barrel and rolls them around in it or drags them into
a cave and crushes them there with the meat machine. Otherwise she
also crushes the children in an iron butter churn. From this she bears
the names *Buttermuhme* (butter aunt), *Bottermäumk* or *Putterlusche*.
The Roggenmuhme also bites and eats children. In order to get hold of

children, she lays out booby traps, throws children into a cauldron of hot water or sucks out their blood. If that is not enough, she slaughters and eats the children or kills and roasts them with the help of her burning breasts and fingers.

Roggenwolf

The *Roggenwolf* (rye wolf) is a wolf-shaped corn demon of German folklore, who stalks the fields and farmlands. To scare children away from the fields, crops or even plum trees (*Pflaumenwolf* = plum wolf), it was said of the Roggenwolf that he would abduct and eat children. Various 19th century proverbs characterize the Roggenwolf as voracious and gluttonous to the point of immobility as a result of excessive gorging. It is also aggressive. The Roggenwolf howls and roars in its greed for food. The shape and nature of the rye wolf are further illustrated by the name forms *großer Wolf* (big wolf), *wilder Wolf* (wild wolf) and *böser Wolf* (angry wolf).

Roggenwolf as wind- and weather-spirit
The Roggenwolf is a *Windgeist* (wind spirit). He is also called the *Windwolf* (wind wolf). Especially when the wind causes the ears of grain to move in waves, the wolf was said to go through or over the grain, to be in the grain or to hunt the sheep in the grain. Sometimes there is also talk of several wolves chasing each other in the grain. The howling of the wind is said to be caused by the Roggenwolf. Within this perception the Roggenwolf could appear as the embodiment of rough weather, fog and rain.

Roggenwolfes as grain demon
The driving of the Roggenwolf in the field is said to either promote the fertility of the field or, on the other hand, reduce the fertility of the field, especially since the Roggenwolfes feed on the grain of the field, in which relation the demon is said to cause *Mutterkorn* (ergot), which is then called *Wolf* or *Wolfzahn* (wolf's tooth). The Roggenwolf is said to sit in the last sheaf of the harvest. This last sheaf is therefore also called *Wolf*. Anyone who comes into contact with the Roggenwolf during the harvest becomes ill.

In addition to the simple name wolf (depending on the dialect also *Wulf*, *Walf*, *Wulp*), various other names for the Roggenwolf also occur, named after the crop of the corresponding field in which the wolf is said to be up to mischief. In addition to Roggenwolf or *Roggenwulf*, these are the other names used for the demon:

- *Getreidewolf* (grain wolf)
- *Kornwolf, Kürnwolf, Koorwolf, Koanwolf, Körwolp* (wheat wolf/grain wolf/corn wolf)
- *Großer Kornwolf* (big corn wolf)
- *Haferwolf* or *Hawerwolf* (oat wolf)
- *Gerstenwolf* (barley wolf)
- *Kartoffelwolf* or *Kantüffelwolf* (potato wolf)
- *Graswolf* or *Grasewolf* (grass wolf)
- *Erbswolf* (pea wolf)
- *Pflaumenwolf* or *Plummenwolf* (plum wolf)
- *Roggenhund* (rye dog)

Rübezahl or Liczyrzepa

Rübezahl, the German name for *Liczyrzepa* is an evil mountain-demon or *Schrat*, also known as *Ducha Gór* (Spirit of the Mountains), *Karkonosz, Rzepiór, Rzepolicz,* Czech: *Krakonoš, Krkonoš, Rýbrcoul*). This figure is still inseparably connected with the folklore of the Karkonosze (Giant Mountains, Krkonoše Riesengebirge, located in the north of the Czech Republic and the south-west of Poland). The legend of the Liczyrzepa or Ducha Gór goes back to the Middle Ages – its origins are probably connected with the pagan cult of the Elbe springs. Initially, he was the personification of the forces of nature in this place, associated with the cult of the Slavic deity *Svantewit*, to whom black roosters were sacrificed. Svantewit (also *Svantovit, Swantewit, Sventevit, Svetovit, Svatovit, Świętowit, Svątevit, Suvid* or Святовит) was a four-headed war god, oracle giver, and supreme deity of the Ranen on the island Rügen and other Elbe and Baltic Sea Slavs, comparable to the supreme god *Perun* of other Slavic tribes. During Christianization, attempts were made to eradicate the old customs by replacing Svantewit with St. Vít, whose attribute, in the Sudetenland region, became a black rooster. The figures of other saints were also used in the Giant Mountains to fight the old beliefs. The St. Lawrence Chapel was erected in 1681 on Śnieżka, and it was an element of "disenchantment" of the pagan genius loci of the Karkonosze (similar with the exorcism of the mountain spirit on the Czech side – at the source of the Elbe). The mountain spirit was also sometimes called *Panem Janem* (Dominus Johannes), which resulted from the introduction of the cult of

St. John the Baptist in place of the pagan rites of the summer solstice. The first known graphic representation of Liczyrzepa (as *Rübenczal*) comes from a map of Silesia made by the Silesian cartographer Martin Helwig in 1561. It is an unusual creature, somewhat resembling a deer standing on its hind legs, and perhaps even a griffin. It has dewy horns and a devil's tail, goat-like hooves, and holds a tall, upright stick in its paws. He is shown in profile, with his mouth turned to the right. Much more popular and well known is the image of Liczyrzepa as an old man supporting himself with an axe, sometimes in hunter's clothes. In later legends he can take on any form he wants.

Liczyrzepa is possibly a corrupt translation of Rübezahl. Maciej Bogusz Stęczyński used the form *Rzepolicz* in his poem *Śląsk*; the form *Rzepiór* (a cluster of the words *rzepa*: "turnip" and *upiór*: "ghost") was also used. Later Józef Sykulski used the term Liczyrzepa. The time of emergence of the name Rübezahl is not clear, though one of the Rübezahl-legends mentions 1512. In 1662 Johannes Praetorius gives different spellings, like *Rübezal, Ribezal, Riebenzahl*. In his collections Rübezahl appears in many guises, sometimes as a giant and guardian of the mountain treasure, as a monk who leads people astray, as a raven, or donkey, and often as Diabolus, Satan. In his first Rübezahl story, Johann Karl August Musäus gave a legendary explanation of the name in 1783. According to this tale, Rübezahl kidnaps the king's daughter Emma, whom he wants to marry, and brings her to his underground kingdom. With turnips that she can transform into any shape she wants, he tries to satisfy her longing for her home. But the turnips wither. Finally, the woman promises him her hand if he tells her the number of turnips in the field. If he does not succeed, he must let her go. Immediately, the mountain-spirit sets to work. To be sure that the number is correct, he counts again, but comes to a different result. Meanwhile, the prisoner escapes on a magic turnip turned into a horse to her prince Ratibor and mocks the spirit by addressing him as Rübezahl. The spirit becomes very angry when he is given this mocking name. This is however not a generally accepted etymology because it seems that the German word Rübezahl or Rübenzahl does not come from the words *Rübe* (turnip, beet) and *zählen* (to count), but is probably related to the words Rabe (raven) and the Old German Zabel (devil). An additional etymology derives *zahl* from the Old High German *Zal, Zagel*, meaning "tail" or "penis", which could refer to the figurative appearance as a tailed or ithyphallic demon (mind his early depiction with horns, a devil's tail, and goat-like hooves, reminding of a *Satyr* or *Faun*). In Czech the spirit is called Krakonoš, which could go back to *krk* or *krak* "mountain pine" and *nosit* "to carry".

Since the 17th century Liczyrzepa/Rübezahl has ceased to be only a demon causing fear, or the "Spirit of the Riesengebirge", and many very diverse folk-legends and entertaining local fairy tales have been created about him in which he figures in many different roles and appearances. A fate that has befallen many medieval or more ancient creatures when modern age emerged after centuries of demonization and Christian "castration" of their original wild nature by the leaders of the church. Only a few relics remain which honor the original mountain-spirit. In the Riesengrund, near the Schneekoppe, a botanical locality with a striking abundance of plant wealth is called *Rübezahls Gärtchen* (Rübezahls little garden), and also some peculiar stone formations are named after him; e.g. the "Rübezahlkanzel" above the Schneegruben.

Runsa

According to a legend from the Pitztal, a valley located in Tyrol, Austria, *Runsa* is a female Alpine spirit who was condemned by God to wander on the alpine pastures of Fundes in the Pitztal. Runsa was once a milkmaid who stole butter and after her death became a gruesome ghostly apparition, an ugly noisy girl with red eyes, who hurls crockery around the house like some kind of *poltergeist*. It remains unclear whether Runsa really is the spirit of a milkmaid or some nature-spirit, as the phenomena she was supposed to manifest include weather changes, strange music (*Hexenmusik*), etc. Johann Nepomuk Ritter von Alpenburg illustrated this in his work *Mythen und Sagen Tirols*, Zurich 1857, with the following recorded story:

> *"60 to 70 Years ago, the "alte Knappeler" (his actual name was Martin Moser) herded the oxen at the so-called Ochsenhütte (oxen hut) above the Rauschbrunnen under the Klamm-Eck. There he sometimes heard beautiful music. Once, however, he felt tempted to whistle the melody of the same music, but then he was up for trouble, because up in the gorge and on the high Wart there was a roar in the air, as if the Runsa was coming, and the oxen and the cattle came roaring wildly from the pasture, the weather turned ghastly, mudflows and*

runes came down, and hail fell in fist-sized pieces. Just then, the Knappeler's boy was drinking from a buttermilk bowl, and his head was violently pushed into the bowl, so that he was almost suffocated. Since then, the Knappeler has become smart and has not whistled again when he heard the Hexenmusik (witch's music) above him."

Rüttelweiber

Rüttelweiber are female demons; in fact the term is used specifically to denote a class of dwarfish forest-spirits, the *Moosweibchen* (little Moss Women), who are hunted down by a figure called *der Nachtjäger* (the Night Hunter), during a storm. They do not belong to the night folk and so can appear during daylight. They are always on the run from fierce hunters and begging for protective shelter. In the area of Kynast and the nearby Riesengebirge (Giant Mountains) as in the Vogtland, the Nachtjäger or *Wilde Jäger* (Wild Hunter) moves with all his noisy entourage, and hunts and torments the Rüttelweiber and *Waldwichtel*. For these there is only one rescue from the Nachtjäger's violence and quick grasp, namely when they come to a cut tree trunk, to which the woodman spoke when cutting it down: *"God forbid!"* – they find asylum and rest there. If they cannot find such a tree, they must flee further and further from their persecutor.

Rübezahl or *Liczyrzepa* on cover of the magazine *Jugend* no 3, 1904

VGEND
No 3 · 1904

S

Salamanders

Salamanders are a group of *Elementals* which form the spirits of fire, who dwell in the invisible Fire-element of nature. Without them, material fire cannot exist; a match cannot be struck nor will flint and steel give off their spark without the assistance of a salamander, who immediately appears (so the medieval mystics believed), evoked by friction. There are many families of them, differing in appearance, size, and dignity. Mostly they are depicted as a creature that looks like a lizard or salamander, residing in the center of a fire. Paracelsus wrote: *"Salamanders have been seen in the shapes of fiery balls, or tongues of fire, running over the fields or peering into houses."* (*Philosophia Occulta*, translated by Franz Hartmann). The Czech magician Franz Bardon and the German occultist Karl Spiesberger give detailed descriptions and functions of several kinds of these Fire-Elementals. Spieberger also mentions the *Feuerfeeën* (fire-fairies), named *Farasilles* and *Schallores*. The different Salamanders described by Bardon can by evoked by the traditional European evocation method using their sigil in a triangle, while standing in a magical circle. One salamander I evoked into materialization myself this way is *Itumo*, who rules abrupt thunderstorms and very heavy rainfall. These spirits have an energy-field like an aura around them, that feels unique and different from the normal atmosphere and is clearly distinguishable. Like many Salamanders described by occultists, Itumo appeared as a creature of about 6 feet in height, slender and – as if designed after a drawing by Austin Osman Spare – reddish, yellowish and orange in color. I included the Salamanders (and *Undines*, *Gnomes* and *Sylphs*) in this encyclopedia, because these nature-spirits are at the base of many creatures which were given their own folkloric existence as local entities. In the context of this book, Elementals in general can be regarded as a godfather-class of beings of which many Fairies, field-, mine-, air- and household-spirits are a derivative. More isolated they do not so much belong to folklore but to the occult traditions of magic and witchcraft.

Salige Frauen

Salige Frauen (Blessed Women), also called *Salkweiber, Salaweiber, Saligen*,
or *Wilde* or *Weiße Frauen*, are figures from the legends of – mainly – the
Alpine region. The Salige Frauen are described as shy but helpful and wise
women. They used to live in rock and glacier caves, or on the banks of
the Drava River. They were shy creatures, but they stood by unexpected
visitors with advice and help. They helped poor farmers and clumsy
people. A legend from Vinschgau reports that in a very dry year they
brought buckwheat, which was still unknown there. At night, when the
moon was bright on the starry canopy, one should not meet the Salige
Frauen. The Salige Frauen also appear in South Tyrolean lore. In one
tale, one of them is described as blond; in another, three of them initially
appear as white doves. Salige Frauen detest noise. According to one legend,
a noisy young peasant was not careful and irritated them, after which the
Salkweiber took him as a love prisoner. They sexually drained him until he
lay soulless on the ground. One day the sound of weapons came from the
valley, and the Salkweiber have not been seen there ever since.

Sandman

The *Sandman* is a figure in European folklore (Germany: *Sandmann*; the
Netherlands: *het Zandmannetje* and *Klaas Vaak*; France: *Le marchand
de sable*; Spain: *El Arenero*; Russia: *Песочный человек*; Denmark: *Ole
Lukøje*; Scandinavia: *Jon Blund*; Austria-Tirol: *Pechmandl*, etc). According
to tradition, he visits children in the evening, sprinkles sleep-inducing
sand in their eyes and causes them to dream. The sleeping sand is rubbed
out of the corners of the eyes in the morning. Celtic religion knows
the Genius *Cucullatus*, a guardian spirit and hooded demon. In Greek
mythology, the *Oneiroi* bring dreams. They are a group of demons, sons
or brothers of *Hypnos*, the god of sleep, who resemble bats. *Morpheus*,
a son of Hypnos, is considered the god in charge of dreams and visions.
He presides over his brothers *Phobetor* (from the Greek *phobia*, φόβος;
"fear") and *Phantasos*. People thus receive messages in their dreams. The
entrance to Morpheus' cave is overgrown with narcotic herbs such as
the opium poppy. For the Teutons, sleep and death were siblings. E.T.A.
Hoffmann's (1776-1822) horror story *Der Sandmann* (The Sandman)
creates a typical traditional child fright figure, whose appearance spreads
fear and terror. It uses sand as a weapon that is dangerous and injurious
to the eyes. An old nurse, in contrast to the somewhat more enlightened

parents, drastically describes the Sandman to an inquiring child as:

> *"...ein böser Mann, der kommt zu den Kindern, wenn sie nicht zu
> Bett gehen wollen und wirft ihnen Händevoll Sand in die Augen, daß
> sie blutig zum Kopf herausspringen, die wirft er dann in den Sack
> und trägt sie in den Halbmond zur Atzung für seine Kinderchen;
> die sitzen dort im Nest und haben krumme Schnäbel, wie die Eulen,
> damit picken sie der unartigen Menschenkindlein Augen auf".*

(...an evil man, who comes to the children when they do not want to
go to bed and throws handfuls of sand into their eyes so that they start
bleeding and then pop out of their heads. He then throws the eyes into
the sack and carries them into the crescent moon to his little children;
they sit there waiting in the nest and have crooked beaks, like owls, with
which they peck open the eyes of the naughty human children.)

In Germany *der Sandmann* joins a multitude of frightening figures,
whose purpose is to make the children go home in the evening or to fall
asleep at home, like the goat-like *Nachtbock* (Night-goat), the *Nachtkrabb*
(Night-crow or Night-raven), the *Nachtgiger* (Night-rooster), the
Bummelux (a German Bogey-phantom that hides behind walls and in
dark places), the *Nachtraben* (Night-raven) or in the Hunsrück-region
the *Naachseil* (Night-owl). Their characteristics have – to varying degrees
– been incorporated in the literary shaping of the well-known Sandman
figure. The friendly figure of the Sandman known today can essentially
be traced back to the Danish fairy tale poet Hans Christian Andersen
(1805-1875). Andersen named the Sandman *Ole Lukøje* (Ole Eye-Closer).
Regularly, before bedtime, he visits the children and closes their eyes with
"sweet milk" and then tells them a bedtime story.

Sauzagel

Sauzagel or *Säuzagel,* a field daemon related to a whirlwind, is discussed
by Wilhelm Mannhardt as prototyping one of the many agricultural
demons in German speaking regions. A whirlwind that blazed a trail
through a cornfield was usually perceived as a field demon making its
appearance. Yearly rituals were performed to keep them friendly and in
turn they would ensure and protect a good harvest. Mannhardt's treatise
on the subject is most interesting:

*"In my "Götterwelt der deutschen und nordischen Völker", I have first
shown that a number of Germanic harvest customs arose from the idea
that in the middle of the grain there is a demonic being which, when
cutting the grain field, withdraws deeper and deeper into it and is finally
caught between the last stalks. This view is clearly recognizable from a
series of harvest rites, which understand that demonic being as a ghostly
pig (sow or boar). In order to give the necessary analogies to the following
compilations about a related mythical figure, it is enough to point out the
following facts. The whirlwind is called Windsau, Sauzagel, Sauschwanz,
Säuarsch (wind sow, sow's penis, sow's tail, sow's ass); the Wilde Jagd (wild
hunt) circumnavigating in the storm carries with it grunting boars. There
is no doubt that the wind was once compared to a boar roaring over the
Earth, and the celestial natural phenomenon was once really considered
to be the vitalization of such a ghostly animal. Widely spread is the speech
"der Eber geht im Korn" (the boar goes in the grain), the wild pigs are in
the grain field, if the wind moves the field wave-like up and down. Again
in many places of Germany one warns the small children not to get lost in
a cornfield, "denn es sitze eine wilde Sau, ein wilder Eber darin" (because
there sits a sow, a wild boar in it). One believed thus really, that Windsau
had her stay in the field. A Belgian spell shows even more clearly that the
poetic comparison of the wind with a boar had developed into a real belief
in a mythical being. There, namely, a countryman blesses his grain against
the lightning, the grain dragon (oorem?), the Bilsenschneider and "tegen
het duivels zwyntje" (against the devilish pig). Just like the natural force
of the wind itself sometimes has a benevolent, sometimes a harmful effect,
also the Windsau, or the Windeber had to have a double side. Sometimes
this demonic being could be thought of as blessing, sometimes angry, that
when a gentle wind fertilizingly shakes up the pollen of the young ears,
but when more violently blowing scatters the same farther and causes
thereby infertility, or when it swelled to the destroying storm, tearing
stalks and grains with itself into the air. The farmer had reason to fear
the wrath "des Windschweines" (of the wind pig), to implore his merciful
disposition. Who mowed the last stalks on the field, captured the wild
boar itself and had the office to carry it into the village and into the barn,
so that it would stay there until the sowing of the coming year. According
to these ideas, in the Bavarian Schwabia dem Schnitter (the reaper), who
cuts the last fruit of the field, is addressed with the saying: "Du hast die
Roggen sau" (You have the rye sow). One binds the last ears in the form
of a pig and lets it be carried home the same under cheering escort."*

The etymology of Sauzagel is interesting. *Sau* means sow and *Zagel* means penis. Hence *Sauschwanz* is also used, where *Schwanz* means tail, but is also slang for penis. As all field daemons were also fertility daemons in the most general sense, the name Sauzagel is likely rooted in that millennia old conception. Sauzagel, as explained above, is also a common name for a whirlwind in Hessian and Thuringian dialects in the form *säuzål, sauzâl*. In Oberhessen, Sauzal was used to mock the Devil as he showed up as a whirlwind in the field (*Zeitschrift fur deutsche Mythologie und Sittenkunde* – erster Band – J.J. Wolf, 1853). Finally the term is used as an abusive word for an unclean person.

Schabbock

The *Schabbock* (short *Schab*) is next to the *Trud* (an *Alp*-type spirit) the best known demon-figure of Weststeiermark (western Styria). This night-spirit is also known in various forms in other parts of Austria and Bavaria (and probably also in Slovenia). In the area around the Koralpe there are still people who claim to have seen this mythical creature. The folklore of western Styria has the following explanation for the origin of a Schabbock: *"If a bride and groom, who have already ordered the banns, do not live demurely and celibate during the last weeks before the wedding ceremony and a child is born from this union, then it has to bear the burden of disturbing the people as a night spirit. If it is a boy, then he appears as a Schabbok and has it on small children. If it is a girl, it appears invisibly as Trud"*. Eyewitnesses told Isabella Wippel – who collected West Styrian legends in the 1980s – the following about the appearance of Schabbock: *"In front the Schabbock has a glowing spike or a glowing head, behind it a glowing birch broom, from which it 'daunigahnt'"* (which probably means sparking). The function of the Schabbock is to kill infants. He flies over the country before midnight or squats on the sour cherry trees next to the farmhouses or immediately on their roof gables. There it waits until parents leave their babies alone and then it kills them.

Defensive measures

As a defensive measure a rosary, a hemp stalk and a man's shirt in the crib were in use. Furthermore it has been recommended to smudge the swaddled children with Schabbockskraut (*Ranunculus ficaria L.*, commonly known as lesser celandine or pilewort) and hemp stalks to ward off the Schabbock, because it is allergic to hemp. Of course, there are also some defensive sayings to drive away the Schabbock. For example this one, which asks God to make the Schabbock pass the house without entering: *"Helf Gott! Mir und dir, Schabbock stoß neben vür"*. It is not known which ancient figure the Shabbock is based on or from which culture it originated. Presumably, the infanticidal night spirit arose from the desire to explain sudden infant death. However, there are also legends about small children who were badly beaten up by the Schabbock or hanged from the door buckle. These were probably crimes that were simply attributed to the Schabbock due to the lack of police prosecution.

Schlitzöhrchen

In local Bavarian folklore *Schlitzöhrchen* is a dangerous water demon. The name Schlitzöhrchen suggests a tiny creature as the ending *"chen"* (Schlitzöhr-*chen*) in the German language is always used as a diminutive, but nevertheless an encounter with the creature could be lethal. People who cross the Streu river below Mellrichstadt were dipped into the river by this water-spirit and often they were drowned. The story of Schlitzöhrchen was recorded in *Deutsche Sagen* by Jacob Grimm and Wilhelm Grimm (Brüder Grimm) in Kassel, 1816/18.

Schrat

Schrat (pl.: *Schrate*; in Bavaria and Austria also *Schrazen*) are considered a kind of nature-spirits. They are known among the Germans and Scandinavians and among the western Slavs. Based on etymology, the Schrat is a spirit creature similar to man (or animal) that dwells in the forests, causes nightmares, and is imitated in masks. Later the Schrat is extended by the meaning *Kobold*. In Carinthia, a Schrat is said to denote a kind of household-spirit. Unlike Elves and the gregarious miners, Schrate are solitary creatures. Depending on their habitat, they can also be named as forest-, stream- or meadow-Schrats (*Wald-*, *Bach-* oder *Wiesenschrate*), etc. The exact etymology of the word *Schrat* is unclear, but it is likely that the word is of Germanic origin. In German-speaking countries, it can be found in Middle High German, for example: *Schraz, Schrate,* or in Old High German *scratto*, Old Norse *skrat(t)i* (sorcerer, giant), Icelandic *skratti* (devil), *vatnskratti* (water-spirit), Swedish *skratte* (fool, sorcerer, devil) and in New English dialect *scrat* (devil). From German, schrat found its way into Slavic languages, for example Polish (before 1500) *skrzat* and *skrzot* (house-spirit, dwarf), and Czech *skřet, skrátek, skřítek* (*Goblin*, gold-bringing devil). The Slovene word *Škrat* (also *Škratelj, Škratec, Škratek*) comes like the Skrat-versions in the other languages and dialects from the Old High German word *scrato* "forest demon". In Slovenia the Skrat is often used as a more generic term for dwarfish spirits or Goblins. In Gorizia it was sometimes called *Kapič* (because of its pointed cap), in the Ter valley *Skarifič*. In some places it was called *Dimek* (because of its grey color), the tree-škrat was a lumberjack. In Dolenjska it was *Gugljaj* (because of its swinging on trees), the *hišnemu škratu* (house skrat) was sometimes also called *Gospodarček* (little master) or *Šetek* (little shepherd). The landscape name of the Schraden at the edge of Lower Lusatia (Niederlausitz) is explained folk-etymologically in this context. A small Schrat is also called *Schretel* or *Schräzel*.

Schrätteli or Schrättele

Female *Waldschräte* (forest-schrats) are known as the *Schrätteli*. The Schrätteli or Schrättele occur in many sagas from the Black Forest, Germany, and are a local variation of the *Nachtmahr*. Here too it is not necessarily an *Alp*-type spirit, but can also be a female person or a witch who leaves her body and enters the bedrooms of her victims through the keyhole in the shape of a straw. Once there, she torments and squeezes her victims until they are completely exhausted, or causes nightmares. The Schrätteli is also said to often squeeze cattle in the barn to get relief there when it cannot squeeze a human victim.

Sgönaunken

Sgönaunken or *Sgönunken* are *Kobolds* of Westphalia, Germany. They are concentrated in the Hüggel, an 225.6 m above sea level high, about 5 km long and 1 km wide mountain range near Hasbergen in the Lower Saxon district of Osnabrück. The Upper Carboniferous outcrop is part of the Ibbenbüren coalfield. It is a place of many legends and tales. There is a legend of the Hüggel blacksmith who ruled over the mountain spirits who mined for gold and silver. There are also stories about the Sgönaunken who lived in the so-called Wüllekeslöckern and, similar to the *Heinzelmännchen*, did a lot of good to the people in the area of the Hüggel.

Slogutis

The name *Slogutis* (pl. *Slogučiai*) is a diminutive and comes from the Lithuanian word *slogus* (oppressive), which comes from a verb *slėgti* (to press, to weigh down). Slogutis generally means pain, fear, misery, bad feelings or nightmare. A Slogutis clearly is an *Alp*-type spirit or demon and was thought to cause sleep paralysis. When this happened one could regain control over one's body by moving the big toe or ring finger and scare Slogutis away. Another defense method was to put a rosary around a the demon's neck (provided one was already out of the state of paralysis). Some folklore tales state that the Slogutis is an evil spirit, visiting its victims predominantly at night, but sometimes also in the daytime. Slogutis is sometimes used as an umbrella term for certain night-spirits instead of denoting a unique species of demon. So the nocturnal visitor could be *Pinčiukas* (a little demon, usually of a good nature), a *Laumė*, a deceased relative, an unbaptized infant's soul, etc. Usually a Slogutis victim exhibits the typical Alp-symptoms of being constantly exhausted and feeling literally "pressed down". He or she is also very unlucky in all matters, during such a period of attacks. It is only natural that in folklore it is believed that an evil spirit is causing these things. Contrary to *Incubus/Succubus* experiences, the attacks of the Slogutis are not of a sexual character. There is no clear understanding how and why a person is chosen by Slogutis as its prey. It is said that Slogutis punishes women that killed their children. The Slogutis is also known to attach itself to a person who does not do what is right. In some tales a person gets Slogutis for a simple act as falling asleep in the wrong place. *Slogučiai,* the souls of unbaptized or murdered infants are said to harass their victim until he or she finds their bones and reburies them. A special defense method was sleeping with a plank on the chest and holding a knife in one hand. It was believed that if a person woke up with a knife stuck into this plank it meant the Slogutis was killed.

Apart from being a separate entity, a Slogutis could be a reversed curse: one's own wrongdoing firing back from the person you had hurt or treated unfairly. In the modern Lithuanian vocabulary *slogutis* is used as a synonym for a light depression. It is also common that Slogutis can tackle someone who simply works too hard and forgets to take care of him or herself. Usually such workaholics get ill, because they do not "see" the signs that they should slow down. Thus instead of just being an Alp or evil spirit, the creature can also act as an anti-burn-out coach.

Sommeltjes

Sommeltjes are a kind of *Goblins* or *Trolls* that would dance in the
moonlight on the Sommeltjesberg, an excavated Dutch burial mound
from Roman times near de river Waal. During the day they are almost
impossible to find. When they come into the sunlight, they petrify. They
can become invisible, but they can also take on the form of all kinds
of animals. In local dialect, a Sommeltje is a kind of ghost or spirit.
In Wieringen the creatures are called *Sammelkes* or *Sammeltjes*, they
live in the *Sammelkeskuul* (Pit of the Sammelkes) on Zandburen near
Hippolytushoef. The creatures could enter through the cracks of a *bedstee*
(bed box), but usually did no real harm. They helped people with little
chores. They liked shiny things and played on small whistles and smoked
a pipe. A pot left outside could be found polished shiny in the pit the
next morning. Other valuables were also collected at night. If one walked
past the pit, silver coins could disappear. In the past, it was told that the
children were brought by the Sammelkes.

Spillaholle

The *Spillaholle* (Silesian German, also: *Spillahulle*, *Spillahole*, *Spillahôle*,
Spiellahole; Standard German: *Spindelholle*) is a legendary ghostly
creature found in the German folklore of formerly German Silesia
including Austrian Silesia. A similar being is found in folktales of
formerly German-speaking Bohemia. The Spillaholle is a Silesian variant
of female German legendary creatures such as *Hulda* or *Perchta,* with
an obsession for spinning activities. In Bohemia, she is simply known
as *Frau Holle*. Other Silesian names are *Satzemsuse*, *Mickadrulle* and
Mickatrulle. Spindelholle is a sallow old woman with short arms and legs.
She appears hooded – characterized by the name *Popelhole* or *Popelhôle*;
Standard German: *Popelholle* (hooded Holle) – or wearing ragged
clothing, as shown by the name variant *Zumpeldrulle* or *Zompeldroll*.
She also can be seen in an old Franconian dress, sometimes wearing a
pelt muff. The Bohemian Frau Holle is depicted as a small and ugly old
woman carrying a bunch of stinging nettles.

Activities

The main activity of the Spillaholle is connected with spinning, for she is
the overseer of spinning taboos and a Bogey used for spinning children.
Therefore, a broad variety of names for Spillaholle shows a connection

to spindles, such as *Spilladrulle, Spillagritte, Spillmarthe, Spillalutsche* or *Spellalutsche*. Spillaholle appears mainly during the winter months, especially during Advent, Christmas or during the Zwölften (twelve nights of Christmas). She goes from house to house to see if the children and spinsters are spinning diligently, looking through the windows or even peeking through gaps in the house wall. When they are still spinning during evening and night, then there will be slight or even severe punishments. When spinsters are not finished with their spinning, then the *Satzemsuse* will sit in their lap during spinning or even give them igniting spindles instead of normal ones. The Spillaholle takes lazy spinsters away. Frau Holle beats them with a bunch of stinging nettles. If all the tow is already spun, then there will not only be no punishment, but one of the nettles will even be left in the house to ward the house against misfortune for the whole coming year. Additionally, in Bohemia all spinning is banned on the night of St. Thomas. If a spinster is working anyway, she will be punished by Frau Holle. To children that are spinning in the night, the Spillaholle says: *"Verzage nicht, verzage nicht, warum spinnst du die Zahl am Tage nicht?"* (Do not despair, do not despair, why do you not spin the number at day?) Then she kills the children or takes them away. To prevent this from happening, children are warned by their parents when at evening the wind is howling in the stove: *"Die Spillaholle kommt!"* (The Spillaholle comes!).

Spoukhoas

In the Lower-Saxonian folklore of East-Groningen (northern Netherlands) the *Spoukhoas* (Ghost-hare) is a ghostly *were-animal*. It looks like a normal, yet over-sized hare, but it is not a normal animal, because as often local farmers or hunters would shoot at the hare, they were unable to kill or wound the creature. The only way to get rid of the hare was by using a silver bullet – just as legend has it that only a silver bullet can kill a *Werewolf*: *"'t Haar 'n spoukhoas west, en dij kinje allinneg roaken mit zulvern koegels."* (It has been a Spoukhoas, and you can only kill them with a silver bullet.)

Stafia

The *Stafia* (pl.: *Stafi*) is described by Claude Lecouteax in his *The Secret History of Vampires* (2010) as a spirit created by masons, or the phantom

of a murder victim or suicide. The masons had a ritual consisting of
secretly measuring the shadow of a person that fell on a wall of a project
they were working on, and burying the measure in the foundations.
This person whose shadow was captured this way usually died soon
afterwards or died when the building was finished. The person then
became a Stafia and remained bound to the building. It was a wide spread
believe in Europe that such a spirit would then prevent the building
from collapsing. In the Baltic regions, especially Lithuania, skeletons of
children are frequently discovered in the walls or under old churches.
In folk-traditions, however, and unlike the belief within the masonic
lore, the Stafia is not by definition bound to a building. The creature is
described as a woman whose hair touched the ground and whose breasts
were immensely long and made of iron. She appeared clad in white or
naked, was very skinny and ugly, with bulging eyes looking like onions
and a head like a bucket. But she was also accredited with shape-shifting
features, as she could appear as a dog, pig, ram, cat, billy- or nanny goat,
horse etc. It could be encountered at night in certain homes, cellars,
churches, and on bridges, but also at abandoned springs, deserted places,
crossroads and in forests. It usually was not aggressive, but could strangle,
scratch or mutilate its victim, steal someone's breath like a *Nightmare*,
blow out candles, or simply look for food in the house. To keep the Stafia
in a friendly mood, people left food and beverages for the creature.

Stalo

Stalo (southern Sami), *Stallo*, *Stállu* (northern Sami) or *Stállo* (Lule Sami),
is a figure in Sami mythology. Stalo appears in several different guises
and is depicted in Sami stories and legends as a *giant*, a *Troll* or a *demon*
or *devil*. The first written reference to Stalo is in the *Lexicon Lapponicum*
(1768/1780), although the term has been used in the Sami tradition for
several hundred years. In the *Lexicon Lapponicum*, Stalo is described
as a one-eyed and ferocious giant, wearing black iron clothes. In later
descriptions, Stalo has been portrayed as – among other things – large,
rich, evil, man-eating and even as a servant of the Devil. However, Stalo
is unintelligent and gullible, and is easily tricked by cunning Sami, often
by the children he intended to eat. The Stalo appears mainly in two types
of tales and legends, either as a man-eating Troll or as a *ghost* or demon
sent by a *noaide* (shaman). The Stalo are evil, bigger and stronger than
human beings, but they are also dumber, so it is often possible to deceive

them. According to Claude Lecouteux, the name Stallo, which can be traced back to the Norwegian and Swedish *stål* (steel), means "the one who is coated with steel". In some folkloric tales he is a cannibal giant of superhuman strength, who comes out at Christmas and is accompanied by a dog: if you kill Stalo, you must also kill his dog, otherwise it will lick the blood of its master and Stalo will rise again. Geographical references to the creature are found in many place names, such as *Stàlo-Javr'i* (Lake Stalo) or *Stàlo-Bak'ti* (Stalo Mountain).

The depiction of the Stalo has shifted over time and there is no entirely consistent view of what a Stalo is. In the 1830s, brothers Lars Levi and Petrus Læstadius speculated whether Stalo was really just a mythological figure, or whether Stalo actually had a historical basis in reality. The brothers looked at several different legends about Stalo and concluded that they were probably Vikings and robbers who roamed the mountain valleys and made a living by stealing reindeer. At the same time, it was thought that the man-eating was merely a way of enhancing the myth up to Bogey-level, to scare children into obedience. No sooner than the 1870s, the theory of Stalo as the 'steel man' emerged, with Stalo being considered the Sami word for 'steel' and the black iron clothes actually being chain mail. During the 20th century, theories developed regarding Stalo as a northerner, i.e. flesh-and-blood people, either in the form of tax collectors, hunters or traders *(birkarlar)*. Norwegian folklorist Marit Anne Hauan argues that Stalo is not derived from any mythological figure outside the Sami world of ideas, unlike, for example, Goblins and giants.

Stampa

The *Stampa* is a strange spirit in Tyrol folklore from the Imst region. The spirit is believed to be some kind of *Wilde Frau* (wild woman) who can shape-shift to scare people. A woman named Benedikta Moll once went with her father at first dawn past the meadows. She walked about a stone's throw behind him, put her foot on a stone wall there, to tie her shoe. Then a snow-white horse's head peered over her shoulders, so that she cried out in horror. Her father rushed towards her, calmed her down and said that it would have been the "Stampa", that wild woman from the Nassereither area, who was especially interested in children and young girls. He kept an eye on his daughter and led her firmly by the hand until the end of the day. The story was recorded in *Imster Geisterbrevier* by Hermann J. Spiehs, Imst 1936.

Steinklammgretel

As mentioned in *Sagen Niederösterreichs* by P. Hillebald Ludwig Seeb, in
a den of the Steinklamm in the Steigraben (Wiesenbach, near Lilienfeld)
lives the ghostly *Steinklammgretel*. She is a female *Wauwua* and drags the
bad children away into her lair so that they disappear forever. It seems
that her main function was that of a *Bogeyman*, useful for parents with
troublesome children.

Steipmännchen

In Luxembourg, near Ehnen, a sinister Unhold, the *Steipmännchen*,
haunted the boatmen in particular, often teasing them and playing
mean tricks on them. When the Steipmännchen sailed up the Ehnener
Wehr on stormy nights, he would make a great splashing sound in the
water with his oar, and you could hear him calling over and over again,
"Hilfe, Hilfe, sonst geh' ich zu Grunde!" (Help, help, I am going down!). If
a merciful boatman, suspecting no harm, arrived at the dangerous spot
with his boat, he not only found no one in need of help, but also heard the
Steipmännchen clapping his hands and laughing at him from the rocky
shore. When the boatman got angry and cursed him, the spirit knocked
over his boat and he had to pay for his insolence with a cold bath.

Stüpp

Stüpp is the name for a kind of Werewolf in the western parts of Rhineland.
The Stüpp differs from the Werewolf as he appears in most Western
European folk traditions, in that he usually did not maul his victims, but
lay in wait for them (usually at a crossroads, a cemetery wall or a stream or
river), jumped at them from behind and let them carry him (in Rhenish
dialect: *pözen* or *hackeln*). This connects him with another figure from
folklore, the *Aufhocker*, who is also frequently represented in the Rhenish
saga world. The Stüpp is represented in numerous folk traditions in the area
between the Rhine and the Eifel, especially in Selfkant, a municipality in the
Heinsberg district, in North Rhine-Westphalia, bordering Dutch Limburg.
In Westphalia, as well as in the bordering provinces of Belgium and the
Netherlands, a similar creature was feared under the name *Klüngelpelz*
or *Böxenwolf*. The Stüpp often accompanied its victim in the guise of a
seemingly playful little dog, but as he did so, he grew larger and larger and
then jumped on their back and could no longer be shaken off. Usually it

grew heavier with each step, while the person carrying it was tormented
by mortal fear and finally collapsed, completely exhausted. Usually people
were said to be scarred by the experience for the rest of their lives, lost their
mind or died soon afterwards.

The Hackestüpp von Düren
Particularly notorious was the *Hackestüpp von Düren*, whose name also
includes the verb *hackeln* (to carry on the back). There are also legends in
which the Stüpp behaves like the Werewolf in other parts of Germany or
Europe does, i.e. it tears its victim apart, but the victim does not become
a Werewolf him – or herself afterwards – the latter actually being a
concept that is absent in European folklore and exclusively a thing of the
Hollywood-werewolf.

The name Stüpp
The Stüpp owes its name to the farmer *Peter Stumpp* (c. 1535-1589),
also spelled as *Peter Stube, Peter Stubbe, Peter Stübbe* or *Peter Stumpf*. He
was a German farmer and alleged serial killer, accused of werewolfery,
incest, witchcraft and cannibalism. He was known as *Werwolf von
Bedburg* (Werewolf of Bedburg). At that time, the wolf in rural areas
was considered a threat and a danger, both to farm animals (e.g. sheep,
goats or cows) and to the people themselves. Fear of wild animals, in this
case the wolf, got a new proxy through the myth of the Werewolf. Peter
Stumpp was executed on 31 October 1589, together with his daughter and
mistress, because he had allegedly made a pact with the Devil and could
transform himself into a wolf. In this guise, he had allegedly cruelly killed
at least thirteen people. The case was described in detail in a voluminous
pamphlet, printed in London in 1590 – the only real source – but the
accounts raise all sorts of question marks. It has been suggested that Peter
Stump was a victim of the Counter-Reformation. There is evidence that
he was executed in a particularly cruel manner (including tearing out his
flesh alive with red-hot tongs) to deter the population of Bedburg, which
had converted to Protestantism, and that the accusation of *Werwolferei*
(werewolfery) was only a pretext that people easily saw through and
understood as a massive warning from the Catholic authorities, especially
from the Kurfürst and Archbishop of Cologne.

Relationships to Revenants and other entities
According to folklore, the Stüpp preferred typical places where

Wiedergänger (Revenants) also appeared, e.g. liminal zones like crossroads, cemeteries, or places where murders had been committed or people had taken their own lives. He either lay in wait for his victims there, or let them carry him to such a place. This suggests that at least the Rhenish variant of the Werewolf was originally conceived as a recurring dead person or as a bearer of the soul of a dead person, and not primarily as a human being who could transform himself into a wolf thanks to magical abilities. A legend in the Eifel reports that a person who commits suicide may appear to people shortly after his or her death as a giant-sized wolf. The figure of the Werewolf, mixed with other squatting haunting figures, especially the *Bahkauv* (Bachkalb), a demonic creature that lay in wait for people along watercourses and let them carry it to the other side of the stream or river. In Aachen and Düren, the Bachstüpp or the Bachkalb was even said to have therapeutic powers, for it cured anyone that had once been ridden by it of drunkenness/alcoholism. Traces of a primitive belief in the returning dead still shine through in the figure of the crouching animal, for the uncanny creatures were actually Revenants that had taken on the form of an animal and preyed on the living – a symbolic action aimed at draining them of their life force. Like all demonic creatures, they shunned contact with flowing water – the symbol of purity – which had to be repugnant to them as impure beings. Other crouching fiends in the Rhineland legends were large dogs with huge, glowing eyes, called *Zubbelsdeer* or *Zotteltier* (shaggy animal), which were probably the fading stage of an original Werewolf. This variant probably only emerged in the last two centuries, after wolves had completely disappeared or been wiped out as a threat to peasant existence in the Rhineland. To the same extent that the Werewolf was replaced by the demonic dog, the belief in a human being that had turned into the threatening animal also faded. Many of the people interviewed by folklorists between 1900 and 1925 knew the Stüpp only as a ghostly creature. In various legends recorded around 1900, the Stüpp had turned into a harmless, if annoying, pest.

Defense against the Stüpp

When a person was attacked by the Stüpp, he could only defend himself to a limited extent. In some legends, however, it is said that a man plunged a knife into the paw of the Werewolf or into the place where the "Werewolf belt" was located and thus put an end to the haunting. If he had a concrete suspicion about the fiend that had attacked him, he

only had to call out its name. The Dürener Hackestüpp was unmasked
because a farmer did not let himself be pushed to the ground but dragged
the fiend into his house and the farmer's wife hit the Werewolf with a
silver crucifix right on the forehead *"where the baptismal water had once
flowed"*. As with every other type of Werewolf, one could defend oneself
against the Stüpp by throwing him a cloth – often an apron – into which
the fiend would then bite. Later, the Werewolf could easily be unmasked
because threads of the torn garment were still hanging between its teeth.
The near-victim of such an attack is often the daughter of the Werewolf.

Sumpurņi

In Latvian folklore *Sumpurņi* (Dog snouts) are Werewolf-like beings that
are taller than humans and live in large forests. Their most distinguishing
feature is having the body of a human covered in fur and the head of a
dog or sometimes a bird, or with one eye or one leg. It used to dress itself
in tree leaves. Sumpurņi also have a tail, and it was believed that they
had a hierarchical society, where the length of the tail would determine
their position in society. When in a state of rage, Sumpurņi would attack
humans and also animals, tearing them apart, eating their flesh and
drinking their blood.

Swan Maiden

The *Swan Maiden* is a mythical creature that shape-shifts from human
form to swan form. The key to the transformation is usually a swan skin,
or a garment with swan feathers attached. In folktales of this type, a
male character spies the maiden, who is usually bathing in some body of
water, then snatches away the feather garment (or some other article of
clothing), which prevents her from flying away (or swimming away, or
renders her helpless in some other manner), thus forcing her to become
his wife. Swan Maiden-tales are common in folklore all over Europe in
Celtic, Germanic, Northern or Slavic regions.

Sylphs

Sylphs are the elemental spirits of the Element Air. In this context air
is not meant as the natural atmosphere of the Earth, but the invisible,
intangible, spiritual medium of Air, an ethereal substance similar in

composition to our atmosphere, yet far more subtle. Manly Palmer Hall quotes the last discourse of the condemned philosopher Socrates, as preserved by Plato in his *Phædo* as follows:

> *"And upon the Earth are animals and men, some in a middle region, others* (Elementals) *dwelling about the air as we dwell about the sea; others in islands which the air flows round, near the continent; and in a word, the air is used by them as the water and the sea are by us, and the ether is to them what the air is to us. Moreover, the temperament of their seasons is such that they have no disease* (Paracelsus disputes this), *and live much longer than we do, and have sight and hearing and smell, and all the other senses, in far greater perfection, in the same degree that air is purer than water or the ether than air. Also they have temples and sacred places in which the gods really dwell, and they hear their voices and receive their answers, and are conscious of them and hold converse with them, and they see the sun, moon, and stars as they really are..."*

While the Sylphs were believed to live among the clouds and in the surrounding air, their true home was upon the tops of mountains, a belief in contrast to modern occultists which describe the Sylphs simply as the inhabitants of the Air-Element, and the rulers of our physical air. They clean polluted air by dismantling poisonous molecules. *Gnomes* and *Undines* use the same method to clean polluted earth and water. To the Sylphs the ancients attributed the labor of modeling the snowflakes and gathering clouds, which they accomplished with the cooperation of the Undines, who supplied the moisture. The winds were their particular vehicle and the ancients referred to them as the spirits of the air. They were believed to have lived for hundreds of years, often attaining to a thousand years and never seeming to grow old. The leader of the Sylphs is called *Paralda*, who is said to dwell on the highest mountain of the Earth. The female Sylphs were called *Sylphids*. By some, the *Muses* of the Greeks are believed to have been Sylphs, for these spirits are said to gather around the mind of the dreamer, the poet and the artist, and inspire him or her with their intimate knowledge of the beauties and workings of Nature. The Sylphs sometimes assume human form, but apparently only for short periods of time. Their size varies, but in the majority of cases they are no larger than human beings and often considerably smaller. While Sylphs are at the base of many creatures of the air, as described in folkloric tales, they are first of all part of the European occult tradition.

Syöjätär

Syöjätär (the Eater) is an evil female creature in Finnish folklore and mythology. She is associated with the origin of some diseases. In a spell against syphilis the disease is called *the progeny of Syöjätär*; in a spell against *"tooth worm"* (*Hammasmato*, gnawer of teeth and bones, was believed to be the cause of tooth decay and infections) the creature's origin is given as coming indirectly from the work of Syöjätär:

> *"The evil mistress Syöjätär, the old mother of iron, Rakehetar, was pulverizing iron grains, was hammering steel points on an iron rock in a mortar of alder wood, with a pestle of alder wood, in a room of alder wood. What she pounded, that she sifted, she gobbled up those groats of hers, bits went astray among her teeth, they settled themselves in the gums to hack the teeth, to rack the jaws."*
> (- John Abercromby (1898), *The pre-and proto-historic Finns: both Eastern and Western, with the magic songs of the West Finns)*

Together with *Hiisi*, Syöjätär is a key element in the creation myth of snakes – in the story Hiisi's sleep drool is swallowed by Syöjätär, but it burns her gums and she spits it out.. after being blown by the wind, it lands and dries, Hiisi then brings it to life. In other variants it is Syöjätär's spittle, and Hiisi who brings it to life. She is also involved in the creation of the lizard – she spits on the sea that forms a bubble – the bubble is swallowed by the girl *Kasaritar* or *Kasarikki* who becomes pregnant for three years, then gives birth to a lizard. A similar creation story for the wolf again involves Syöjätär spitting on the sea – then *Kuolatar* appears from the sea on a bare island – this creature rubs its palms to create some land whereon the wolf was reared. In a song describing the origin of stone, it is described as the heart's core of Syöjätär, amongst several other allusions; she is also the originator of the fir tree (in one version), together with *Maajatar*, *Pellervoinen*, and *Naservainen* who develop it.

Together with *Ajatar* (huntress) and *Akka* (old woman), Syöjätär fulfills similar roles in Finnish folklore as does *Baba Yaga* in Russian lore. There are also some similarities between Syöjätär and Russian folkloric depictions of the Devil – such as both being the origin of creatures like snakes and toads. Syöjätär lacks the positive side of the ambiguous Baba Yaga – this positive role is fulfilled by Akka in Finnish myth. In some folktales she takes the role of wicked mother. Syöjätär can be translated as *man-eater*, as well as *seductress*. In fairy tales and legends, Syöjätär is a traditional character, resembling a witch or an evil and dangerous adult or old woman. In some stories she is capable of incredible magic by means of which she can devour many people in an instant, in others she is content to just seduce and scheme. In a song for the purpose: *"To Still Violence"*, Syöjätär is referenced as the *"Ogress"*, and is portrayed as an element in the consumption of persons that are consumed by violence or anger:

> *".. there is the Ogress (Syöjätär) in the sea with a mouth in the middle of her head, a tongue in the middle of her throat, who has eaten a hundred men, destroyed a thousand full-grown men; may she now also eat thee up, as the bread she eats, as the feast she holds."*
> (- John Abercromby (1898), *The pre-and proto-historic Finns: both Eastern and Western, with the magic songs of the West Finns)*

In *Mythologia Fennica*, the dictionary of Finnish mythology originally published by Kristfrid Ganander in 1789, Syöjätär is a female *Devil* and a *half-Elf*. She is one of the anthropophagi, a cruel and large carnivore and a *stone-fairy*. In Elias Lönnrot's collection *Ancient spell casters of the Finnish people*, Syöjätär is an evil spirit or witch, mentioned along with other evil spirits such as *Hiisi*, *Perkelee* and *Louhe*.

T

Tatzelwurm or Stollenwurm

In the folklore of the Alpine region of south-central Europe, the *Tatzelwurm, Stollenwurm* or *Stollwurm* is a legendary lizard, with a serpent-like body of around 1 to 7 feet in length which may be slender or stubby, and with two, four or six legs. It has a cat-like face, especially in Switzerland. The Tatzelwurm of Austria and Bavaria was believed to have a poisonous breath, which could be lethal. The Stollenwurm has also been characterized as poisonous in Swiss lore. The creature is said to make a shrieking sound or utter whistles and hisses. The creature is known in the Austrian, Bavarian, French, Italian and Swiss Alps under many regional names, including *Bergstutz, Springwurm, Praatzelwurm*, and in French: *Arassas*. The name Tatzelwurm is not traditionally used in Switzerland, as the creature is usually known by the Swiss as Stollenwurm or Stollwurm (tunnel worm or dragon of the mine-tunnels), especially in the Bernese Alps. Stollenwurm may also be interpreted to mean a "serpent with short, thick feet". Tatzelwurm was the term localized in Bavaria, Germany, next to *Daazlwurm* and *Praazlwurm*. Apart from Tatzelwurm, *Bergstutz*, *Birgstutz* or *Birgstuz'n* (mountain-stump) were the local names used in some places in Austria, such as the state of Styria, parts of the Tyrol, Salzburg and the Salzkammergut regions, and some parts of Bavaria (specifically Berchtesgaden). In the valleys of the Traun and Alm rivers of Austria the name was simply *Stutzn*.

Encounters

An anecdotal "cat-headed serpent" with a black-gray body and no legs was said to have been encountered by Johann and Thomas Tinner at a place locally known as "Hauwelen", on the Frümsen mountain in the Barony of Altsax, Switzerland. It was alleged to measure 7 feet or more in length. Residents in the neighborhood were complaining that their cows' udders were being mysteriously sucked on but the incidents stopped after this creature was killed. A four-legged lizard with a crest on its head was allegedly seen by Johannes Bueler of Sennwald Parish. A dragon with an enormous head and two forelimbs, was claimed to have been encountered by 70-year-old Johannes Egerter of Lienz on Mt. Kamor; when it exhaled its breath, the man said, he was overcome with headache and dizziness. A four-legged, cat-faced "mountain dragon" was described by one Andreas Roduner in the year 1660 on the Wangersberg in Sarganserland and when it reared up on its hind legs it became tall as a man, with boar-like bristles running down its back.

A 1779 legend describes an encounter with the Tatzelwurm by farmer Hans Fuchs. According to the story, while in the mountains, he allegedly saw two of these creatures in front of him. Frightened for his life, he fled to his home and died of a heart attack from the experience. Supposedly before he died, he told his family of the encounter, describing the creature as 5 to 7 feet in length with a serpent-like body, two clawed front legs and a large feline-like head. In 1811, a Stollenwurm with a forked tongue, a serpent-like but rather wide head, and two stubby feet was reported by a Schoolmaster Heinrich. He claimed to have seen the creature in Guttannen-tal, Canton Bern, Switzerland. He described it as measuring one "klafter" in length, with a body about the thickness of a man's leg. (The klafter is a historical measurement unit, used in Central Europe based on the span of a man's outstretched arms – traditionally around 6 feet) This encounter happened a few years before Hans Kehrli, from Allmentli in Trachselwald, claimed to have killed a quite small, hairy Stollenwurm, carrying ten young Stollenwurms. The writer Johann Rudolf Wyss, explicitly stated that while the dragon was fabulous, the Stollenwurm was dubious. To the standard description of the Stollenwurm as a sort of snake with a cat's head and short feet, he added that it was sometimes said to be hairy, and having not just 2 or 4, but multiple limbs, like a caterpillar.

Modern sightings

It is unclear whether the Tatzelwurm should be catalogued under "folklore" or "cryptozoology", as even in modern times the Tatzelwurm has been sighted again and again. To date, there are about 80 eyewitness accounts. In 1950, various people saw it in the Jura, in 1948 and 1968 in the French Alps, in the early 1980s in South Tyrol, and in 1984 near Aosta. In 1935, a Tatzelwurm was reportedly photographed in the Aareschlucht gorge in the eastern Bernese Oberland, according to a multi-page report in the *Berliner Illustrierte Zeitung*. A reward for a captured specimen was also offered by the newspaper. Even today, the Tatzelwurm is the mascot of the Aare Gorge. In the summer of 1963, a Tatzelwurm was seen several times near Udine in northern Italy. It was described as a 13 feet long snake with a head the size of a child's head and a body the size of a telegraph pole. Before the Tatzelwurm appeared, a high-pitched whistle was said to have sounded.

Tobelhocker

In Liechtenstein folklore, *Tobelhocker* are earthbound souls of bad people in a state of terminal depression:

> *"Folk legend exercises its own justice against the Brenners, who, not good enough for hell, are banished to a dark Tobel (ravine); the gorge you have to pass through if you want to reach the Alp Lawena. There they sit at tables of stone dumb and rigid, because their hearts were also hard as stone and implacable, and their lying mouths are closed forever. The people call them 'Tobelhocker'".*
> (- *Sagen aus Liechtenstein*, Otto Seger, Nendeln/Liechtenstein, 1966/1980, no. 56.)

U

Uldra

In the folklore of Lapland *Uldras* are creatures living underground, exclusively in Lapland, resembling *Brownies* or *Pixies*. They are said to have pointed teeth as well as a black hairy face and – according to mythology – are the rulers of the reindeer and other large animals. In winter, they would feed the bears that were in hibernation, and do so very delicately, so that the bears would not wake up from it. They came out only at night, being unable to see anything in the daytime, and lived in extended families or tribes. Although Uldras are initially very friendly creatures, they can take revenge in terrible ways on people who disturb or offend them. The most terrible act of revenge on their part is the spreading of a powder over the reindeer moss, which causes the reindeer to die in rows. They were also known to replace babies with changelings that had hairy black faces and long teeth. There is also a Norwegian version of the Uldra, which is descibed as a water-sprite: – see *Spirit Beings in European Folklore* – Compendium 1.

Undine

An *Undine* (rarely also: *Undene*, French *Ondine*) is a (usually) female, virgin water-spirit. Like the *Salamander*, *Gnome* and *Sylph*, she belongs to the so-called *Elemental spirits*. The name is therefore mostly used as a generic term, and is derived from both the Old High German *undia* (Common Germanic *unþi*, New High German die *unde*) and the Latin *unda*, with the identical meaning of "wave", for which a common Indo-European root is assumed. They are the archetypal source of many (mostly feminine) water-spirits and often identical with *Water-Nymphs* and *Mermaids*. In the occult tradition a distinction is made between *water* and the *Water-Element*. Manly Palmer Hall writes:

> *"... the Undines (a name given to the family of water elementals) function in the invisible, spiritual essence called humid (or liquid) ether. In its vibratory rate this is close to the element water, and so the Undines are able to control, to a great degree, the course and function of this fluid in Nature. Beauty seems to be the keynote of the water spirits. Wherever we find them pictured*

in art or sculpture, they abound in symmetry and grace. Controlling the Water-Element – which has always been a feminine symbol – it is natural that the water spirits should most often be symbolized as female."

Undines appear in European folklore mainly as Water-Nymph-like creatures. The figure of Undine first appears in a legend of the Upper Rhine knightly dynasty of the Staufenberg, in a poem written around 1320, which has been adapted many times afterwards. According to Paracelsus, it is an elemental creature belonging to the mythological genus of Nymphs and embodying the element of water. According to him, it can usually be discovered in forest lakes or waterfalls. Like the more malicious *Sirens* they have a beautiful voice or luring call, sometimes heard above the sound of the rushing water. What is special is that the Undine has no soul. However, by marrying a human, Undines could gain a soul and even give birth to a child. The motif of mortality when Undines give birth to a child is one that inspired many romantics and tragedies (to an unfaithful spouse, the Undine brings death) in art, music and literature.

Unkatl

In Tyrol, the term *Unkatl* is commonly used for a mischievous poltergeist that sometimes manifests itself as a teasing *Kobold*, sometimes resembles a Revenant with eyes like burning coals, and sometimes as a house spirit that looks like a tiny little woman. The Unkatl often appears during the Ember Days and on the eve of all major religious holidays. There are also more specific, place-bound Unkatl. One of them who haunted Zwingenstein moved to a Dornach homestead. He settled in a farmhouse, where it haunted so badly that the farmer sent for a pious priest from Bolzano, to bless the unholy thing away. The priest came, and as soon as the bell rang and the exorcism text was spoken, the *Spuk* (ghost) slipped into the barn and onto the grain floor. A quiet night seemed to be the result. The farmhands and day laborers had come home, eaten their supper, and all lay down together in the hay to sleep. However, as midnight approached, they were awakened by a loud noise and teasing giggling in the barn. The hay was knocked over and everywhere it rattled, things moved and thumped in such a disturbing way that the residents all ran to the room cursing. In the morning the Dornacher farmer fetched the priest again to banish the Unkatl from the stable and barn back into the house. *"I'd rather have him in there"*, the farmer said.

V

Vadātājs

In Latvian folklore a *Vadātājs* (leader) is the spirit of a prematurely deceased person. It is a ghost who kills people by creating the same situation or condition that caused its own death. The Vadātājs was also a demon who led travelers astray by confusing their mind so that they were unable to find their way home. They especially lured people into following them to the nearest body of water, where they eventually drowned them.

Vanapagan

The *Vanapagan* (Old Pagan) or *Vanatühi* (Old Void) is a figure from Estonian mythology. Appearance and interpretation of the Vanapagan are very different, without a unified system being shown so far. In numerous folk tales recorded from the 19th century onwards, the Vanapagan stands for the Devil of Christian dogma or simply the underworld god as a figure with negative connotations. In others, he is a giant peasant of simple mind who is regularly tricked by his subordinate, the mischievous *Kaval-Ants* (Clever Hans). The Vanapagan is the greatest enemy of the giant *Suur Tõll*, the hero of the island of *Saaremaa*. He also stole a magic pipe from the Estonian thunder god Pikne, with which the latter brought rain. Attribute of Vanapagan is sometimes a "hat made of nails", which makes him invisible. In other tales, *Vanapaganad* (pl.) appear, living in bogs, in the forest or in caves, and occasionally visiting the villages (especially during important festivals such as weddings or baptisms). Now and then a woman is said to have become pregnant by a Vanapagan. Furthermore, the Vanapagan appears as a demiurgic entity, the shaper of the earth, creating mountains and lakes or moving large stones. He often tries to build cities or bridges; however, his works always remain unfinished. He fears wolves and thunderstorms. The text editions of the folklorist Matthias Johann Eisen (1857-1934) have popularized the Vanapagan again in Estonia. There are only speculations about the pre-scriptural meaning and its place in the original Estonian mythology. It seems probable that in more recent times various very different figures and ideas were personified under the name Vanapagan.

Veen emonen

Veen emonen (Water Mother), *Veden emo* or *Vedenemo*, is a *Mermaid*-like *water-sprite* or goddess, known in Karelian-Finnish folklore. Fishermen used to offer their first catch to appease Veen Emonen, but spotting her was regarded as a bad omen. In Mikael Agricola's 1551 list of 'idols', the Karelian goddess, *Wedhen Eme*, the Water-Mother, is said to guide the fish into the nets of the fishermen. Veen Emonen should not be confused with *Väinämöinen*, usually a distinctly male character, the central figure of the Kalevala. He is a creative god, cultural hero, shaman, sea hero, a great sage and an accomplished blacksmith, singer and cantor. The name Väinämöinen is believed to be derived from the word *väinä*, meaning a wide, slow-flowing river or strait.

Vėlės

Vėlės (Latvian: *Velis*) – were the spirits of the dead in ancient Baltic mythology. It was believed that when a person dies, the *Vėlė* separates from the body and wanders among the living for a while (settling on a high place, in a tree, etc.). The Vėlės of good people were believed to help the living, while the Vėlės of bad people (criminals, suicides) were believed to harm them. The living, in order to appease the Vėlės and believing that they live like the living, would place a pile of bones in the grave of the deceased and bring them food (hence the tradition of the Long Day or All Souls Day). It was believed that the Vėlės would eventually go to the other world *(dausas, kapines, vėlių kalnelį)*.

The imagination of Vėlės has evolved over the centuries: in the earliest times they were imagined as reincarnated animals (birds, bees, mice, etc.), and later as a ghost; a blurred human figure. With the beginning of the custom of burning the dead (second millennium BC), the image of the Vėlė became less clear, less material. The cult of Vėlė-worship is mentioned by Jan Dlugosz, Motiejus Strijkovskis, Jonas Lasitsky and other historians. In Christian times, the image of the Vėlės was confused with the Christian idea of the immortal human soul. The word vėlė comes from the Indo-European root ṷel-, meaning death. From this root also comes the word Velnias (Devil – the ruler of the world of the dead).

Vellamo and Athi

The Finnish folk-belief of the fisherman, working on the great lakes, dangerous rivers or at sea, the Chief of the *water-sprites Athi* or his wife *Vellamo* was invoked for protection against all kinds of accidents, for tranquilizing the waves and the force of the water and guiding the boats safely along the protruding rocks. Another water-sprite, *Litvetti* (also *Livetti*), was the King of the waters beneath the surface. Along with Athi or Vellamo he was invoked to make the rocks just beneath the surface soft as moss, so that fishing boats would not be damaged by them.

Velns

The Latvian term *Velns* (pl.: *Velni*) or Lithuanian *Velnias*, also known as *Jodu* and *Jupi*, has two distinct meanings. On the one hand it is a devil or *the* Devil in Latvian and Lithuanian mythology, the ruler of the underworld, although the Baltic Devil was not the Prince of Evil as in the European tradition, but more a creature the size of a human with animal features and not very clever. In the other definition Velns are beings whose young are portrayed as roughly half the size of a human. The young Velni are not physically powerful, but are still mischievous and sometimes even stupid. All Velni have black fur and occasionally horns on their head. Adult Velni are strong, greedy and sometimes they have more than one head, this is best portrayed in the famous fairy tale *Kurbads*. They live in a place called *Pekle*, later referred to as *Elle*. To get to Pekle you have to find a very deep hole, usually in a cave, swamp, or under the roots of a large tree, as Pekle is not another realm, but simply a place beneath the surface of the Earth.

Vetevana

In Estonian folklore the *Vetevana* is a male water creature in the beliefs of various peoples. The term is however vague and can include both deities (e.g. *Ahti*) and male Mermaids. In general the Vetevana can be compared to the English *Merman*, German *Wassermann*, Finnish *Vetehine*n, or the Russian *Vodjanoi*. He was regarded as mostly hostile to humans.

Vogelhannes

– See *Jasiek-Ptasiek* in *Spirit Beings in European Folklore* – Compendium 3

W

Waldweibchen von Wilhelmsdorf

Waldweibchen (Little Forest Woman) is often used as a synonym for
Moosweiblein (Little Moss Woman). One story in *Das Große Deutsche
Sagenbuch* tells of a Waldweibchen in Wilhelmsdorf that had taken up
residence with a farmer, and did more in the household than the best
maid. In the evening, after work, she always sat on her place behind the
stove and from there gave the people all sorts of wisdom:

*"Piep dein BrotPiepen = mit den Fingerspitzen vor dem Backen ein
Kreuzzeichen in das Brot machen,
Schäl keinen Baum,
Erzähl keinen Traum,
Back keinen Kümmel ins Brot. Von stark riechenden Würzkräutern wie
Kümmel, Lauch, Thymian wollen solche unterirdische Wesen nichts wissen.,
So hilft dir Gott in aller Not."*

(Peep your breadpeep = make a sign of the cross in the bread with your
fingertips before baking it...,
Don't peel a tree,
Don't tell a dream,
Don't bake caraway seeds into the bread. Such subterranean beings do
not want to know anything about strong smelling herbs like caraway,
leek, thyme,
So God helps you in all need.)

But sometimes the farmer's wife had to get angry with the Waldweibchen;
without asking, she took the dumplings out of the pot and the bread out
of the oven, all scolding and bickering did not help. At last the farmer's
wife thought that she wanted to get rid of this mischief, so she baked
cumin seeds into the bread and peeped it properly. As soon as the little
creature had tasted the new bread, she became angry and ran away from
the house into the forest, screaming:

*"Sie haben mir gebacken Kümmelbrot,
Das bringe diesem Hause lauter Not."*

(You have baked me caraway bread,
It will bring misery to this house.)

Since then, the prosperity of the people went downhill; they fell into
poverty and hardship and were soon among the poorest people in
the village. Later, the farmer's wife often regretted bitterly that she did
not follow the advice of the Waldweibchen. Within this context it is
a fascinating fact that (whole) black cumin seeds ("nigella", and not
the oil or dry powder) are regarded as a miracle herb against a myriad
of diseases (even in the Koran) and in occult lore every disease has a
corresponding demon or entity which causes this disease. This vision
is shared all over the world and used by shamans to heal people. See
also the Greek/Jewish *Testament of Solomon*. This German lore of the
Waldweibchen (and more German spirit beings) responding badly to
cumin suggests that the herb has certain exorcism qualities – seemingly
on all kinds of spirit beings.

Walen

Walen or *Venediger* (also *Walhen, Wahlen, Wälsche* or *Welsche,
Venedigermandln, Vennizianer, Venezianer, Venetianer* and similar
spellings) appear in German legends as foreign ore- and mineral seekers.
They possibly searched for minerals needed for glass production, but
there is a lot of uncertainty about this. Just like it is uncertain the Walen
were foreign people or some ghostly *Fairy*-race. The Walen, due to their
foreign language and incomprehensible actions in the mountains, have
inspired the creation of legends throughout Central Europe. Magical
properties were also attributed to them. In southern German-speaking
areas, the legendary Walen are called *Venedigermandl* or *Mandl* for
short, because of their proximity to the *Bergmännchen* (little mountain
men) and *Berggeistern* (mountain spirits), and in Thuringia they are
also called *Erzmännchen* (little ore-men). The Walen were attributed the
authorship of the so-called *Walenbücher*, books containing directions
to hidden treasures and rich veins of ore. These books still exist. In the
Hauptstaatsarchiv in Dresden, there is still a handwritten *Walenbuch*
(in German) from the year 1590. It seems to me that the most plausible
explanation for the Walen is that they were simply the people from
Wallonia (*Walen* in Dutch), who were widely known for their mining
skills, traveled or migrated for this reason to other European nations

(even Sweden), spoke a unique language, and who later got somehow confused with *Fairies* or *mountain-spirits*.

Wassermann

Wassermann is a commonly used term in the folklore of German-speaking countries and regions to refer to a *Nix* or *Nixe*. It involves the same creature (Water-sprite), but when it comes to the male version, Wassermann is used much more in folklore sources than Nix, as opposed to the female version *Wasserfrau*, in which case Nix or Nixe prevails.
– See under *Nix*.

Wechselbalg

Wechselbalg is the most used term in German speaking countries/regions for a changeling, the baby of a spirit-being that was put in place for an abducted human baby.
– See under *changeling* in *Spirit Beings in European Folklore –* Compedium 1

Wehklage

Die *Wehklage* (the Lamentation) is a kind of German *Banshee*, but in contrast to the Irish death announcer, this phantom is not bound to a particular family, but only to certain regions of Germany. On the Lüneburger Heide (Lüneburg Heath), *das Klageweib* (the Lamentation Woman), a huge, hollow-eyed, deathly pale ghost, wanders around on stormy nights in a blowing corpse robe, and howls through the nights with ghastly wailing. The ghost stretches her long bony arm over the houses where someone is destined to die soon, and before the moon is full, this fatal prophecy will be fulfilled. The people of Thuringia also know this night spirit and call it *die Wehklage*, as in the cities of Weimar, Erfurt and the Harz Mountains. The origin of the specter is as obscure as the time in which it appears, shrouded in a chilly wind. There are few specific legends about her.

Werewolf

The word *Werewolf* derives from the Proto-Germanic *wera-wulfa*. *Wera* meant man; *wulfa* wolf. A Werewolf is thus a manwolf. Other sources derive the word from *warg-wolf*, where *warg* (later *werg* or *wero*) is related to the Old Norse *vargr* meaning knave or bandit or, used euphemistically, 'wolf'. A *Werewolf* is now worldwide used as a generic term, to describe a human with the ability to shape-shift into a wolf, either purposely or after being placed under a curse or affliction (in Eastern Europe there are many varieties, often fused with Vampire-type creatures). Nowadays the Werewolf phenomenon is linked, in occult circles, to very dense etheric doubles used by shamans or witches for astral travel and created by them. Early sources for belief in this ability, or affliction (called *lycanthropy*), are Petronius (27–66) and Gervase of Tilbury (1150–1228). The Werewolf is a concept in European folklore, existing in many variants, which are related by a common development of a Christian interpretation of underlying European folklore developed during the medieval period. In the early modern period, Werewolf beliefs also spread to the New World with colonialism. In the course of the Late Middle Ages and the Renaissance period, parallel to, or as part of the witchcraft trials as a whole, the trials of supposed Werewolves emerged in what is now Switzerland (especially the Valais and Vaud) in the early 15th century and spread throughout Europe in the 16th century, peaking in the 17th and subsiding by the 18th century. Thus the persecution of supposed "Werewolves" and the associated folklore is an integral part of the witch-hunts, albeit a marginal one, accusations of lycanthropy being involved in only a small fraction of witchcraft trials. During the early period, accusations of lycanthropy (transformation into a wolf) were mixed with accusations of wolf-riding or wolf-charming. The case of Peter Stumpp (1589) led to a significant peak in both interest in and persecution of supposed Werewolves, primarily in French-speaking and German-speaking Europe. The phenomenon persisted longest in Bavaria and Austria, with the persecution of wolf-charmers recorded until well after 1650, the final cases taking place in the early 18th century in Carinthia and Styria.

How to change into a Werewolf

Several methods for becoming a Werewolf have been reported, one of the simplest being the removal of clothing and putting on a belt made of wolf skin, probably as a substitute for the assumption of an entire animal skin (which also is frequently described). In other cases, the body is rubbed

Werewolf (1685) - Depicted is the Werwolf of Neuses, now Ansbach, Germany

with a magic salve. Drinking rainwater out of the footprint of the animal in question or from certain enchanted streams were also considered effectual ways of accomplishing metamorphosis. The 16th century Swedish writer Olaus Magnus says that the *Livonian Werewolves* were initiated by draining a cup of specially prepared beer and repeating a set formula. Ralston in his *Songs of the Russian People* gives the form of incantation, still familiar at the time (19th century) in Russia. In Italy, France and Germany, it was said that a man or woman could turn into a Werewolf if he or she, on a certain Wednesday or Friday, slept outside on a summer night with the full moon shining directly on his or her face. In other cases, the transformation was supposedly accomplished by Satanic allegiance for the most loathsome ends, often for the sake of sating a craving for human flesh. In his *Restitution of Decayed Intelligence* (1628) Richard Verstegan wrote:

> *"The Werewolves are certayne sorcerers, who having annoynted their bodies with an ointment which they make by the instinct of the devil, and putting on a certayne inchaunted girdle, does not only unto the view of others seem as wolves, but to their own thinking have both the shape and nature of wolves, so long as they wear the said girdle. And they do dispose themselves as very wolves, in worrying and killing, and most of humane creatures."*

Cursed Werewolves

The curse of lycanthropy was also considered by some scholars as being a divine punishment. Werewolf literature shows many examples of God or saints allegedly cursing those who invoked their wrath with "werewolfism". Such is the case of Lycaon, who was turned into a wolf by Zeus as punishment for slaughtering one of his own sons and serving his remains to the gods as a dinner. Those who were excommunicated by the Roman Catholic Church were also said to become Werewolves. The power of transforming others into wild beasts was attributed not only to malignant sorcerers, but to Christian saints as well. *Omnes angeli, boni et mali, ex virtute naturali habent potestatem transmutandi corpora nostra* (All angels, good and bad have the power of transmutating our bodies) was the dictum of St. Thomas Aquinas. St. Patrick was said to have transformed the Welsh King Vereticus into a wolf. Natalis supposedly cursed an illustrious Irish family whose members were each doomed to be a wolf for seven years. In other tales the divine agency is even more direct, while in Russia, again, men supposedly became Werewolves when incurring the wrath of the Devil.

Werewolves fighting the Devil

The Werewolf was not always regarded as evil in the Baltics. A notable exception to the association of lycanthropy and the Devil, comes from a rare and lesser known account of an 80 year-old man named Thiess of Kaltenbrun, which has been associated with the *Benedanti* batteling *Maledanti* by Carlo Ginsburg. In 1692, in Jürgensburg, Livonia, Thiess testified under oath that he and other Werewolves were the *Hounds of God*. He claimed they were warriors who went down into hell to do battle with witches and demons. Their efforts ensured that the Devil and his minions did not carry off the grain from local failed crops down to hell. Thiess was steadfast in his assertions, claiming that Werewolves in Germany and Russia also did battle with the Devil's minions in their own versions of hell, and insisted that when Werewolves died, their souls were welcomed into heaven as reward for their service. The court tried to make Thiess confess that he had made a pact with the devil and that the Werewolf was in the service of Satan, but they did not succeed, and he was sentenced to whipping on October 10, 1692. He received ten lashes for idolatry and superstitious belief.

Etymology

The word *wera-wulfa* continues in the late Old English wer(e)wulf. The only Old High German testimony is in the form of a given name, *Weriuuolf*, although an early Middle High German werwolf is found in works of Burchard of Worms and Berthold of Regensburg. The word or concept does not occur in medieval German poetry or fiction, gaining popularity only from the 15th century on. Middle Latin: *gerulphus*, Anglo-Norman: *garwalf*, Old Frankish: *wariwulf*. Old Norse had the cognate *varúlfur*, but because of the high importance of Werewolves in Norse mythology, there were alternative terms such as *ulfhéðinn* ("one in wolf-skin", still referring to the totemistic or cultic adoption of wolf-nature rather than the superstitious belief in actual shape-shifting). In modern Scandinavian also *kveldulf* (evening-wolf) is used, presumably after the name of Kveldulf Bjalfason, a historical berserker of the 9th century who figures in the Icelandic sagas.

Lycanthropy

The term lycanthropy, referring both to the ability to, and the act of transforming oneself into a wolf, comes from the ancient Greek λυκάνθρωπος *lukánthropos* (from λύκος *lúkos* "wolf" and ἄνθρωπος, *ánthrōpos* "human"). The word does occur in ancient Greek sources, but only in Late Antiquity, and only rarely and only in the context of clinical lycanthropy described by Galen, where a patient had the ravenous appetite and other characteristics of a wolf; the Greek word attains some currency only in Byzantine Greek, featuring in the 10th century encyclopedia *Suda*. Use of the Greek-derived lycanthropy in English occurs in learned writings, beginning in the late 16th century (first recorded 1584 in *The Discoverie of Witchcraft* by Reginald Scot, who argued against the reality of Werewolves; *"Lycanthropia is a disease, and not a transformation"*). Thus lycanthropy is treated clinically, i.e. a type of insanity, where the patient imagines to have transformed into a wolf, and not in reference to supposedly real shape-shifting. Use of the term lycanthropy for supposed shape-shifting started much later, and was introduced around ca. 1830.

Slavic terms for the Werewolf

The Slavic peoples use the term *Vlko-dlak* (Polish: *Wilkołak*, Czech: *Vlkodlak*, Slovak: *Vlkolak*, Serbo-Croatian: вукодлак/*Vukodlak*, Slovenian: *Volkodlak*, Bulgarian върколак/Vrkolak, Belarusian: ваўкалак/*Vaukalak*, Ukrainian: вовкулака/*Vovkulaka*), literally "wolf-skin", paralleling the Old Norse *Ulfhéðinn*. However, the word is not attested in the medieval period. The Slavic term was loaned into modern Greek as *Vrykolakas*. Baltic has related terms, Lithuanian *Vilkolakis* and *Vilkatas*, Latvian *Vilkatis* and *Vilkacis*. The name *Vurdalak* (вурдалак) for the Slavic *Vampire* (Ghoul, Revenant) is a corruption due to Alexander Pushkin, which was later widely spread by A.K. Tolstoy in his novella *The Family of the Vourdalak* (composed in French, but first published in a Russian translation in 1884).

Hungarian Werewolves

In Hungarian folklore, Werewolves used to especially live in the region of Transdanubia, and it was thought that the ability to change into a wolf was obtained at the infant age after suffering from abuse by the parents, or by a curse. At the age of seven the boy or girl leaves the house and goes hunting by night and can change from person to wolf and vice versa whenever he or she wants. The ability to change into a Werewolf can also be obtained in adulthood, when the person passes three times through an arch made of a birch branches, with the help of a wild rose as its spine. The Werewolves were known to slaughter all kinds of farm animals, especially sheep. The transformation usually occurred at the Winter solstice, at Easter and on full moon nights. Later, in the 17th and 18th centuries, the Church trials in Hungary were not only conducted against witches, but also against Werewolves, and many records exist creating connections between both kinds. Vampires and Werewolves are also closely related in Hungary, and both were feared equally in antiquity.

Kashub and Serbian Werewolves
Among the South Slavs, and also among the Kashubs (northern Poland), there was the belief that if a child was born with a more than normal amount of hair, a birthmark or a caul over their head, they were supposed to possess shape-shifting abilities. Although capable of turning into any animal they wished, it was commonly believed that such people preferred to turn into a wolf. Serbian Vulkodlaks traditionally had the habit of congregating annually in the winter months, when they would strip off their wolf skins and hang them from the trees. They would then get hold of another Vulkodlak's skin and burn it, releasing the Vulkodlak from whom the skin came from its curse.

Lycaon, the first Werewolf
Few references to men changing into wolves are found in Ancient Greek literature and mythology. Herodotus, in his *Histories*, wrote that the Neuri, a tribe he places in northeastern Scythia, were all transformed into wolves once a year, for the duration of several days. In the second century BC, the Greek geographer Pausanias related the story of Lycaon, the King of Arcadia and father of Callisto, who was transformed into a wolf because he had ritually murdered a child. In accounts by the *Bibliotheca* (3.8.1) and Ovid (*Metamorphoses* I.219-239), Lycaon serves human flesh to Zeus, wanting to know if he is really a god. Lycaon's transformation, therefore, is a punishment for his crimes (murder, cannibalism and impiety). Ovid also relates stories of men who roamed the woods of Arcadia in the form of wolves. Others believed that Lycaon is the constellation of the Wolf and that in him were united the qualities of wolf, king and constellation. In addition to Ovid, other Roman writers also mentioned lycanthropy. Virgil wrote of human beings transforming into wolves. Pliny points out that the origin of transformation into wolves was due to Evanthes, a Greek author of good repute, who tells the story of Antheus, the Arcadian, whose relative is chosen by fate and then taken to a certain lake in the district, which he swims across and turns into a wolf for nine years. Similarly, Demæntus, during a sacrifice of human victims, tasted the entrails of a boy who had been slaughtered, upon which he

turned into a wolf, but ten years later he triumphed in the pugilistic (fist fighting) contests at the Olympic games. In the *Satyricon*, a Latin work of prose, written circa 60 AD by Gaius Petronius Arbiter, one of the characters, Niceros, tells a story at a banquet about a friend who turned into a wolf. He describes the incident as follows:

> *"When I look for my buddy I see he'd stripped and piled his clothes by the roadside… He pees in a circle round his clothes and then, just like that, turns into a wolf!… after he turned into a wolf he started howling and then ran off into the woods."*

202
W **The woman of Saintonge and Eliphas Levi's commentary on lycanthropy** Another story in which a human being suffers from a wound inflicted while being a Werewolf concerns a woman of Saintonge, who used to wander at night in the forests in the shape of a wolf. One day she ended up with her paw in a trap set by the hunters. This put an end to her nocturnal wanderings, and afterwards she had to keep a glove on the hand that had been trapped, to conceal the mutilation of two of her fingers. Eliphas Levi, the occultist, has endeavored to explain this sympathetic state between man and his animal appearance:

> *"We must speak here of lycanthropy, or the nocturnal transformation of men into wolves, histories so well substantiated that skeptical science has had recourse to furious maniacs, and to masquerading as animals for explanations. But such hypotheses are puerile and explain nothing. Let us seek elsewhere the solution of the mystery, and establish—First, that no person has been killed by a werewolf except by suffocation, without effusion of blood and without wounds. Second, that werewolves, though tracked, hunted, and even maimed, have never been killed on the spot. Third, that persons suspected of these transformations have always been found at home, after the pursuit of the werewolf, more or less wounded, sometimes dying, but invariably in their natural form…. We have spoken of the sidereal body, which is the mediator between the soul and the material organism. This body remains awake very often while the other is asleep, and by thought transports itself through all space which universal magnetism opens to it. It thus lengthens, without breaking, the sympathetic chain attaching it to the heart and brain, and that is why there is danger in waking up dreaming persons with a start, for the shock may sever the chain at a blow and cause instantaneous*

A Werewolf incident of 1588

The peculiarity of a wound inflicted on a Werewolf being reproduced in
man, is highlighted by an incident that took place around 1588 in a tiny
village in the mountains of Auvergne. A gentleman was gazing one evening
from the windows of his castle when he saw a hunter he knew passing
on his way to the chase. Calling to him, he begged that on his return he
would report what luck he had had. The hunter, after pursuing his way, was
attacked by a large wolf. He fired his rifle without hitting the animal. Then he
struck at it with his hunting knife, severing one of the paws, which he picked
up and put in his knapsack. The wounded wolf quickly disappeared into the
forest. When the hunter reached the castle, he told his friend of his strange
fight with the wolf, and to add strength to his story he opened his knapsack,
in which to his shock and surprise he found, not as he had expected, a wolf's
paw, but the hand of a woman, with a gold ring on one of the fingers. The
castle owner recognized the ring as belonging to his wife, rushed to the
kitchen to question her, and found her with one arm hidden beneath the
folds of a shawl. He drew it aside and saw she had lost her hand. Then she
confessed that it was she who, in the form of a wolf, had attacked the hunter.
Soon afterwards she was arrested and burnt to death at Ryon.

Livonian Werewolf trials

In Livonia, throughout the 17th century, the indigenous peasantry – in
contrast to the Baltic-German citizens and nobility – often continued to
hold Pagan worship services, in defiance to the Christian Church, the

authorities and the nobility. Generally, the Livonians did not believe in Satan and therefore not in witches or Satanic pacts. They did, however, believe in malevolent magic, as well as in the existence of Werewolves, but did not associate them with Satan, as the Church and authorities did. In order to eradicate paganism, in at least 18 trials between 1527 and 1725, 18 women and 13 men were accused of having caused harm in the shape of Werewolves. The accused often confessed that they had gotten their "wolf skin" from another person, or from a demon, sometimes after having eaten something special, and that they usually hid the skins under a rock, when not using them. In 1636, for example, a woman from Kurna claimed to have been taken into the woods by an old woman and given berries to eat, after which they started to hunt together in the woods as wolves. People did not only turn into wolves, but also into bears. The testimony of Gret of Pärnau claimed that while Kanti Hans and his spouse had turned into wolves, a female accomplice of them had taken the shape of a bear (1633). The accused never voluntarily claimed to have had any ties with Satan, but through leading questions and torture, the authorities adapted confessions about Werewolves into confessions about witchcraft, resulting in convictions and executions of the alleged Werewolves as witches. As late as 1696, Greta, the daughter of Titza Thomas, testified that an entire pack of eleven Werewolves, led by their leader Libbe Matz, was hunting in the forests around Vastemoisa.

Sixth century Lebanese Werewomen
In sixth-century Lebanon, villagers attacked by *Werewomen* were advised by a local holy man to be baptized and take collective ritual preventive measures.

Vseslav of Polotsk 1044
From 1044 to 1101 AD, Vseslav was the ruler of Polotsk, a region that is now part of Belarus. History records him as a strong leader and warrior, but he was also said to be a sorcerer. (In fact, in Russian literature, he is called "Vseslav the Sorcerer".) Soon after his death, he was referred to as a Werewolf in folktales; this reputation was recorded in an Old Slavic poem, that translates as *The Tale of Igor's Campaign*, in which the prince was said to race from town to town as a wolf.

Pierre Bourgot and Michel Verdun, 1521
The "Werewolves of Poligny" were three men accused of lycanthropy in France in 1521. Someone was traveling through the area when he was

suddenly attacked by a wolf. The traveler injured the wolf, then tracked it
to Michel Verdun's house, where Verdun was found wounded, dripping
with blood. He was arrested and under torture not only confessed
to being a Werewolf himself, but also implicated Pierre Bourgot and
Philibert Montot. Bourgot in turn confessed, and told a tale of making
a deal with three mysterious men dressed in black, to protect his sheep.
Bourgot said he only found out later that the deal entailed renouncing
God and nullify his baptism. He said that in the years that followed,
Michael Verdun gave him an ointment that turned him into a wolf, and
together they killed at least two children. It is not clear whether Philibert
Montot ever confessed, but he was executed along with the other two.

Gilles Garnier, 1573

Around the year 1572, in the town of Dole, France, several children
went missing and were later found mortally wounded in the woods. The
children had died, and some townspeople were charged with the task of
finding the Werewolf responsible for this dreadful event. In November,
a hunting group witnessed a wild animal attack on a child, and someone
noticed that the beasts features resembled the local hermit, Gilles Garnier.
A week later, when another child had disappeared, Garnier and his wife
were arrested. Fifty witnesses testified against Garnier, and he was put on
the rack. He confessed to being a lycanthrope and also to hunting, killing
and eating children who ventured into the woods, saying that he shared
the meat with his wife. In January 1573, Garnier was burned at the stake.
Modern speculation is that Garnier was guilty of murder and cannibalism
(he likely found children easier to catch than wildlife), but the Werewolf
confession is attributed to either mental illness or torture.

Peter Stubbe, 1590

The only actual record of the case of Peter Stubbe, or "the Werewolf
of Bedburg", is a pamphlet – supposedly a translation in 16th century
English from some now-lost German original – that had been circulating
in London in 1590. According to the pamphlet, Stubbe was a lecherous
and murderous person, who had received a special belt from the Devil,
which could turn him into a strong, mighty and devouring wolf. The
pamphlet depicted Peter Stubbe as a serial killer who murdered and
sometimes ate his victims over a 25-year period. He was also accused of
incest with his daughter, as well as killing and eating his son. However,
modern historians have speculated that Stubbe could also very well have

been misused for political purposes, or to calm those who were terrified of the demons that were killing the townspeople. Since confessions from this period so often involved torture, making anyone "confess" to all sorts of things , we simply don't know. When he was arrested, Stubbe told all about his deal with the Devil and the magic belt that turned him into a wolf, confessing to murder, incest and cannibalism. Stubbe's execution, on October 31, 1589 in Bedburg, Germany was an exceptionally gruesome process: He was first lashed to a wheel, where the flesh was torn from his body with red-hot pincers; next, his arms and legs were broken; then, his head was chopped off; finally, his body was burned. Stubbe's girlfriend (a distant relative) and daughter, both accused of incest, were also tortured and then burned alive. After the executions, a wolf's body was set up in public, its head replaced with Stubbe's, as a warning to anyone else that might be contemplating lycanthropy.

Georg Kress, 1591
A 1591 broadside, *Werewolves of Jurich*, printed by Georg Kress, tells the story of the terrorizing of the town of Jurich by hundreds of Werewolves and depicts a number of male and female Werewolves being executed, including some apparently wearing nun's shrouds.

Johan Martensen van Steenhuisen, 1595
In 1595, an explicit Werewolf witch trial was conducted in Arnhem (Gelderland, the Netherlands). Johan Martensen van Steenhuisen confessed to having been made a Werewolf by the Devil three years previously, and to have been part of a party of eight to ten other wolves, commanded by Satan, to harm people and animals. He also claimed to have bewitched people and animals. During his periods as a wolf, he claimed to have been aware, but unable to speak. He was executed; first strangled and then burned at the stake on August 7, 1595.

Jacques Roulet, 1598
Jacques Roulet – who was known as *The Werewolf of Angers* or *The Werewolf of Caud* after two French towns – comes to us via an 1865 account by Sabine Baring-Gould. The story goes like this: In 1598, the mutilated body of a teenage boy was discovered in the woods – and wolves were spotted nearby. Not far away, Roulet was found wounded and half-naked. After he was arrested and confessed to the murder, Roulet revealed that he had been given an ointment that turned him into a wolf.

The boy wasn't even his first kill, he said – he had murdered and eaten others. Unlike other cases, there appears to be no clear record of Roulet having been tortured into making a confession, and he did not confess to making a deal with the Devil. Roulet was sentenced to death for murder, lycanthropy and cannibalism, but after an appeal he was judged mentally ill or "feeble-minded" and instead was admitted to an insane asylum with religious instruction for two years.

A woodsman in 1615
In 1615, the French physician Jean de Nynauld reported in *De la lycanthropie, transformation et extase des sorciers* (On lycanthropy, transformation and ecstasy of wizards) the case of a woodsman who had been attacked by a wolf, but had managed to cut off one of its legs. Immediately the wolf turned into a woman, who was subsequently burned alive.

Hans the Werewolf, 1651
Dozens of people were accused of supernatural crimes in a series of witch- and Werewolf trials, that took place in 17th century Estonia. One 18-year-old teenager named Hans was convicted of both lycanthropy and witchcraft. Although he denied making a pact with the Devil, Hans admitted that he had been a Werewolf for two years, and had become one of these beasts after he was bitten by a man dressed in black who was, of course, a Werewolf himself. The court decided that Hans must have made a satanic deal, which also made him guilty of witchcraft, and so he was put to death.

The wolf of Ansbach, 1685
There exists one notorious Werewolf case, which involved an actual wolf instead of a person. In 1685, the Principality of Ansbach (now a district in Germany) was part of the Holy Roman Empire. It was plagued by a wolf that preyed on livestock – and eventually moved on to eating people. The citizens thought they were being terrorized by a Werewolf, and they knew exactly who it was: their unnamed, hated (and dead) mayor, who had returned in the guise of a wolf. A hunting party with dogs drove the wolf into a well, where it was killed. Still believing it was a Werewolf, the citizens chopped off the wolf's nose, dressed it in a man's clothing, added a human mask, and hung the body from a pole. The carcass was later installed in a local museum.

Armenia, recorded in 1920

Lewis Spence, in his 1920 work *An Encyclopaedia of Occultism*, recorded that in Armenia it was thought that a demon would present himself to a sinful woman and command her to wear a wolf's skin, after donning which she would spend seven years as a wolf during the night, devouring her own and other children and acting generally as a wild beast, until the morning, when she would resume her human form.

Winselmutter

A *Winselmutter* or *Klagemutter* (Wailing Mother) is a legendary figure that appears in various regions of Germany – in the Ore Mountains, in Vogtland as well as in Eastern Thuringia. She is usually described as an elderly woman (a mother) who cannot find peace. In the stories she appears as a white figure or a walking light. The creature stays in eerie places or in the homes of the seriously ill and emits plaintive sounds. An encounter with a Winselmutter is always considered an omen of a person's imminent death. Examples of tales in which a Winselmutter appears are *Die Winselmutter am Oswaldbach, Die Winselmutter in der Mutzmühle* or *Die Winselmutter bei Grünhain*. The appearance of the *Weiße Frau* (White Woman), which – according to folklore – can be found in the Bavarian district of Ebersberg, is sometimes said to be similar to the Winselmutter. A Weiße Frau, also known as *Weiße Maria* (White Maria) is said to haunt the Ebersberger forests, mainly at night.

The Winselmutter of the Oswaldbach

According to local folk-belief, when midnight approaches, a ghostly shadow flits along the edge of the river Oswaldbach near Grünhain, whimpering and wailing. Then the people know that the Winselmutter is on the loose. She is believed to be the mother of a young man whose lover betrayed him one day. Deeply saddened by this, he went to the Oswaldbach and drowned himself in a deep waterhole of the raging river. For seven long days the mother searched in vain for the body of her son. And when she did not find him, she died of exhaustion and a broken heart. But because she quarreled with God during the search and rebelled against His providence, by swearing not to rest until she had found her son, she found no peace after her death. Now it is her fate to walk around at midnight on the edge of the Oswaldbach and search for the body of her drowned child accompanied with loud wailing and whimpering.

Wichtel or Wichtelen

In German legends and folklore *Wichtel* (also *Weichtelen*, *Wichtlein* or *Wichtl*; singular *Wichtel*) are mostly described as being similar to humans, but significantly smaller and living in their own communities. They usually appear in groups, live underground, in caves or in hidden corners of houses. In general, they are friendly towards humans and help them with their daily chores, usually without being asked. Sometimes, however, they in turn ask the humans for help. Of the Wichtel it is also believed, they occasionally exchange a human child for one of their own. Contradictory to the legends that describe contacts between humans and the Wichtel, there are legends that claim a Wichtel will leave and not come back – as soon as they are discovered. In the collection of *Hessian legends* by Karl Lyncker, the Wichtel are described as small, thumb-sized creatures with thick heads, who help people but also tease them and who can make themselves invisible. Newborns are said to be protected by a small burning light, like a candle, so that they would not be replaced by a changeling. Lyncker collected a good twenty accounts of the appearance of Wichtel in Hesse.

Wichtel or *Wichtelmännchen* (little Wichtel men) is a diminutive of *Wicht*, a term which in Old German generally stood for a living being, a creature. According to the Brothers Grimm, it is used almost exclusively in the sense of *Kobold, Zwerg* (Goblin, dwarf). The grammatical gender is neuter. In Dutch a *booswicht*, for example, is an evil intended person, not specified as male or female – while in many Dutch dialects *wicht* means girl. Furthermore, the term *Wichtelzopf* is mentioned as a term for matted head hair. Some belief the term *Wichtel* comes from the pre-Christmas *Wichteln*. In Germany, *Wichteln* (Secret Santa) is a popular pre-Christmas tradition. Small gifts are distributed before Christmas Eve. Various legends tell that Wichtel who were on good terms with the human inhabitants of an area sometimes presented them with gifts in the form of gold, money or other valuables. Hence possibly the link between Wichtel and Wichteln. The Brothers Grimm referred to mentions of the Wichtel in German dictionaries of the 15th and 16th centuries, such as Luther describing them as *a small spirit who lives in the kitchen*, Salomo Franck as a *kleines Bergmännlein* (little miner) or *Schrätlein*, and Stephan Agricola describing them as *Teufelein* (little devils). The Church assigned the Wichtel to the realm of superstition – in its political campaign to wipe out every trace of pre-Christian European religion, lore and folk beliefs. The *Heinzelmännchen* are considered to be closely related to the Wichtel.

Wichtel in Luxembourg

In 1883, the Luxembourg philologist Nikolaus Gredt presented a
collection of about sixty folk tales about the appearance and work of the
Wichtel in the Luxembourg countryside. These tales always mention
the specific places where a Wichtel appeared. There are reports about
so-called *Wichtellöcher* (Wichtel holes), about passages through rocks
and caverns, but also about tiled buildings, or beautifully whitewashed
square rooms that were found under the earth when ploughing. Here,
too, the Wichtel are always helpful to the people, especially the simple
people from the lower classes, in carrying out their daily work, but they
disappear if they are approached too closely. This often happens through
well-meaning attentions such as the provision of food. On their part, the
Wichtel give bread or cakes to individuals, but they also stop doing so
when this secret is betrayed. In these Luxembourg tales we sometimes
find the motif of time extension, experienced by the person that stays for
some time in the world of the Wichtel.

Wichtelhöhlen

Some places specifically point to geological features for which there are
stories about Wichtel and which, as entrances to *Wichtelhöhlen* (Wichtel
caves and passages), have also become a tourist attraction, such as the
Wichtelhöhlen near Bad Kissingen or the Wichtelhöhlen in Uttershausen
and in Ziegenhain.

Wichtel-customs formed the basis of Santa's Elves

In Denmark and other Scandinavian countries, the *Weihnachtswichtel*
(Christmas Elf) (Danish: Julenisse) is part of the pre-Christmas tradition
in families, especially when dealing with smaller children. This is
now also widespread in Germany and other European countries. The
Weihnachtswichtel wears a red pointed hat and red shoes with a lace and
comes riding at Christmas-time on the "Julbock", which is also part of the
Christmas tradition. Family traditions also include the *Wichteltür* – Danish:
Nissedør (Wichtel door) – a small painted or handmade door above the
doorstep, that is placed as an entrance for the Wichtel into the house. In the
evening, the child can place small things in front of the door – a residue of
a sacrifice to nature/home spirits – that he or she thinks the Wichtel could
use. If, together with the parents, the child finds a small gemstone or a treat
in the morning, it can create the idea that the Wichtel were there during
the night and brought him/her a present. The child never gets to see the

shy Wichtel, which is part of the game. Some children's books also refer to the Weihnachtswichtel (Christmas Wichtel) and *Wichteltüren* (Wichtel doors). The commercial side of these customs consists of a wide range of Christmas Wichtel-figures and extensive accessories, as well as instructions for handicrafts to be given to or made by children.

Stallwichtelen

In *Sagen aus Innsbruck's Umgebung, mit besonderer Berücksichtigung des Zillerthales,* collected and edited by Adolf Ferdinand Dörler, Innsbruck, 1895, a story from Tyrol (Inzing, Innsbruck region) is recorded about Wichtelen that lived in stables:

"In Inzing in the Oberinnthal region, there used to be kleine Männlein (little men) called Wichtelen who lived in the stables. Where they stayed, the cattle remained healthy, gave plenty of milk and no witch could get power over them. However, they were only visible to a few people, most of whom only occasionally heard their sweet singing in the barn, one moment about this cow and the next about another. But despite their good-natured attitude, they could not refrain from teasing.

Once, a farmhand, while milking early in the morning, noticed that the most beautiful cow was sticking her head out through a very narrow "gap" in the barn door. He hurriedly ran back into the house and informed the farmer. The farmer ran with the farmhand to the barn, but could not see anything unusual, because the cow was now standing quietly in its place. The two of them, however, heard the Wichtelen giggling and laughing from all corners, since their successful little play had given the farmer and farmhand such a fright.

Another farmhand in Inzing, who listened to the song of such a Wichtel almost daily, wanted to show his gratitude, bought a piece of red cloth and had a skirt made for it. But when he had hung it up in the stable, the Wichtel left it crying loudly, and he has not seen or heard it again since."

Wiedergänger

Various ghostly phenomena, from many different cultural areas, are referred to as Revenants. In German speaking countries and regions they are called *Wiedergänger*, sometimes also spelled *Widergänger*. Central to the Wiedergänger-folklore is the idea of a deceased person returning to the world of the living – often as a physical apparition or "undead" figure. Wiedergänger are usually malicious, either because they want revenge for injustices suffered, the disturbance of their resting place, or because their souls were not redeemed by their way of life. The Wiedergänger usually resembles a living person, but there is also the "macabre type" of the living corpse, which shows various stages of decomposition. In different parts of Germany, until the early 20th century, the belief was widespread that the dead still lived on after death and exerted an ominous influence from the grave. Sometimes this was done through sorcery, so that the fiend known as the Nachzehrer did not have to rise from the grave and could nevertheless suck the life-force out of the living through its open mouth, an open eye and by chewing on its shroud. Other undead, according to popular belief, rose from their grave and jumped on the backs of nocturnal wanderers. They were called an *Aufhocker*, and could also take on different forms, for example in the Rhineland that of the *Werewolf*, and had to be carried by the person, often to the cemetery wall or to the place where the corpse was buried or entombed. In the process, the Aufhocker (also called *Huckop* or *Huckupp*) became heavier and heavier, and the victim finally collapsed, exhausted or even dead. In some legends, the afflicted person succeeded in banishing or redeeming the fiend by means of a spell or prayer. It has been suggested that the Aufhocker could not be a ghost, because he had a tangible body that also increased in weight from step to step, which would not have been possible for a discarnate spirit. The problem is, that this would not have been possible for an incarnate spirit either. The Revenant, or returning corpse, is also widely known in Slavic and Nordic cultures, and via the Balkan also in Greece.

Wilde Jagd or Wilde Goich

The *Wilde Jagd* (Wild Hunt) or *Wilde Goich* is the German name for a folk belief found in many parts of Europe, usually referring to a group of supernatural hunters who hunt across the sky. In the past centuries people were very afraid of the Wild Hunt. It moved through the air especially in the time of the *Rauhnächte* (Christmas to *Three Kings' Day*), but also at Carnival and even on Good Friday. The spooky procession was led by the *Hetzjäger*, *Perchta*, *Diana*, *Wotan* or a mysterious figure like *Hellequin*, or *Hennequin*, and was followed by a pack of yapping dogs,

Wilder Mann (1649) by Conrad Meyer (1618-1689)

Con. Meijer fecit.
A.º 16+9.

and with a terrible clatter of screams, howls, wails, groans and moans, the ghosts whizzed through the air. Men, women and children took part in it, especially those who had died a "premature" death, whether by misfortune or violence. In fact, the procession consisted of the souls of those who died "before their time". Animals, especially horses and dogs, also moved along. People had to stay indoors, and those who were outside and felt the Wild Hunt roaring over them had to lie flat on the ground if they wanted to remain safe. Anyone who provoked or mocked the Wild Hunt was inevitably harmed, and of anyone who deliberately looked out the window, the head became so swollen that they could not pull it back.

Wild Man

The *Wild Man* (also *Woodwose, Wodewose, Woodehouse, Wudwos, Wodwos*; German:*Wilder Mann*) is an anthropomorphic being in the folk-beliefs of the Germanic and Slavic linguistic area from the early Middle Ages to the beginning of modern times. The first part of the name Woodwose has been explained etymologically as derived from *wudu* (wood, forest), or is a derivative of the Proto-Germanic *widuz* (woodland, wood, tree). The second element has been identified as a hypothetical noun *wāsa* (being), from the verb *wesan, wosan* (to be, to be alive) to be compared to the Dutch *wezen* (to be, being). In Lombardy and the Italian-speaking parts of the Alps the terms Salvan and Salvang are used for the Wild Man, which derive from the Latin Silvanus, the name of the Roman tutelary god of gardens and the countryside. In Tyrol the Wild Man was often called *Orke, Lorke,* or *Noerglein.* Tyrol and German-speaking Switzerland also included a Wild Woman known as *Fangge* or *Fanke* until the 20th century, which is believed to come from the Latin *Fauna,* the female *Faun.* Medieval German sources also give *Holzmoia* and *Lamia* as names for the *Wilde Frau* (Wild Woman); the latter refers to the Greek wilderness demon Lamia, while the form can possibly by traced back to the Greco-Roman earth and fertility goddess *Maia* who is also identified with Fauna and who exerted a great influence on medieval Wild Man/Wild Woman lore. The Wild Man was described or depicted as a huge, muscular hairy loner, endowed with giant strength, naked or merely clad in moss or a string of leaves. From the 12th century onward, they were consistently depicted as covered with hair. In pictures and in the narratives, the Wild Man is always barefoot and – unlike the animals

– armed with a club or a severed tree trunk. His way of life was considered semi-animal and primitive on the one hand, but also paradisaical and close to nature on the other. Uninhabited or dense forest and mountain areas were considered his preferred place of residence. The Wild Man appears in the art and literature of medieval Europe, comparable to the *Green Man*, the *Satyr* or Faun type, to *Sylvanus* in classical mythology, or the Slavic *Leshy* and the *Basajaun* of the Basques. Renaissance engravers in Germany and Italy were particularly fond of Wild Men, Wild Women, and Wild families, with examples by Martin Schongauer (died 1491) and Albrecht Dürer (1471-1528) among others. The image of the Wild Man is often found on heraldic coats-of-arms, especially in Germany.

Fertility demon

Wild Men, especially in parts of Germany and Tyrol, can have characteristics of ghosts and nature demons, such as the Basajaun and the descendants of Sylvanus, although in many cases Wild Men/Women are humans rather than transcendent beings. Hypertrichosis (a rare condition in which hair grows all over the body) will certainly have played a role in the lore of the Wild Man/Woman. However, there are some important exceptions. Wild Men, may possess magical powers, super human strength or visionary abilities according to some lore, but many folkloric tales tell of mortal Wild Men/Women, who may have sexual and family lifes and can be killed and hurt. This is however all anecdotal scattered information.

In contrast, Wilhelm Mannhardt, writes in his volume 1 of *Walt und Feldkulte* (Berlin 1875), that in the 18th century in the German speaking area of Etschlande, Ulten and Vintsgau (South Tyrol, Italy) there was a tradition of *das Wildemannspiel* (the Wild Man-game). This was held annually and every Tuesday (Shrove Tuesday) before Fastnacht. Festively dressed schoolgirls wearing white aprons went to a forest near the town of St. Felix, where there was a hidden den, and searched for the Wild Man there. It was a man whose clothes consisted solely of moss and hair, even his face which was so overgrown with moss that only his eyes were visible. Around his neck he wore chains of snail shells, which made a lot of noise when he jumped up. In his right hand he held the trunk of a young tree. The Wild Man always had two sons with him who looked like their father and had to be taken out of the den. The father and sons were tied together with red silk ribbons by the singing girls, and led to the village.

There the father and his sons made all kinds of jokes, and after that the Wild Men and the girls were given bread, wine, cheese, and fruit. Emperor Joseph (Benedict Anthony Michael Adam, 1741-1790) was Holy Roman Emperor from August 1765 and the sole ruler of the Habsburg lands from November 1780 until his death. He banned this ritual, after which it was later resumed in a more modern form. Mannhardt also mentions a festival with a Wild man and Wild Woman that was held in Nuremberg between late February and early March, during the *Fastnachttage* (Shrove Days).

Windgspral

The *Windgspral* or *Windsbraut* (wind-bride) is a so called "wind-woman", where *gspral* means "a woman with long legs". Around Waldthurn, Bavaria she is also called *Windgspreidra*. She is the female part of the wind. It is best to avoid her, for she grabs everything that comes her way. So that the *Windgspreidra* does not harm you, you should throw something into her, whatever it may be. A legend of Neudorf tells of a little boy who was walking towards his parents' farm on a cloudy, rainy November night at the back of the Bohemian border. There a Windgspral, a wind-bride, passed by. *"Komm nur wieder her, du Hexe!"* (Come back here, you witch!) the lad shouted and threw his knife in the air. Immediately the wind took him and carried him off to a faraway place. In front of an inn he slid to the ground. Here a one-eyed man was already waiting for him, and he was angry: *"Schau, was du mir angetan hast!"* (Look what you have done to me!) and showed him his eye and knife. Then he warned him and let a new wind bride lead him home.

Witte wieven and Weiße Frauen

In lower Saxon folklore *Witte wieven* (eastern and northern parts of the Netherlands) or *Weiße Frauen* (northern part of Germany), are local mythical varieties on the *White Lady* theme. In the Netherlands they are also known as *Witte Juffers* (White Maidens), *Joffers, Jomfers, Widde Juffers, Juvvers, Wiefkes, Olde Witten, Guede Holden* or *Telewitten*. *Het Moerasvrouwtje* (the little Swamp Lady) has overlap with the Witte wieven (White Wives). She is a creature found in folk tales and fairy tales. The little swamp lady brews the vapors and mists above the swamp. She rules the underworld, is a kind of witch or sorceress, the aunt of the Elves, and she lures people to her swamp. Witte wieven can have a benevolent or a malevolent nature. Often seen as related with witches and/or ghosts, they show many similarities with the *Banshee*, the *Fairy*, and the *Elf*. As malevolent beings, they kidnap or switch newborns, abduct women, and punish people who have mistreated them. As benevolent beings, they may help with childbirth or give good advice. Although the adjective *witte* means "white", it may originally refer to the Germanic word *wid*, related to the English *"wit"* and *"wise"*, and thus may be better understood as *"wise women"*, as they are known in Germany, where they are associated with the *Völva*. The belief in Witte wieven may have its origins in Germanic times, although we don't know for sure. Similar phenomena in popular folk beliefs can be found in Indo-Germanic cultural areas, including Romance languages and Gaelic. Megalithic monuments such as long graves, burial mounds (tumuli) and dolmens (*hunnebedden* in Dutch) were considered by some to be their place of residence. The burial mounds often lie together in groups of three and are also called *"wievenbelter"*. Witte wieven were sometimes thought to be the spirits of witches or other women who had done evil. At night, they would leave their mounts, floating slowly across the fields. In some sagas, Witte wieven are Fairies that appear as white mists on moors and marshes. They seduce people to follow them, with the result that these people disappear forever. The Witte wieven dance across the moors or in the woods, have stored their money in megaliths and know exactly where in the woods valuables are hidden. Ghostly-looking wisps of ground mist and fog banks are sometimes called Witte wieven. In German folklore, the *Weiße Frauen* (meaning White Women) are *Elf*-like spirits that may have been derived from Germanic paganism in the form of legends about *Light Elves* (Old Norse: *Ljósálfar*). The Dutch Witte wieven date back at least to the 7th century. They are described as beautiful and enchanted creatures who not only appear at dusk but also at noon and can be seen sitting in the sunshine brushing their hair or bathing in a brook.

According to Jacob Grimm, the association of Weiße Frauen with the color white and their appearance in sunlight originated from the original Old Norse and Teutonic mythology of *Alven* (Elves), specifically the bright white *Ljósálfar*. These "light Elves" lived in *Álfheim* (a part of heaven) under the fertility god Freyr. As mythology evolved, Elves no longer lived in Álfheim but instead lived on earth, in nature. The Weiße Frauen may also stand for the ancient belief in ancestral spirits or older native goddesses and nature-spirits. Jacob Grimm noted in particular they might come from *Holda*, *"Berhta, white by her very name"* and *Ostara*. According to

Grimm's *Teutonic Mythology* and to the *Mythology of All Races* series, the enchantment under which they suffer *"may be a symbol of the prohibition imposed by Christianity on the deities of the older faith"*. The Witte wieven in Dutch folklore, and the German Weiße Frauen may have come from the Germanic belief in *Disen* or *Land wights* and *Alven*. There are also many legends in German folklore about Weiße Frauen, which are actually similar to the legends of White Ladies; ghosts of the United Kingdom. In the alpine Regions of Austria and southern Germany they are called *Salige Frauen, Salige, Salkweiber* or *Salaweiber*. In France they are called *Dames blanches*.

Wolpertinger

The *Wolpertinger* is a Bavarian mythical creature whose exact origin is unclear. It is described and depicted as a hybrid creature in various forms, for example as a squirrel with a duck's beak or a rabbit with duck's wings. Its current name may vary somewhat, depending on the area it is also called *Wolperdinger*, *Woipertinger*, *Woiperdinger*, *Volpertinger*, *Walpertinger* or *Wulpertinger*. In parts of Lower Bavaria the mythical creature is called *Oibadrischl*, in the Upper Palatinate *Rammeschucksn*, in Lower Austria and parts of Salzburg the term *Raurackl* is common in various spellings. The writer Ludwig Ganghofer referred to the creature as *Hirschbockbirkfuchsauergams*. The brothers Grimm make mention of a creature called *Kreißl* in their German collection of legends and sagas in 1753. The origin of the name *Wolpertinger* is unclear. Bernd E. Ergert, director of the *Deutsches Jagd- und Fischereimuseum* (German Hunting and Fishing Museum) in Munich traces the name back to glass-makers from the town of Wolterdingen with Donaueschingen. These made schnapps glasses in the form of animal figures, which were generally called "Wolterdinger". Due to linguistic wear, Wolpertinger would have originated from this. Another explanation of the word is provided by the *Großer Brockhaus* of 1994, Vol. 24. According to this, *Wolpertinger* is related to *Walper* in dialect, a corruption of *Walpurgisnacht*.

Wouzl

A similar forest-spirit to the Bavarian *Hoymann* is the *Wouzl* or *Böycherlbär* (beech bear), who is dressed in a bear skin, growls *"wou, wou"* and is a frightening figure to children. He lives in hollow beech trees and always roams the beech forests.

Z

Zmora

In Prussian folklore the Zmora (pl.: *Zmorami*) or *Smora* is a female half-demonic creature of the *Alp*-class, with many local features. The Zmora is the Prussian version of the German *Mare* or *Moor(t)*, the *Mara* (demon of death) – which appears in Bulgarian, Czech and Polish folklore; the Ukrainian *Mapa* or *Mára*, the Russian *Mara*, *Morok* or *Zmora*, the Bulgarian *Marok* or *Mapa*, the Polish *Marzanna*, *Dusiołek*, *Gnieciuch*, *Macek*, *Siodełko*, the Czech *Mařena*, etc. Although the Zmora is essentially the same creature, represented by the many national and local European variants of the Mare or Nightmare, it is quite unique in the sense that it does not only prey on humans and horses, but also sucks the life force out of stones, plants (they drink sap from trees), water and even thorns.

The Zmora was usually described as a tall woman with unnaturally long legs and a transparent body and in very rare cases in the form of a human skeleton. She could be seen by moonlight, when the rays of the moon shone through her body. She therefore looked like a *specter*, not a "living corpse" like a *Ghoul* or *Vampire*, which in later accounts were often mixed with primitive views of Zmorami's appearance. The creature may sit with its knees on the chest of a sleeping person at night, causing excessive blood flow to the head. It drinks the blood flowing from the nose, or it cuts a vein in the temple or neck with its teeth and sucks it dry. It may also leave claw marks on the chest of the sleeping person. The Zmora's victim loses strength and energy, which he or she later regains naturally. As a rule Zmorami are unable to kill their victims directly, an exception is made, however, for a severely starved Zmora who deprives her victim of too much vitality. A man tormented by a Zmora moans, sweats and throws himself on the bed, finally fainting and lying as if paralyzed. The person's condition just after waking up was characteristic; a poignant feeling of fatigue, of *"being crushed all night"*. When the person attacked by the Zmora wakes up, she immediately flees. The attacked person is *"pale as a nightmare"* the next day. Having eaten its fill, the Zmora goes to a stable, where it mounts a horse and forces it to gallop, taking care to always be illuminated by the moon's rays.

A Zmora is a person, living or dead. According to folk tales, Zmorami
were the souls of sinful women, people wronged, those who died without
confession, and the damned. The seventh daughters from a given
marriage, or people whose names were distorted during baptism often
turned into Zmorami. Becoming a Zmora could also be a side effect
of people having eyebrows crossed over their eyes – this was especially
believed in Poland near Kalisz and in Bohemia and Lusatia – or eyes
of different colors. A neighbor/wife could be a Zmora. If a woman was
promised to marry a man, but he then married another, the spurned
woman could also become a Zmora during the night. She would than
leave her body at night to torment her competition. A child of a pregnant
woman who meets two pregnant friends or happens to cross their
paths could also become a Zmora. There are beliefs (e.g. in central and
northwestern Poland) that a person becomes a Zmora if, on the deathbed,
while reciting the Angelic Salutation, commits a slip of the tongue and
says *Zmoraś Mario* instead of *Zdrowaś Mario* (Bane Mary instead of
Hail Mary). In addition to a human appearance, the Zmora could also
transform into various animals: a cat, marten, frog, dog, mouse, as well as
inanimate objects:
• a blade of grass (central and western Poland)
• an ear of grain or a needle (Ziemia Chełmińska)
• a wire, ribbon, string or cord (Wielkopolska, Pomerania, Silesian
  Beskid)
• a ball of yarn (Masuria)
• a feather (Łowicz)
• an apple or pear (Slowenia)
• a shapeless, black mass (Upper Silesia).

Activities such as going out to the stable with damp hair, or washing
dishes on Thursday after dinner, might result in a Zmora being brought
into the house. Many German and Polish folk myths describe the Zmora
as a creature that loves to harass farm animals, especially horses or
cows. A horse visited by a Zmora at night would be sweaty and visibly
exhausted in the morning. To keep it away from the stable, people
placed an axe under the doorstep. People could also protect themselves
from Zmorami by fumigating the bedroom with special herbs, keeping
holy water close to the bed, or going to sleep with an axe or another
sharp metal object close-by. In an old tale from Hohenstein/Olsztynek,
chronicled in *Superstitions in Masuria* (1867) by the German folklorist

Max Toeppen, two traveling journeymen discover that the three daughters of the innkeeper where they are staying are all Zmora, as the women are sleepless and can be overheard talking about their harsh fate of being forced to draw life energy from humans, cattle and trees. Eventually, the sisters are healed by their father, who baptizes them again, expelling the evil.

Protection against Zmorami

- In Poland or the former Prussia in order to help a sleeper tormented by a Zmora, one had to approach with a bottle in one's right hand and with one's left hand move the bottle from the sleeper's head to his/her feet, then cover it with one hand and quickly cork the vessel. The bottle with the seized Zmora was to be drowned or thrown into the fire. In the water you heard a long wail, similar to that of a small child. In the fire, when the glass broke, you could hear the screeching of the scorched Zmora, which along with the smoke escaped up the chimney like a black streak.
- Another effective method of protection oneself against the Zmora was to change one's sleeping position. One had to lie in bed upside down, with one's head in the foot of the bed, or not on one's back. Additionally, one could sleep with one's legs crossed.
- A common method was to put a bundle of straw on the bed while the owner went to sleep in another room. An angry Zmora could poke into the bed and never come back.
- One could drink coffee grounds before bedtime (village of Wojciechowo).
- One could take the Zmora's hat, which it usually leaves on the quern in the hallway (village Czarna).
- A belt which once belonged to a hanged man could be thrown at a Zmora (Lipnica Dolna village).
- On could sleep in a wedding leather belt or with a scythe by his/her side (Krakowskie).
- Inviting a Zmora to breakfast, is another Polish method.
- Various tools could be useful. One could put a crossed axe and a broom on the threshold, or stick an awl in the door, or sleep with a nail and hammer to beat the Zmora.
- A rather filthy way of Zmora-prevention was to smear the door with feces, or eat while taking care of one's physiological needs (Upper Silesia and others).

Various methods of protection against Zmorami were also used for farm animals tormented by the creature. One way to protect stables from the Zmorami was to nail a magpie or a bird of prey killed on Christmas Eve above or on the door. Red ribbons were braided into the horses' manes, a circle was drawn around the stable with chalk and a mirror was hung above the manger. The horse's back could also be greased with a smelly substance. The braided mane was cut off, put on a stone and beaten with another stone to *"beat the Zmora's fingers"*.

Zonnet

In Paracelsian alchemy a *Zonnet* (pl.: *Zonnetti*) is defined as *"the fantastic body of a Fairy"* or the *"fantastic bodies of the Gnomes or Pigmy-spirits"*. A Zonnet is clearly an earth-spirit. According to Pinnell: *"To the Earth doe belong Gnomes, Lemurs, Sylphs, Montans, Zonnets, whose Monsters (offspring) are the Pigmyes."* Thus, it is more likely that the Zonnet was regarded as a less dense homeostasis of the Pigmy and conversely that the Pigmy was a more compacted form of the Zonnet.

Abyzou

In the myth and folklore of the Near East and later in parts of Europe
as well, *Abyzou* (also: *Abizou, Obizu, Obizuth, Obyzouth, Byzou* etc.;
Akkadian: 𒁭𒉿𒍪 *Dap.bi.zu*) is the name of a female demon. Abyzou
was held responsible for miscarriages and infant mortality and was
said to be motivated by envy (Greek: φθόνος *phthonos*), as she herself
was infertile. In the Coptic Egypt she is identified with *Alabasandria*,
and in Byzantine culture with *Gylou* (see under *Gello*), but in various
texts surviving from the syncretic magical practice of antiquity and
the early medieval era, she is said to have many or even virtually
innumerable names. Abyzou is pictured on amulets with fish- or serpent-
like attributes. Her most complete literary description is found in an
estimated second or third century grimoire: the *Testament of Solomon*.

Alfons Ascher Barb (1901-1979) connected Abyzou and similar female
demons to the story of the primeval sea, *Abzu*, in ancient Mesopotamian
religion. Barb argued that although the name "Abyzou" appears to be a
corrupted form of the Greek ἄβυσσος *ábyssos* "abyss", the Greek itself
was borrowed from Akkadian *Apsu* or Sumerian Abzu. This primeval sea
(*Binah* in the Jewish mystical tradition) was originally an androgyne or
asexual, later dividing into the male Abzu (fresh water) and the female
Tiamat (seawater, appearing as the *Tehom* in the *Book of Genesis*). The
female demons, among whom *Lilith* is the best-known, are often said to
have come from the primeval sea. In ancient Greek religion, female sea
monsters that combine allure and deadliness may also derive from this
tradition, including the *Gorgons* (who were daughters of the old sea god
Phorcys), *Sirens, Harpies*, and even *water Nymphs* and *Nereids*. In the
Septuagint, the Greek version of the *Hebrew Bible*, the word Abyssos is
treated as a noun of feminine grammatical gender, even though Greek
nouns ending in -os are typically masculine. Abyssos is equivalent in
meaning to Abzu as the dark chaotic sea before Creation. The word also
appears in the Christian New Testament, occurring six times in the *Book
of Revelation*, where it is conventionally translated not as "the deep" but
as "the bottomless pit" of Hell. Barb argues that in essence the Sumerian
Abzu is the "grandmother" of the Christian Devil.

Abyzou (as Obizuth) in the *Testament of Solomon*
In the *Testament of Solomon*, Abyzou (as Obizuth) is described as having
a *"greenish gleaming face, with disheveled serpent-like hair"*; the rest of her
body is covered by darkness. King Solomon encounters a series of demons,
binds and tortures each in turn, and inquires about their activities; then
he metes out punishment or controls them as he sees fit. Put to the test,
Abyzou says that she does not sleep, but rather wanders the world looking
for women about to give birth; given the opportunity, she will strangle
newborns. She claims also to be the source of many other afflictions,
including deafness, eye trouble, obstructions of the throat, madness, and
bodily pain. Abyzou (Obizuth) can also find no rest until she steals a child
each night. Solomon therefore orders that she be chained by her own hair
and hung up in front of the Temple in public view.

225
—
A

Agrat bat Mahalath

Agrat bat Mahalath or *Agrat bat Mahlat* (אגרת בת מחלת, Achrat daughter
of Mahlat), is the "Queen of the Demons" in Talmudic legend. In
Jewish mythology she is associated with destruction, sorcery and sexual
seduction. In the rabbinic literature of Yalḳuṭ Ḥadash it was taught that
*"a person should not go out alone at night, on Wednesdays and Sabbaths,
because 'the Dancing Roof-demon' who haunts the air, Agrat bat Mahalath
and 180,000 destroying angels go forth, and each has permission to wreak
destruction independently"*. Ḥanina ben Dosa limited her power to these
nights; Abbaye further reduced it *(Pes. 112b)*. Another authority states
that the following sentence, whispered repeatedly, is effective against
witchcraft: *"Agrat bat Mahalath came and caused the death, by arrows, of
[two other female demons,] Asya and Belusia"* (Pes. 111a; see *Ein Ya'akov*
version). According to *Numbers Rabbah 12:3*: *"Thou shalt not be afraid
of the terror by night"* (Ps. 91:5), refers to Agrat bat Mahalath and her
chariot. Some scholars hold that Agrat bat Mahalath is identical with
Lilith, but Lilith is also seen as her mother, or even her grandmother. The
view that the name "Agrat" is derived from the Persian *A(n)gra*, meaning
"enemy" or demon"", and Mahalath from the root *mḥl* (מחל; dance)
therefore meaning "the dancing witch or demon," has been proposed
to explain her name, but is regarded as controversial and not generally
accepted. The kabbalists identify Mahalath with the daughter of Ishmael
(Gen. 28:9), who gave birth to demons and evil spirits. The Midrashic
source for this is now lost (cf. Maharsha Pes. 112b).

In Zoharistic Kabbalah, she is a queen of the demons and an angel of sacred prostitution, who mates with Archangel *Samael*, along with Lilith and *Naamah*, sometimes adding *Eisheth Zenubim* as a fourth mate. According to legend, Agrat and Lilith visited King Solomon disguised as prostitutes. The spirits *Solomon* communicated with via Agrat were all placed inside a brazen vessel and put inside a cave near the Dead Sea. Later the spirits were discovered by King David. According to the Kabbalah and the School of Rashba, Agrat bat Mahlat mated with King David and gave birth to a cambion son *Asmodeus*, the *King of Demons*, who is identified with *Hadad the Edomite* (a cambion is a creature half human, half demon; often used for a human/succubus or incubus-hybrid). The spiritual intervention of Hanina ben Dosa and Rabbi Abaye curbed her malevolent powers over humans. In another Kabbalistic treatise – by Nathan Spira (died in 1662) – it is explained that Mahlat was daughter to *Ishmael* and his wife Mahlat, who was herself daughter of the Egyptian sorcerer *Kasdiel*. Mahlat was exiled to the desert, where the demon *Igrathiel* mated with Mahlat and engendered Agrat or Igrat. Mahlat later became Esau's wife.

Alabasandria

Alabasandria is the same female demon as *Gello* and related to *Abyzou* and akin child harming specters. At the monastery of St. Apollo in Bawit, Egypt, a wall-painting depicts the childbirth demon under the name of Alabasandria (or *Alabasdria*), while she is being trampled under the hooves of a horse. The rider wears a belted tunic and trousers in the Parthian manner, and an inscription, now faded, was to be read at the time of its discovery as *Sisinnios*. This central image is surrounded by other figures, including a *Centaur*, the piercing of the evil eye, and the demon's daughter, winged and reptile-tailed, identified by the inscription.

Alukah

According to the German orientalist Julius Wellhausen (1844-1918) *Alukah* (Prov. xxx. 15; A. V. "horseleech"), the bloodsucker or Vampire, whose two daughters cry *"Give! Give!"* is none other than the flesh-devouring Ghoul of the Arabs, named by them "Aluk". (Wellhausen, l.c. pp. 135-137). In Jewish mythology she has been rendered the

demon of the netherworld, and the names of her two daughters have
in all probability, as familiar names of dreaded diseases, been lost. In
Ashkenazi folklore Alukah is a type of leech with many teeth, that feeds
on the throats of animals. According to biblical scholars, Alukah can
mean "blood-lusting monster" or Vampire. Alukah is first referred to
in *Proverbs 30:16*. The most detailed description of the Alukah appears
in *Sefer Chassidim* (Hebrew: ספר סידים = Book of the Pious), where the
creature is understood to be a living human being, but one who can
shape-shift into a wolf. The *Sefer Hasidim* or *Sefer Chassidim* is a text by
Judah ben Samuel of Regensburg, a fundamental work of the teachings
of the *Chassidei Ashkenaz* (Pious Ones of Germany). It offers an account
of the day-to-day religious life of Jews in medieval Germany and their
customs, beliefs and traditions, in presenting the combined teachings
of the three leaders of German Hasidism during the 12th and 13th
centuries; Samuel the Chassid, Judah the Chassid of Regensburg (his
son), and Elazar Rokeach.

Of the Aluka it was believed it could fly by releasing its long hair and
that it could eventually die if prevented from feeding on blood for a long
enough time. Once dead, a Vampire could be prevented from becoming a
demon by being buried with its mouth stuffed with earth. King Solomon
refers to a female demon named "Alukah" in a riddle he tells in Proverbs,
involving Alukah's ability to curse a womb bearing seed. Historically,
Alukah has been closely associated with Lilith, or thought to be her direct
descendant. The name Alukah may, additionally, merely be another title
for Lilith. R.E.L. Masters describes the Alukah as *"a Hebrew succubus and
Vampire derived from Babylonian demonology"*.

Dybbuk or Dibbuk

In Ashkenazic Jewish folklore a Dybbuk (Yiddish: דבק, dāḇaq) is an
evil spirit which enters into a living person, clings to his soul, causes
mental illness, talks through his mouth, and represents a separate and
alien personality. Dybbukim (pl.) were generally considered to be souls
which, on account of the enormity of their sins, were not even allowed to
transmigrate, and as "denuded spirits" they sought refuge in the bodies
of living persons. The entry of a Dybbuk into a person was a sign of
this person having committed a secret sin which opened a door for the
Dybbuk. Belief in Dybbukim was very common in Eastern Europe.

Dybbuk by Ephraim Moshe Lilien (1874-1925)

The term Dybbuk appears neither in Talmudic literature nor in the Kabbalah, where this phenomenon is simply called "evil spirit". In Talmudic literature it is sometimes called *ruaḥ tezazit*, and in the New Testament "unclean spirit". This term was introduced into literature only in the 17th century, from the spoken language of German and Polish Jews. It is an abbreviation of *dibbuk me-ruaḥ raʾah* (cleavage of an evil spirit), or *dibbuk min ḥa-ḥizonim* (dibbuk from the outside). So the act of the attachment of a spirit to a body became the name of the spirit itself. However, the verb *davok* (cleave) is found throughout kabbalistic literature, where it denotes the relations between the evil spirit and the body, *mitdabbeket bo* (it cleaves itself to him).

When possessed by a Dybbuk, only a specially trained rabbi is able to cast out this evil spirit, which usually leaves the body of its victim through the small toe, where a little orifice from which blood oozes marks the exact point of its exit. The kabbalistic literature of Yitzchak Luria's disciples contains many stories and "protocols" about the exorcism of Dybbukim. Numerous manuscripts present detailed instructions on how to exorcise them. The power to exorcise Dybbukim was given to a baʾalei shem, or accomplished Ḥasidim. They exorcised the Dybbuk from the body it had attached itself to and simultaneously redeemed the soul by providing a tikkun (restoration), either by transmigration or by causing the Dybbuk to enter hell. Moses Cordovero defined the Dybbuk as an "evil pregnancy". According to the *Jewish Encyclopedia*, full descriptions of successful acts of exorcism – where however the Dybbuḳ is still called by its older name "ruakh" – are given in Manasseh ben Israel's *Nishmat Hayyim* (part iii., ch. 14; part iv., ch. 20). Another detailed description of a similar incident is reported in *Ha-Shakhar* (vi. 459, 697) from Moses Prager's (Graf) *Zeraʾ Ḳodesh* (Fürth, 1696). This is remarkable because of the fact that R. David Oppenheim – the celebrated book-collector, who at the time was rabbi of Nikolsburg, Moravia – is one of the signatories to the narrative. Dr. S. Rubin, in his *Gilgul Neshamot*, the German title of which is: *Die Metempsychose in Mythus und Kultur Aller Völker* (Cracow, 1898), points out the connection between the ancient belief in the transmigration of souls and in possession by evil spirits, and that of the Dybbuḳim of modern times. He says at the end of his work (p. 29) that the belief in the wanderings of the soul *"has come down to our time among the ẓaddikim and saints of the Ḥasidim, who cast out 'gil-gulim' and 'Dyibbuḳim' from insane people"*.

In modern Judaism some rabbi's take the Dybbuk seriously while others regard the phenomenon as superstition. The thing is, that although not called Dybbuks in the 20th century, a lot of literature by non-Jews was written about the spirits of deceased people taking possession of the living and causing a lot of trouble. One of the best books on the subject is *Thirty Years Among the Dead*, the monumental work of Dr. Carl Wickland, a Swedish-American psychiatrist, dating back to 1924. In non-European cultures, diseases, bad luck and mental illnesses are almost without exception linked to evil spirits, demons or possession by spirits of the dead. This belief was once common among all Jews. See for example the *Testament of Solomon*. Christ and his disciples healed people by casting out the demons that made them ill.

The Dybbuk in theater plays and movies
The Dybbuk, or *Between Two Worlds* (Russian: Меж двух миров [Дибук] -*Mezh dvukh mirov* [Dibuk]; Yiddish: דער דִבּוק – צווישן צוויי וועלטן, *Tsvishn Tsvey Veltn – der Dibuk*) is a play by S. Ansky, authored between 1913 and 1916. It was originally written in Russian and later translated into Yiddish by Ansky himself. The Dybbuk had its world premiere in that language, performed by the Vilna Troupe at Warsaw in 1920. A Hebrew version was prepared by Hayim Nahman Bialik and staged in Moscow at the Habima Theater in 1922. The play, which depicts the possession of a young woman by the malicious spirit of her dead beloved, became a canonical work of both Hebrew and Yiddish theater, being further translated and performed around the world. The Dybbuk-theme also inspired several movie directors. *The Dybbuk* (Yiddish: דער דיבוק, *Der Dibuk*; Polish: *Dybuk*) is a 1937 Yiddish-language Polish fantasy drama directed by Michał Waszyński. It is was based on the play *The Dybbuk* by S. Ansky. We also find the Dybbuk theme in *The Possession,* a 2012 American-Canadian horror film directed by Ole Bornedal. Dayan D. Oualid created *Dibbuk* in 2019, a 33 minutes horror movie. Dan, a pious man, is tasked by Sarah to examine her husband Eli. Dan thus brings together a "Minyan", a group of ten Jewish individuals, in order to perform an exorcism according to a strict and tiresome ritual.

Eisheth Zenunim

In Jewish lore *Eisheth Zenunim* is a soul-eating demon of prostitution and a *Succubus*. In the Kabbalah Eisheth Zenunim (Heb. אֵשֶׁת זְנוּנִים, Woman of Prostitution) is found in one of the Zohar-versions as *Isheth zennanim* or *Qodeshah* (Holy female one). She is said to eat the souls of the damned, or to function as one of the four angels of prostitution, the mates of Samael. Her fellow Succubi are *Lilith, Naamah,* and *Agrat bat Mahlat,* although in the Zohar-version I own myself (the 3 volumes, 1598 pages thick, *Wisdom of the Zohar – An Anthology of Texts,* London 1994 – by Fischel Lachower, Isaiah Tishby and translations by David Goldstein) the Sitra Achra and demon-sections in the book only mention Lilith, Naamah, and Agrat bat Mahlat. S.L. MacGregor Mathers does mention her though, in his translation of *Kabbala Denudata – The Kabbalah Unveiled:*

> *"[...] Their prince is Samael, SMAL, the angel of poison and of death. His wife is the harlot, or woman of whoredom, AShTh ZNVNIM or Isheth Zenuni; and united they are called the beast, CHIVA or Chioa. Thus the infernal trinity is completed, which is, so to speak, the negative side and caricature of the supernatural Creative One Samael, and considered to be identical with Satan..."*

No need to say that under the blanket of any Abrahamitic religion, any woman engaged in sexual activity or even a woman that is simply beautiful, is associated with a "whore", whilst theonic or angelic forces like *Satan* and *Samael* are often completely misunderstood and wrongly profiled. This is simply because of the anti-vitalist and dualist character of these religions and the deeply smoldering sexual frustrations they cultivate, which of course in turn needs a scapegoat as an outlet of distorted and misogynous energies (the woman, witch or "female demon of whoredom" as the origin of evil and the enemy of God). On the other side of the spectrum, many modern occult groups only make it worse, as these beings are idolized (half rebellious, half feminist) by which means they still remain *politicized.* In order to understand the true nature of any being, it is of course essential that it gets depoliticized first. In contrast to Lilith, Naamah and Agrat, Eisheth Zenunim mostly remains a mystery. I was able to trace her in a rather pythonesque and revised Hebrew text in the *William Davidson Talmud : Pesachim 87-A,* which does not bring us any further either; (The cursive text underneath it is the direct translated Hebrew; the bold text mentions *Eisheth z'nubim w'yaldei z'nubim* (a woman of prostitution and children of prostitution):

אָמַר הַקָּדוֹשׁ בָּרוּךְ הוּא: מָה אֶעֱשֶׂה לְזָקֵן זֶה? אוֹמֵר
לוֹ: לֵךְ וְקַח אִשָּׁה זוֹנָה וְהוֹלִיד לְךָ בָּנִים זְנוּנִים, וְאַחַר
כָּךְ אוֹמֵר לוֹ שַׁלְּחָהּ מֵעַל פָּנֶיךָ. אִם הוּא יָכוֹל לְשַׁלּוֹחַ
— אַף אֲנִי אֲשַׁלַּח אֶת יִשְׂרָאֵל. שֶׁנֶּאֱמַר: "וַיֹּאמֶר ה׳
אֶל הוֹשֵׁעַ לֵךְ קַח לְךָ **אֵשֶׁת זְנוּנִים וְיַלְדֵי זְנוּנִים"**,
וּכְתִיב: "וַיֵּלֶךְ וַיִּקַּח אֶת גֹּמֶר בַּת דִּבְלָיִם". "גֹּמֶר", אָמַר
רַב: שֶׁהַכֹּל גּוֹמְרִים בָּהּ. "בַּת

*"The Holy One, Blessed be He, said: What shall I do to this Elder
who does not know how to defend Israel? I will say to him: Go and
take a prostitute and bear for yourself children of prostitution. And
after that I will say to him: Send her away from before you. If he is
able to send her away, I will also send away the Jewish people."*

This deliberation provides the background of the opening prophecy in
Hosea, *as it is stated: "The Lord said to Hosea: Go, take for yourself a woman
of prostitution and children of prostitution"* (Hosea 1:2). *And then it is
written: "So he went and took Gomer the daughter of Dibelim"* (Hosea 1:3),
and the Sages interpreted her name homiletically as "Gomer" (Last one);
Rav said she was so called because everyone would finish having relations
with her and satisfy their desires with her. "The daughter of Dibelim".

Estrie

Estries are seen as a kind of female *Vampire*. The *Vampire* in Hebrew is
usually called an *Arpad* or *Alukah* (Bible, Prov. 30:15). However, the earliest
explicit reference to a vampiric creature occurs in a text of Late Antiquity,
the *Testament of Solomon*. A boy gets thinner and thinner, although *King
Solomon* offers him more than enough food. On questioning the child, the
boy tells him that every day a demon takes away half of his food and wages
and also sucks blood out of his thumb. After hearing this story, Solomon
responds to this threat by constructing a magic ring with which he enslaves
this demon and, subsequently, higher orders of demons. In the end, the king
uses these demon-slaves to help him construct the Temple. Later, a very
different kind of Vampire appears among the Jews of medieval Rhineland.
Instead of Alukah, the Yiddish term *Estrie* was used for the creature.

Estries are female Vampires of Jewish folklore that were believed to prey on Hebrew citizens. The name derives from the French *Strix*, a term for *night owl*. In some accounts they are considered identical with *Succubi*: both were portrayed as beautiful, blood-thirsty female demons, but only Succubi were thought to favor babies and young children as prey. Estries, like other Vampires, also needed to feed on blood to survive, but were more indiscriminate in their choice of victims. Succubi were said to kill pregnant women and babies out of jealousy or spite, and to seduce (or in some cases rape) men. Estries and Succubi were both said to be able to appear as humans or in spirit form at will. Estries were also described as able to turn into birds or cats and various other animals. They were able to fly if their hair was unbound, while binding an Estries hair would keep it grounded. The *Sefer Hasidim*, stated about the creature:

"1465 There are women that are called estrie... They were created at sunset [before the first Sabbath before creation]. As a result of this, they are able to change form. There was one woman who was a estrie and she was very sick and there were two women with her at night; one was sleeping and one was awake. And the sick woman stood up and loosened her hair and she was about to fly and suck the blood of the sleeping woman. And the woman who was awake screamed and woke her friend and they grabbed the sick estrie, and after this she slept. And moreover, if she had been able to grab the other woman, then she, the estrie, would have lived. Since she was not able to hurt the other woman, the estrie died, because she needs to drink the blood of living flesh. The same is true of the werewolf. And since....the estrie need to loosen their hair before they fly, one must adjure her to come with her hair bound so that she cannot go anywhere without permission. And if a estrie is injured or seen by someone, she cannot live unless she eats of the bread and salt of the one who struck her. Then her soul will return to the way it was before.

1466: There was a woman who was suspected of being an estrie, and she was injured when she appeared to a Jew as a cat and he hit her. The next day she asked him to give her some of his bread and salt, and he wanted to give it to her. An old man said to him (Eccl. 7:16) "Be not overly righteous." When others have sinned one must not show kindness, for if she lives, she will harm people. Thus the Holy One, blessed be He created her for you [as a test]. This is similar to Amalek and Saul. Saul was punished for saving Amalek's life. [1 Sam. 15]"

The nature of these Vampires is strangely indeterminate. In the beginning of the passage, they are identified as demonic spirits, as in the *Testament of Solomon*. On the other hand, the end of the passage suggests that this is an ordinary woman (apparently, she has a soul) living within her community. Other passages in the *Sefer Hasidim* convey that same idea. Perhaps the resolution of this puzzle is that vampirism was understood to be a kind of demonic possession, though this is never stated explicitly. An Estrie wounded while in monstrous form would die, unless she was able to acquire bread and salt from the assailant while in human form. There is also one example of a judicial proceeding being conducted against a suspected Estrie. Not surprisingly, conviction results in a death sentence. Apparently killing an Estrie presents no particular challenge, but there is a potential post-mortem complication:

> *"When an estrie that has eaten children is being buried one should observe whether her mouth is open, if it is, she will persist in her vampirish pursuits for another year unless it is stopped up with earth."*
> (cf. Sefer Hasidim 5) (Toldot Adam v'Havah 28)

Estries were considered undeterred by religious iconography, distinguishing them from other mythological demons. Estries were believed to be able to walk into holy places, and sometimes to seek prayer for healing from unsuspecting religious people seeking to do good. But blessing an Estrie was considered an evil act in ancient cultures.

Ghoul

The *Ghoul* (Arabic: *Ghūl*) is a humanoid, demon-like being, originating in pre-Islamic Arabian religion, associated with graveyards and the consuming of human flesh. Ghoul is from the Arabic ghūl, from ghāla (to seize). In Arabic, the term is also sometimes used to describe a greedy or gluttonous individual. There may also be a link with the etymology of *gal* and *gala* (to cast spells, scream, crow), and its association with *warlike ardor*, *wrath* and the Akkadian *gallu*, which refer to demons of the underworld. The term was first used in English literature in 1786 in William Beckford's Orientalist novel *Vathek*, which describes the Ghūl of Arabic folklore. In Arabic folklore, the Ghoul is said to dwell in cemeteries and other uninhabited places. A male Ghoul is referred to as *Ghul* while the female is called *Ghulah*. One figure called *Umm Ghulah* translates as "Mother Ghoul" and is portrayed in tales wherein she lures men into her home to eat them. In some lore the Ghoul is a desert-dwelling, shapeshifting demon or *Jinn* that can assume the guise of an animal, especially a hyena. It lures unwary people into the desert wastes or abandoned places to slay and devour them. The creature also preys on young children, drinks blood, steals coins, and eats the dead, then taking the form of the person most recently eaten. One of the narratives identified a Ghoul named *Ghul-e Biyaban*, a particularly monstrous character, believed to be inhabiting the wilderness of Afghanistan and Iran. Although a being of the Arabic world, Ghoul-like creatures – under other names – belong to the European tradition as well and can be found in almost every part of the continent, although eastern Europe and the Slavic regions have the highest concentrations.

Lilith and the Lilin

Legend has it, that the child-protecting angel *Sandalphon* forced *Lilith* to confess all her names and describe all her appearances, in order to render her powerless. From this, the following 17 names derived (collected by F.C. Conybeare): *Abeko, Abito, Amizo, Batna, Eilo, Ita, Izorpo, Kali, Kea, Kokos, Lilith, Odam, Parthasa, Patrota, Podo, Satrina, Talto*. In *Folklore of the Holy Land*, J.E. Hanauer lists 27: *Abro, Abyzu, Ailo, Alio, Alu, Amiz, Amizu, Ardad, Lili, Avitu, Bituah, Gallu, Gelou, Ik, Ils, Kalee, Kakash, Lamassu, Lilith, Partasah, Petrota, Pods, Paphi, Satrinah, Thiltho, Zahriel, Zefonith*.

The demonology of *Lilith* and *Lilin* – although rooted in the Middle-East – lived on through the centuries via the Jewish communities in Europe. Lilin (Hebrew: לילין) is an adopted Akkadian and Sumerian term for nocturnal female spirits, who attacked men to sexually rob them from their vital energies. In Hebrew texts, the term *Lilith* or *Lilit* is translated as "night creature", "night monster", "night hag", or "screech owl". The Lilin are regarded as dangerous creatures in Jewish folklore and according to some stories, the Lilin are the daughters of Lilith (Hebrew: לילית), Adam's first wife, born to *Samael*, who was often (very) wrongly identified as *Satan*. Samael, who in kabbalistic lore presides over the 5th Hekhalah (Sanctuary, here: Mars-sphere) is also the guardian of *Araboth*, the 7th *Hekhalah* or heaven, or more precise: the Saturn-sphere ruled by the archangel *Cassiel*, who is not the *Angel of Death*, but carries a lot of sorrow and suffering from the world, which would otherwise afflict humans. Samael is a fiery *Shiva*-like force and represents absolute immunity to any sort of obsession or parasitical entity that wants to obsess, possess or manipulate. On an esoteric level, Lilith, in Jewish folklore often regarded as the queen or mother of the Lilin, was indeed an ideal match for Samael, because she represents the "refusal" or right to refuse, ignore, or not to bend over for any authority, not even the one of God himself. She therefore became the only female creature in God's creation endowed with the divine gift of the *Ha-Shem*, i.e. she could directly create, just by uttering the words, as if they were God's own words and powers.

Lilith is mentioned in the *Babylonian Talmud* (*Eruvin 100b*, *Niddah 24b*, Shabbat 151b, *Baba Bathra 73a*), in the *Book of Adam and Eve* as Adam's first wife, and in the *Zohar Leviticus 19a* as *"a hot fiery female who first copulated with man"*. In the satirical *Alphabet of Sirach* (c. 700-1000 AD), Lilith appears as Adam's first wife, who was created at the same time (at Rosh Hashanah) and from the same clay as Adam. The legend of Lilith developed extensively during the Middle Ages, in the tradition of *Aggadah* (legends used to give insight in the complexity of life and God-man relationships), the *Zohar*, and additional texts of Jewish mysticism. For example, in the 11th century writings of Isaac ben Jacob ha-Cohen, Lilith left Adam after she refused to become subservient to him and then would not return to the Garden of Eden after she had coupled with the archangel Samael.

In Jewish folklore Lilith was reduced to a single Lilin-demon. She was feared by men traveling and forced to spend the night in the wilderness, abandoned areas or buildings, as a *Succubus* that wanted to steal their seed, and by both women and men for her habit of abducting or harming babies and children. Special amulets and magical formulas were used to protect a child from getting stolen or hurt, and a prayer was said, invoking the three special anti-Lilith angels: *"Senoi, Sansenoi* and *Samangeloph"*. So these *Mazikim* (harmful spirits) as the Lilin and Lilith, had various roles; the one who preyed on males became also known as the *Ardat-Lilith*, while others imperiled women in childbirth and their children. A predecessor of the latter kind was *Lamashtu*, against whom incantation formulas have been preserved in Assyrian. Winged female demons that strangle children are known from a Hebrew or Canaanite

inscription found at Arslan-Tash in northern Syria and dating from about
the 7th or 8th century BC. Lilith was feared as the nocturnal seducer
of men, because it was believed that from their wet dream emissions
she bore an infinite number of demonic children. In this latter role she
appears at the head of a vast host of Lilin, who share in her activities.
Belief in her erotic powers led some Jewish communities to adopt
the custom of sons not accompanying their dead father's body to the
cemetery, because they would be shamed by the hovering presence of
their demon step-siblings, born of their father's seduction by Lilith.

Samuel Noah Kramer published in 1938 his translation of *ki-sikil-lil-
la-ke* as Lilith in "Tablet XII" of the *Epic of Gilgamesh*, dated c.600 BC.
(Tablet XII is not really part of the Epic of Gilgamesh, but a later Assyrian
Akkadian translation of the last part of the Sumerian Epic of Gilgamesh.)
Suggested translations include *ki-sikil* as "sacred place", *lil* as "spirit",
and *lil-la-ke* as "water-spirit", but also simply as "owl" – given that the
lil is building a home in the trunk of a tree, and she in general has been
associated with the screech owl. Akkadian, Sumerian and Babylonian
texts mention *Lilu* (masculine), *Lilitu* (female) and *Lili* (female). A *Lilu*
or *Lilû* is a masculine Akkadian word for a spirit, related to *Alû* (demon).
In Akkadian and Sumerian mythology, Alû is a vengeful spirit of the
Utukku (an ambiguous class of demons, who were sometimes thought of
as good and sometimes as evil) that goes down to the underworld *Kur*.
The demon has no mouth, nor ears. It roams at night, terrifies people and
disturbs their sleep, and possession by an Alû results in unconsciousness
and coma; in this manner it resembles creatures such as *Alps* and the
Incubus/Succubus, which are notorious for causing sleep paralysis. In
Akkadian and Sumerian mythology, Alû is associated with other demons
like *Gallu* and Lilu. It is disputed whether, if at all, the Akkadian word *Lilu*
is related to the Hebrew word *Lilith* in Isaiah 34:14, which is thought to
be a night bird (screech owl) by some modern scholars. The Babylonian
concept of Lilu may be more strongly related to the later Talmudic
concept of Lilith and Lilin. In *Targum Sheni Esther 1:3* King Solomon
had Lilin dance before him. In the Syrian *Apocalypse of Baruch*, the Lilin
come from the desert and they are similar to the *Shedim*. The Shedim
are often regarded as the offspring of Lilith, from her union with Adam,
or other men. They are not always regarded as demons, but nevertheless
labeled as evil, simply because they are seen as not of God's creation. In
Academic circles a connection between the Jewish Lilith to an Akkadian

Lilītu is generally accepted. In the *Dead Sea Scrolls (4Q510-511)*, the Lilith first occurs in a list of monsters. Jewish magical inscriptions on bowls and amulets from the 6th century AD onwards identify Lilith as a female demon and provide the first visual depictions of her. In the *Testament of Solomon*, a Greek work of about the second or third century, based on Judeo-Hellenistic magic, Lilith is called *Obizoth*, and it is related that one of the mystical names of the angel *Raphael,* inscribed on an amulet, prevents her from inflicting injury.

Mazzikin

The *Mazzikin* (harmful spirits) are said to have been created on the eve of the Sabbath of creation *(Avot 5:6)* but this late reference is the only one made to demons in the entire *Mishnah*. In Jewish mythology, Mazzikin (also written as Mazzikim) refers to a class of invisible demons that can create minor annoyances or major dangers. The Hebrew term mazzikin (מַזִּיקִין, also spelled mazzikim מַזִּיקִים), found in the *Talmud*, means "harmful" or "those who harm". It is generally understood to refer to harmful invisible demons that a person might encounter in everyday life. Demons or evil spirits do not occupy a prominent place in Jewish religion. Rather, they were seen as under the command of God, who sent his punishment through them.

Naamah

Naamah (Hebrew נַעֲמָה), also known as *Nachem, Nahema, Naamah, Nhama, Naamáh, Nammah* or *Na' Ammah* (pleasant, charming or pleasing, or pleasing to the gods) is a legendary demoness, introduced in Europe through Jewish lore, who depicts her as the *demon of Prostitution*. She is said to have been a *Succubus*, and like *Lilith* has had relations with Adam. The demoness is described in more detail in the Kabbalistic book *Zohar* as the mother of the *Shedim*, the friend of *Asmodeus* and temptress of the angels. Later (in western occultism) Naamah became the ruler of the Qlippoth (demons) of Malchuth (physical world) on the Etz haChayim (Tree of Life), analogous to the diapositive of the *Shekhinah* (the immanence of God in creation, or female side of God). Naamah was depicted as a woman of fire or as a naked woman with bat wings. According to tradition, Naamah and Lilith lived on the shore of the Red Sea, where they had ended up after leaving *Eden*. Naamah is similar in appearance to Lilith. Demonology shows Namaah as one of the women of *Shaitan* (Satan), and she is mentioned in the *Zohar* as one of the four angels of sacred prostitution (along with *Lilith*, *Agrat bat Mahlat* and *Eisheth Zenunim*), consorts of *Samael*. She is sometimes mentioned as the mother of Asmodeus and often confused with Lamech's daughter, who is also called Namaah. According to the *Zohar*, after *Cain* kills *Abel*, *Adam* separates from *Eve* for 130 years. During this time, Lilith and Naamah seduce him and bear his demonic children, who became the plagues of mankind. She and Lilith cause epilepsy in children. In another story from the *Zohar*, Naamah and Lilith are said to have corrupted the angels *Ouza* and *Azazel*. The text states that Namaah also attracts demons, as she is continuously (every night) chased by the demon kings *Afrira* and *Qastimon*, but she leaps away every time and takes multiple forms to entice the men:

> *"She makes sport with the sons of man, and conceives from them through their dreams, from the male desire, and she attaches herself to them. She takes the desire, and nothing more, and from that desire she conceives and brings forth all kinds of demons into the world. And those sons she bears from men visit the women of humankind, who then conceive from them and give birth to spirits. And all of them go to the first Lilith and she brings them up."*

Onoskelis

Onoskelis (she with the mule's legs) was a beautiful female demon mentioned in the apocryphal text of the *Testament of Solomon*: *"Her body was that of a woman with a fair complexion, but her legs were those of a mule"* – TSol 4:2. Onoskelis is usually associated with the Hobgoblin *Empusa*, who was able to assume various shapes, however in this case Onoskelis is a *Satyra* or female *Satyr*. According to the *Testament of Solomon*, Asmodeus, subjected by the King-Magician with his magical ring, was forced to bring Onoskelis to his court. When Solomon asked Onoskelis what her purpose was, she stated:

> *"I am a spirit which has been made into a body. I recline in a den on the earth. I make my home in caves. However, I have a many-sided character. Sometimes I strangle men; sometimes I pervert them from their true natures. Most of the time, my habitats are cliffs, caves, and*

ravines. Frequently, I also associate with men who think of me as a woman, especially with whose skin is honey-colored, for we are of the same constellation. It is also true that they worship my star secretly and openly. They do not know that they deceive themselves and excite me to be an evil doer all the more. For they want to obtain gold by remembering (me), but I grant little to those who seriously worship me."

She also describes her creation:

"from an unexpected voice which is called a voice of the echo of a black heaven, emitted in matter."

Onoskelis travels by the full moon and Solomon commands her to spin hemp to construct the ropes used for the Temple. She travels stealthily and kills indiscriminately but she is also a shy creature, a half hermit, barely daring to protrude her head out of her caves.

Se'īrīm

Se'īrīm (Hebrew: שעירים, singular *Sa'ir*) is a genus of demons, in the form of a hybrid creature with goat-like characteristics, from Judaism. Sa'ir was the ordinary Hebrew word for "he-goat", and it is not always clear what the word's original meaning might have been. Se'īrīm are frequently compared with the Shedim of Hebrew tradition, along with *Satyrs* of Greek mythology and *Jinn* of Arab culture. Biblical scholar Samuel Bochart identified the Se'īrīm with the Egyptian goat gods. (Jerome of Stridon, (circa 342/347-420) equated them with the Satyrs. They are mentioned in the *Tanakh* and are also mentioned once in *Leviticus 17:7* probably a recalling of Assyrian demons in the shape of goats. Samuel Bochart and other Biblical scholars identified the Se'īrīm with Egyptian goat-deities. *Leviticus 17:7* admonishes Israel to keep from sacrificing to the Se'īrīm. Texts from the *Dead Sea Scrolls* describe the underworld as full of Se'īrīm. *Isaiah 34:14* declares: *"Wildcats (ziim) shall meet with hyenas (iim), goat-demons (se'īrīm) shall call to each other; there too Lilith (lilit) shall repose and find a place to rest."* The Talmud says the Se'īrīm can harm humans and would be as swift as the wind. There were also spells in use to ward off these demons. In the Qumran fragments, they are referred to as the children of angels and men and have horns. In the Latin Vulgate translation of the Old Testament, *Sa'ir* is translated as *Pilosus*, which also means "hairy".

Shedim

Shedim (pl. of *Shed*, Hebrew: שֵׁדִים, protecting spirits) refers to a type of demon in Judaism. They were often understood as foreign gods, independent, but inferior in power to God. They do not represent a competitor or antithesis to God, but because they are worshipped as idols, looked upon as reprehensible. Although they are attributed as the cause of disease, they can also be pious, or even friendly. When Hebrew texts were translated into Greek, the term Shedim was always translated as *Daimonion* with implied negative connotations as foreign invisible powers. Their whereabouts were also thought to be near tombs. Shedim are said to have had the feet and claws of a rooster. To see if the Shedim were present, ashes were thrown to the ground or floor, which made their footsteps become visible. Shedim can shapeshift and assume a human form. The Talmud tells of Asmodeus assuming King Solomon's form and ruling in his place for some time. However, he was never seen barefoot, because he could not disguise his feet. The Zohar has a passage where a female Shed, a *Shedah*, takes the form of a woman:

> *"The Shekhinah hid Esther from Ahasuerus and gave him a Shedah*
> *(a she-devil) instead while she returned to Mordechai's arms. [...]*
> *This is why a man must speak with his wife before he mates with her,*
> *because she might have been exchanged with a female demon."*

In the Tanakh, the word Shedim is used twice (*Psalm 106:37* and *Deuteronomy 32:17*) and refers to non-gods to whom sacrifices were presented. The Hebrew term is a loanword from Akkadian. The *Torah* (*Deut 32:17*) explicitly speaks of Shedim as "non-gods" and asserts that there are no supernatural powers apart from the one and only YHWH, the God of Israel (*Deut 4:35*). The term non-gods in the Torah has a deliberately sarcastic undertone. Among others, the *Se'irim* (hairy beings) are still distinguished from the Schedim. The Christian theologian Woyke claims that in Jewish tradition pagan gods are generally also referred to as Schedim. According to the *Midrash*, Shedim have wings like angels and can reach the borders of heaven to hear what will happen in the future, but likewise they must take nourishment, multiply and die, like humans. In popular belief, they are sometimes said to be the children of *Samael* and *Lilith,* whereas the *Zohar* describes them as the offspring of the demons *Azazel* and *Naamah.* According to another legend, Shabbat dawned even before God created their bodies that were supposed to become like humans, but since God rested on Shabbat, their bodies were never completed. The Talmud describes the Shedim as possessing some traits of angels, and some traits of humans:

> *"In three ways they are like ministering angels: they have wings like ministering angels and they fly from one end of the world to the other like ministering angels and they know what will be in the future like ministering angels. And in three ways they are similar to humans: They eat and drink like humans; they multiply like humans; and they die like humans."*

Shedim were thought to cause sickness and misfortune, follow the dead and fly around graves. Supposedly, sinful people sacrificed their daughters to the Shedim, but it is unclear if the sacrifice consisted in the murdering of the victims or in the sexual satisfaction of the demons. There are many things that one is admonished not to do in order to avoid invoking the Shedim, such as whistling or even saying the word "Shedim". The 2nd and 3rd century mystic Judah ben Samuel of Regensburg wrote in his will and testament that one should not seal up windows completely because it may trap Shedim in the house. The Shedim are not always seen as malicious creatures and are also considered to be helpful to humans. They are said to be even able to live according to the *Torah*, like Asmodeus did.

Sheid beit ha-Kisset and Šulak

Sheid beit ha-Kisset (demon of the privy) is a lavatory demon that takes the form of a goat in the *Talmud (Shabbat 67a, Berachot 62a)*. The "demon of the privy" appears also in the *Babylonian Talmud*:

> *"The Rabbis taught: on coming from a privy a man should not have sexual intercourse till he has waited long enough to walk half a mile, — because the demon of the privy is with him for that time; if he does not follow this rule, his children will be epileptic."*

This demon that lurks in the toilet is a type of unclean spirit that in the early Christian era was regarded as causing both physical and spiritual afflictions. In the Middle East the "Toilet Lurkers" were especially associated with epilepsy and stroke. Related is the *Šulak*, who besides the privy also lurks in the bathroom. Šulak appears in the *Babylonian Diagnostic Handbook (Tablet XXVII)*, in which various diseases are described and attributed to the "hand" of a god, goddess, or spirit. A *Lurker* is a type of demon that lies in wait in places where a potential victim is likely to be alone. When one has to urinate or defecate, one is exposed and hence vulnerable: *"Šulak will hit him!"* The *hit* may be a type of *stroke* (mišittu). According to Marten Stol *(Epilepsy in Babylonia,* 1993) an even earlier reference to this demon is found in a Hittite diagnostic text. Ancient folk etymology held that the name *Šulak* derived from a phrase meaning *dirty hands,* due to his dwelling in the *bīt musâti –* literally *house of rinse-water*, i.e. lavatory. The appearance of a Šulak is described in Akkadian sources as a "rampant" or bipedal but otherwise normal looking lion. Protective amulets in the form of the Lion Centaur *Urmahlullu,* or cuneiform tablets inscribed with spells to ward off Šulak, were often buried under the doorways of lavatories, in the foundations of the house, or deposited in drainage pipes.

LITERATURE AND DIGITAL SOURCES

- Abercromby, John – *The Pre- and Proto-historic Finns, both Eastern and Western with the Magic Songs of the West Finns – in two volumes*, published by David Nutt in the Strand, London, 1898
- Árnason, J.; Powell, G. E. J. and Magnússon, E. trans. – *Icelandic Legends* – Richard Bentley, London, 1864
- Arrowsmith, N. – *Field Guide to the Little People: A Curious Journey Into the Hidden Realm of Elves, Faeries, Hobgoblins & Other Not-so-mythical Creatures* – Llewellyn Worldwide., 1970/2009
- Barb, A.A. – *Antaura. The Mermaid and the Devil's Grandmother: A Lecture* – Journal of the Warburg and Courtauld Institutes, 1966
- Bardon, Franz – *Die Praxis der Magische Evokation* – Rüggeberg Verlag Wuppertal, 2003
- Bartsch, Karl – *Sagen, Märchen und Gebräuche aus Meklenburg*, vol. 1 – Vienna, Wilhelm Braumüller, 1879
- Beaumont, William Comyns – *Britain The Key To World History* – London, 1948
- Benwell, G. and Waugh, A. – *Sea Enchantress: The Tale of the Mermaid and her Kin* – Hutchinson, London, 1961
- Blau, Lajos (Ludwich) – *Das Altjüdische Zauberwesen* – 1897-98 Budapest / Graz, 1974
- Blécourt, W. de, – *"I Would Have Eaten You Too": Werewolf Legends in the Flemish, Dutch, and German Area* – 2007
- Bonnefoy, Yves, – *Asian Mythologies* – University of Chicago Press, 1993
- Bottiglioni, Gino – *Leggende e tradizioni di Sardegna (testi dialettali in grafia fonetica)* – 1922
- Briggs, Katharine – *An Encyclopedia of Fairies – Hobgoblins, Brownies, Bogies and Other Supernatural Creatures* – Pantheon Books, USA, 1976
- Calmet, Dom Augustine – *The Phantom World: The History and Philosophy of Spirits, Apparitions &c. Two Volumes in One* – Philadelphia: A Hart, Late Carey & Hart, 1850
- Campbell, J.G. – *Superstitions of the Highlands and Islands of Scotland* – James MacLehose and Sons, Glascow, 1900
- Conway, Moncure Daniel -*Demonology and Devil-Lore 1 & 2* – revised publication of the 1897 editions by VAMzzz Publishing, Amsterdam, 2015
- Conybeare, Frederick Cornwallis – *Testament of Solomon* – *Jewish Quaterly Review of October 1889* – revised edition VAMzzz Publishing, Amsterdam, 2015
- Corstorphine, Kevin & Kremmel, Laura R – *Horror in the Medieval North: The*

Troll, The Palgrave Handbook to Horror Literature – ed., 2018
- Courtney, M.A. – *Cornish Feasts and Folklore* – Beare and Son, Penzance, 1890
- Craigie, W.A. – *The Oldest Icelandic Folklore,* 1893
- Davidsson, O. *The Folk-lore of Icelandic Fishes,* 1900
- Dennison, W. Traill – *Orkney Folklore, Sea Myths* – Edinburgh University Press, 1891
- Dörler, Adolf Ferdinand (collected and edited by) – *Sagen aus Innsbruck's Umgebung, mit besonderer Berücksichtigung des Zillerthales* – Innsbruck, 1895
- Edmondston, Thomas – *An Etymological Glossary of the Shetland & Orkney Dialect* – Adam and Charles Black, 1866
- *Encyclopedia Brittanica online*
- Folkard, Richard – *Plant Lore Legends & Lyrics* – 1884, revised edition by VAMzzz Publishing, Amsterdam, 2021
- Frazer, Sir James George – *The Golden Bough: A Study in Magic and Religion* – edition 1906-15
- Genesin, Monica & Rizzo, Luana (Hrsg.) – *Magie, Tarantismus und Vampirismus; Eine interdisciplinäre Annäherung* – Verlag Dr. Kovač, Hamburg, 2013
- Gibbings W. W. – *Folk-lore and Legends* – *Germany,* London, 1892
- Gieysztor, Aleksander – *Mitologia Słowian* – Warszawa: Wydawnictwo Uniwersytetu Warszawskiego, 2006
- Gill, W. Walter – *A Second Manx Scrapbook* – Arrowsmith, London Bristol, 1932
- Grimm, Jacob – *Deutsche Mythologie* – Göttingen: Dieterich, 1835
- Hageland, A. van – *La Mer Magique* – Marabout, Paris, 1973
- Hall, Manly Palmer – *The Secret Teachings of All Ages: An Encyclopedic Outline of Masonic, Hermetic, Qabbalistic and Rosicrucian Symbolical Philosophy* – 1928
- Hanaur, J.E. – *Folk-Lore of the Holy Land* – *Moslim, Christian and Jewish* – Edited by Marmaduke Pickthall, London Duckworth & Co, 1907
- Henderson, William – *Notes on the folk-lore of the northern counties of England and the borders* – Longmans, Green, 1866
- Hlidberg, J. B. and Aegisson, S.; McQueen, F. J. M. and Kjartansson, R., trans. – *Meeting with Monsters* – JPV utgafa, Reykjavik, 2011 .
- Huizinga-Onnekes, E.J. – *Groninger Volksverhalen* – bewerkt door K. ter Laan, J.B.Wolters' Uitgevers Maatschappij N.V. Groningen – Den Haag, 1930
- *Jewish Encyclopedia online*
- Johnston, Sarah Iles – *Restless Dead: Encounters Between the Living and the Dead in Ancient Greece* – University of California Press, Berkeley-Los Angeles-London, 2013

- Karakurt, Deniz – *Türk Söylence Sözlüğü* (*Turkish Mythological Dictionary*) (OTRS: CC BY-SA 3.0), 2011
- Kivilson, Valerie A. & Worobec, Christine D. – *Witchcraft in Russia and Ukraine, 1000–1900: A Sourcebook* – Cornell University Press, Northern Illinois University Press, 2020
- Kreuter, Peter Mario – *Der Vampirglaube in Südosteuropa. Studien zur Genese, Bedeutung und Funktion. Rumänien und der Balkanraum* – Weidler, Berlin, 2001, (Dissertation Universität Bonn, 2001)
- Lachower, Fischel & Tishby, Isaiah; translations by David Goldstein – *Wisdom of the Zohar – An Anthology of Texts* – London, 1994
- Landt, George – *A description of the Faroe Islands, containing an account of their situation, climate, and productions, together with the manners and customs of the inhabitants, their trade etc.* – 1810
- Lawson, John Cuthbert, M.A. – *Modern Greek Folklore and Ancient Greek Religion – A Study in Survivals* – Cambridge: at the University Press, London: Fetter Lane, E.C., 1910
- Lecouteux, Claude:
  - *Witches, Werewolves and Fairies: Shapeshifters and Astral Doubles in the Middle Ages*, Inner Traditions (Rochester, Vermont) transl. Clare Frock, 2003
  - *The Return of the Dead: Ghosts, Ancestors and the Transparent Veil of the Pagan Mind*, Inner Traditions (Rochester, Vermont) transl. Jon E. Graham, 2009
  - *The Secret History of Vampires: Their Multiple Forms and Hidden Purposes*, Inner Traditions (Rochester, Vermont) transl. Jon E. Graham, 2010
  - *Phantom Armies of the Night: The Wild Hunt and Ghostly Processions of the Undead*, Inner Traditions (Rochester, Vermont) transl., Jon E. Graham, 2011
  - *The Tradition of Household Spirits. Ancestral Lore and Practice*, Inner Traditions (Rochester, Vermont) transl. Jon E. Graham, 2013
  - *Demons and Spirits of the Land: Ancestral Lore and Practices*, Inner Traditions (Rochester, Vermont) transl. Jon E. Graham, 2015
  - *The Hidden Historie of Elves and Dwarfs – Avatars of Invisible Realms*, Inner Traditions (Rochester, Vermont) transl. Jon E. Graham, 2018
- Libera, Roberto – *Storie di streghe, fantasmi e lupi mannari nei Castelli Romani, Genzano di Roma* – Consorzio SBCR editore, 2010
- Lindley, Charles, Viscount Halifax – *Lord Halifax Ghost Book* – first edition Glasgow, 1936
- Lomas, Adriano Garcia – *Mitología y supersticiones de Cantabria* – 1964
- Luzel, François-Marie – *Contes populaires de Basse-Bretagne* – 1881
- Mackenzie, Donald Alexander
  - *Wonder Tales from Scottish Myth and Legend* – Blackie and Son Limited,

London, Glasgow, Bombay, 1917

- *Scottish Folk-Lore and Folk Life. Studies in Race, Culture and Tradition* – 1935

- *Elves and Heroes* – 1909

- *Teutonic Myth and Legend* – 2nd Ed. 1934

• Mannhardt, Wilhelm:

- *Roggenwolf und Roggenhund – Beitrag zur Germanischen Sittenkunde* – Verlag von Constantin Ziemssen, Danzig, 1865

- *Die Korndämonen, – Beitrag zur Germanischen Sittenkunde* – Harrwitz und Gossmann, Berlin 1868

- *Wald- und Feldkulte. Band 1: Der Baumkultus der Germanen und ihrer Nachbarstämme: mythologische Untersuchungen* – Gebrüder Borntraeger, Berlin, 1875

- *Wald- und Feldkulte. Band 2: Antike Wald- und Feldkulte aus nordeuropäischer Überlieferung erläutert* – Gebrüder Borntraeger, Berlin, 1877

- *Mythologische Forschungen* – Karl J. Trüber, Strassburg – London 1884

• Marliave, Olivier de – *Trésor de la mythologie pyrénéenne* – Toulouse, Esper, 1987

• Marliave, Olivier de et Pertuzé, Jean-Claude – *Panthéon Pyrénéen* – Toulouse, Loubatières, 1990.

• Masani, R.P., M.A – *Folklore of Wells, being a study of Water Worship in East and West* – Bombay, D.B. Takapokevale Sons & Co, 1918

• Mathers, S.L. MacGregor / Knor von Rosenroth – *Kabbala Denudata / The Kabbalah Unveiled* – Samuel Weiser Inc. York Beach, Maine, 1989

• McAnally, David Russell – *Irish Wonders: The Ghosts, Giants, Pookas, Demons, Leprechawns, Banshees, Fairies, Witches, Widows, Old Maids, and other marvels of the Emerald Isle* – The Riverside Press Cambridge, 1888

• McIntosh, A – *Faerie Faith in Scotland* (2005) in *The Encyclopaedia of Religion and Nature* – edited by Bron Taylor, 2006

• McPherson, Rev. J. M. – *Primitive Beliefs in the North-East of Scotland* – London, New York and Toronto – Longmans, Green and Co., Ltd., 1929

• Meyer, Elard Hugo – *Mythologie der Germanen*, Straszburg, Verlag von Karl J. Trübner, 1930

• Nadmorski, Dr – *Kaszuby i Kociewie. Język, zwyczaje, przesądy, podania, zagadki i pieśni ludowe w północnej części Prus Zachodnich* – Poznań, 1892

• Paracelsus – *Four treatises of Theophrastus von Hohenheim, called Paracelsus* (1493-1541) – English translation of the German, Baltimore: Johns Hopkins Press, 1941

• Petiteau, Frantz-E. – *Contes, légendes et récits de la vallée d'Aure* – éditions Alan Sutton, 2007

- Plancy, Collin de, – *Dictionnaire Infernal* – 1818
- Podgórscy Barbara and Adam – *Wielka Księga Demonów Polskich. Leksykon i antologia demonologii ludowej* – Katowice: KOS, 2005
- Rajki, Andras – *Mongolian Ethymological Dictionary* 2006-2009 – via *academia. edu*
- Ralston, W. R. S., M.A.
  - *Russian Fairy Tales – A choice collection of Muscovite folk-lore* – New York: Hurst & Co., 1872
  - *The songs of the Russian people, as illustrative of Slavonic mythology and Russian social life* – London, Ellis, 1872
- Ritter, Johann Nepomuk von Alpenburg – *Deutsche Alpensagen* – Vienna, 1861
- Rose, C. – *Giants, Monsters, and Dragons* – W. W. Norton and Co., New York, 2000
- Rosenthal, Bernice Glatzer (editor) – *The Occult in Russian and Soviet Culture* – Cornell University, 1997
- Rhys, John – *Celtic Folklore Welsh and Manx* – Library of Alexandria, 2020
- Ryan, W.F. – *The Bathhouse at Midnight – An Historical Survey of Magic and Divination in Russia*, Pennsylvania State University Press, 1999
- Sacaze, Julien – *Le dieu Tantugou, légende du pays de Luchon* – (in Revue de Comminges, Tome III, 1887, p. 116-118), texte « patois » et traduction littérale
- Saxby, Jessie Margaret Edmondston – *Shetland Traditional Lore* – Edinburgh, Grant and Murray, 1932
- Sébillot, Paul – *Le Folk-Lore de France, Tome Premier: Le Ciel et la Terre* – 1904
- Sikes, Wirt – *British Goblins: Welsh Folk-Lore, Fairy Mythology, Legends and Traditions* – London, 1880
- Simpson, J. – *Icelandic Folktales and Legends* – University of California Press, Berkeley and Los Angeles, 1972
- Sinastrari of Ameno – transl. Liseux, Isidore 1876 – *Incubi and Succubi or Demoniality – A Historical Study of Sexual contacts with Demons* – Revised edition by VAMzzz Publishing, Amsterdam, 2017
- Sluijter, P.C.M. – *IJslands Volksgeloof* – H. D. Tjeenk Willink & Zoon N.V., Haarlem, 1936
- Spada, Dario – *Gnomi, Fate e Folletti e altri esseri fatati in Italia* – SugarCo, Milano, 2007
- Spiesberger, Karl – *Naturgeister wie Seher sie schauwen – wie Magier sie rufen* – Richard Schikowski Verlag, Berlin 1978
- Stefánsson, V. – *Icelandic Beast and Bird Lore* -1906
- Summers, Montague – *The Vampire in Lore and Legend* – Toronto 2001 (previously published as: *The Vampire in Europe*, London, 1929)

- Ter Laan, K. – *Groninger Overleveringen* – Erven B. van der Kamp, Groningen, 1930
- Thompson, Francis – *The Supernatural Highland* – Robert Hale, London, 1976
- Thorpe, Benjamin – *Northern mythology : comprising the principal popular traditions and superstitions of Scandinavia, North Germany, and the Netherlands* – 1852
- Veen, Abe J. van der – *Witte wieven, weerwolven en waternekkers – Een beschrijving van alle geesten, elfen en andere wondere wezens uit Nederland –* 2017
- Vries, A. de, – *Flanders: a cultural history* – Oxford University Press, Oxford, 2007
- Wippel I. – *Schabbock, Trud und Wilde Jagd* – Verlag für Sammler, Graz 1986
- Wikimedia Commons Licence folklore data via *Armenian, Austrian, Basque, Belarusian, Catalan, Dutch, Estonian, Danish, German, Finnish, Icelandic, Italian, French, Latvian, Lithuanian, Norwegian, Polish, Portuguese, Russian, Spanish, Swedish, Swiss, Turkish, and Ukrainian* Wikipedia-files
- Wlislocki, Dr Heinrich von – *Volksglaube und religiöser Brauch der Zigeuner –* Aschendorffsche Buchhandlung, Münster, 1891

FROM THE SAME SERIES

Spirit Beings in European Folklore 1
*Ireland, England, Wales, Cornwall,
Scotland, Isle of Man, Orkney's, Hebrides,
Faeroe, Iceland, Norway, Sweden and
Denmark*
by Benjamin Adamah, 250 pages,
Paperback, ISBN 9789492355553
www.vamzzz.com

Compendium 1 of the *Spirit Beings in European Folklore*-series covers
the northwestern part of the continent where Celtic and Anglo-Saxon
cultures meet the Nordic. This book catalogs the mysterious creatures of
Ireland, the Isle of Man, England, Wales, Cornwall, Scotland, Hebrides,
Orkneys, Faroe Islands, Iceland, Norway, Sweden and Denmark. For
centuries, the peoples of these regions have influenced each other in
many ways, including their mythologies and folklore. The latter is
perhaps most evident in the various species of *Brook-horses* or *Water-
horses*. These semi-aquatic ghostly creatures come in all kinds of varieties
and are typical of the English or Gaelic speaking parts of Europe and
Scandinavia. Many other ghostly entities occur only in specific areas or
countries. Some even became cultural icons, such as the Irish *Leprechaun*,
the *Knockers* from Wales, the Scandinavian *Trolls* and *Huldras* or
the Icelandic *Huldufólk*. England has its *Brownies*, several kinds of
Fairies and locally famous *ghost dogs*. Iceland and Scandinavia seem to
"specialize" in spirit beings who appear fully materialized, such as the
different species of *Illveli* (Evil Whales) and *Draugr*, the returning dead.

Compendium 1 discusses 292 spirit beings in detail, including their
alternative names, with additional references to related or subordinate
beings and a unique selection of illustrations.

252

Compendium 3 of the *Spirit Beings in European Folklore*-series offers an overview of the mysterious, sometimes beautiful and often shadowy entities of the Slavic countries, the Balkans, the Carpathians, Albania, Georgia, and the Turkish and Romani peoples. Many types of *Vampires* and vampiric *Revenants* are included – in their original state and purged of later applied disinformation. The undead are prominent in the folklore of Eastern Europe and Albania. Also typical are farm- and household-spirits such as the *Domovoy*, water-spirits and forest demons like the Russian *Leshy*, the *Chuhaister*, or the evil Polish *Bełt*, who like the Ukrainian *Blud*, leads travelers off their path until they are lost in the deepest part of the forest. Unique is the Russian *Bannik* or spirit of the bathhouse. Amongst the Slavs, some 'demons', like the *Boginka* for example, originally belonged to the pre-Christian pantheon. Eastern Europe, in contrast to its returning dead, is rich in seductive female spirits such as the Romanian *Iele*, the Russian *Russalka*, the *Vila* of the Eastern and Southern Slavs and the Bulgarian *Samodiva*. Via the Balkans, Greek influences entered Slavic culture, while there are also spirits that intersect Germanic and Nordic folklore.

Compendium 3 discusses 255 spirit beings in detail, including their alternative names, with additional references to related or subordinate beings and a unique selection of illustrations.

CONTENTS:

253

Spirit Beings in European Folklore 4
France, Brittany, Wallonia, Portugal,
Italy, South Tyrol, Malta, Greece,
Spain – Basque Country, Asturias,
Catalonia, Cantabria, Galicia, Valencia
by Benjamin Adamah, 250 pages,
Paperback, ISBN 9789492355584
www.vamzzz.com

Compendium 4 of the *Spirit Beings in European Folklore*-series covers an area that starts with Wallonia and continues via France and the Pyrenees, through the Iberian Peninsula, to Italy and Greece. This results in a very diverse and colourful collection of spirit beings, due to the many included Basque nature-spirits or *Ireluak*, the Spanish *Duendes*, the Celtic spirits of Brittany, the prankster Italian *Folletti* and the creatures from Greece. Some creatures from Breton folklore are particularly gruesome, such as the hollow-eyed *Ankou*, the *Werewolf*-like *Bugul-nôz*, or the ghostly and *Will-o'-the-wisp*-like *Yan-gant-y-tan*, who roams the night roads with his five lit candles. Most Italian ghosts are less gloomy, while the Iberian Peninsula is home to everything ranging from the 'Beauty' to the 'Beast'. Compendium 4 contains – amongst other things – many kinds of dwarf-spirits or *Goblins* (*Lutins, Nutons, Folletti, Farfadettes, Korrigans, Minairons*) various seductive and feminine spring creatures, *Wild Man*-varieties (*Basajaunak, Jentilak*) and an extensive section on the *Incubus-Succubus*. It is fascinating to discover how many types of European spirit beings (from *Kobold* to many female spring-spirits), described in the other Compendiums, can be traced back to creatures from Ancient Greece.

Compendium 4 discusses 270 spirit beings in detail, includes their alternative names, additional references to subordinate beings and a unique selection of illustrations.

255